What to Do  Shit Hits the Fan

What to Do When the Shit Hits the Fan

2014–2015 Edition

Dave Black

Skyhorse Publishing

Skyhorse Publishing books may be purchased in bulk at special discounts for sales promotion, corporate gifts, fund-raising, or educational purposes. Special editions can also be created to specifications. For details, contact the Special Sales Department, Skyhorse Publishing, 307 West 36th Street, 11th Floor, New York, NY 10018 or info@skyhorsepublishing.com.

Skyhorse® and Skyhorse Publishing® are registered trademarks of Skyhorse Publishing, Inc.®, a Delaware corporation.

Visit our website at www.skyhorsepublishing.com.

10 9 8 7 6 5 4 3 2 1

Library of Congress Cataloging-in-Publication Data is available on file.

ISBN: 978-1-62636-109-6

Printed in the United States of America

Contents

Introduction

What constitutes a "disaster" for a person experiencing it is going to be relative to a number of factors: that person's background and lifestyle, his or her financial situation, the nature of the event, where he or she is when the event occurs, and how well that person has prepared for catastrophic events.

"Disaster" is commonly defined as an event causing widespread destruction and distress. A grave misfortune. A crisis event that surpasses the ability of an individual, community, or society to control or recover from its consequences.

Disasters are often divided into two categories, natural and man-made. Natural disasters include earthquakes, volcanoes, floods, cyclones and hurricanes, tornadoes, droughts, and slope failures. We are essentially powerless against these events except for mitigation and effective response; natural disasters often produce horrific effects well outside the immediate area they first occur in. During these events, impoverished areas suffer grossly higher death tolls due to their architectural inferiorities and defects in their health care systems. After the main event, disease and famine often follow.

The three big killers are flooding, famine, and infectious disease. They often work in brutal combination. Aside from the initial drownings, floods mix sewage and waste with the local drinking water. Rotting corpses add to the pollution and disease inventory. Gastrointestinal diseases run rampant, commonly leading to severe dehydration (e.g. cholera), which, in turn, cannot be relieved adequately because of the lack of clean water.

Infectious disease is an interesting villain that tends to emerge in a wide area over a long period of time. Outbreaks are not often treated as disasters until the media picks ups on the situation, and then public opinion forces government officials to take action. By the time the full gravity of the situation is realized, the disease can be out of control.

Man-made disasters are those caused by humans through negligence, technological failure, fanaticism, or sheer meanness. These disasters include war, structure fires, civil unrest, building collapse, industrial accidents, transportation accidents, and hazardous material incidents. As we urbanize and our capacity to produce, store, and transport hazardous materials and technologies grows, so does the potential intensity of a disaster.

For most North Americans a disaster is something nasty that happens to somebody else. That's our attitude, and people in other parts of the world know it and resent it. Most of us living in the Western World, especially those of us from the US and Canada, are spoiled and exceptionally prosperous. Our poorest are considered blessed compared to the average person in Third World countries. Our prosperous lives and governments shield us from discomfort and discontinuity. The sheer size, geographic diversity, and wealth of our nation makes catastrophes seem like somebody else's problem, not ours. When a hurricane in New Orleans laid the city bare and killed a thousand people, the rest of us watched it in decadent comfort, snacking in luxury on the sofas in front of our big-screen LED TVs. Video from the Indian Ocean tsunami kept us captivated for weeks. We

are a complacent and distracted group of generations, easily entertained by the horrific events that others go through.

In the early 2000s I made several trips to the Republic of Georgia to present disaster management training to mid-level government officials and to develop a cadre of community emergency response trainers. On the final evening of one trip during the traditional dinner for the departing guest, after endless toasts and lots of wine, one politician's wife looked across the table at me and asked "Have you ever been in a *real* disaster?" It was a skeptical ambush that caught me off guard. Like a drowning man with his life flashing before his eyes, my memory raced through dozens of bloody scenarios I had encountered as a firefighter and paramedic, desperately searching for something that would qualify as a disaster in her eyes. The Georgians were in a perpetual financial crisis.

Poverty was extreme and rampant. Since the end of the Soviet Union, the country's infrastructure was in complete shambles. Healthcare was primitive and inaccessible to most. Terrorism, invasion, corruption, and civil war loomed on the horizon. These people knew hardship; it was painfully obvious that hotel fires and simple multi-casualty incidents that killed a few rich people and took a couple of days to clean up would not qualify as disasters here. I suddenly fell victim to survivor guilt.

For most of us it's time to wake up. Here are some searing truths about disaster and catastrophe: events since the turn of the century should remind us that even in our protected cocoons of technological sophistication and group prosperity, we are virtually powerless in the face of the laws of science and human psychology. We humans, regardless of where we live, are constantly on the verge of one disaster or another. From earthquakes to tsunamis, asteroids to pandemics, nuclear war to computer terrorism, disasters are a constant threat; for people in many parts of the world they are almost a daily occurrence.

Here in the United States we have not been visited by major disasters since the World Wars and the flu pandemic of 1919. Small disasters yes, but nothing major, and we're getting spoiled by it. For the younger generation in particular, our relationship with disasters is more about entertainment than preparation. Our media is overflowing with war games, disaster movies, living-dead zombies and vampires. "Reality" shows expose us for what we are: whiney spoiled brats who think a disaster is when our hair is out of place or we don't get invited to a party. And we wonder why the rest of the world doesn't take us seriously. Sooner or later, though, the odds are that it will all catch up to us. Somewhere out there lurking is the new most horrible disaster ever, and it could happen here in America just as easily as anywhere else.

Let's take a look at some real modern disasters. We'll stick with events that have occurred since 1900.

First on the list is war, and for our purposes we'll list World War I and II together. Starting in 1914 until the Japanese surrender in 1945, this disaster resulted in the deaths of 70 million people, most of them civilians. It included some amazingly cruel stuff: the Rape of Nanking, the Holocaust, the bombing of Dresden, the sinkings of the Lusitania and the Wilhelm Gustloff, the atomic bombings of Hiroshima and Nagasaki. The effects of these disasters will linger for centuries. Lesson learned: man has developed the technology for instant genocide and is not afraid to use it.

In 1918 an influenza pandemic broke out. It may or may not have started in Europe, but it really took hold when it was spread by troops fighting or preparing to deploy for combat. By 1919 it had killed 70 million people, tying with the World Wars as second only to the plague, another pandemic in the Middle Ages that in its worst episode killed 75 million in 13 years. Lesson learned: the healthcare system faces collapse when the medical personnel who are tending the sick fall prey to the disease themselves.

Another virus, HIV (AIDS), will kill 90 million in Africa alone by 2025, and malaria continues to kill a million each year.

Pandemics are nothing new and are ever-present; as viruses and bacteria become immune to our antibiotics and antivirals, the potential is high for devastating events in the near future.

The Hwang He and Yangtze rivers flooded in 1931 and killed 140,000 Chinese; another 3 million died from the resulting famine and disease. Another Chinese famine in the late 1950's killed an estimated 40 million. Next to the World

Wars it could be considered the worst man-made disaster of the 20th century because it was caused in large part by agricultural reforms imposed by the Chinese government.

Floods kill with remarkable effectiveness. The 1970 Bangladesh cyclone produced a storm surge responsible for killing half a million people. The Indian Ocean Tsunami just after Christmas of 2004 killed a quarter of a million, many of them Westerners on vacation. It was the worst tsunami ever recorded and was caused by a large undersea earthquake.

Another earthquake in 2011 off Tohoku, Japan, produced a killer tsunami that drowned 12,000 of the 15,000 confirmed casualties. Another 3000 are still missing. This event frightened us all as we watched a series of earthquake- and tsunami-caused nuclear incidents that included serious radiation releases, shattering the concept of "safe" nuclear power.

Hardly a day goes by without news of an earthquake. The Kashmir and Pakistan earthquake of 2005 killed

100,000, and the Haiti quake of 2010 killed a quarter of a million.

As you think about these kinds of events, try to imagine what it would be like if they occurred in your area. Also, take note that large disasters are never as simple as here today, gone tomorrow. There is an enormous list of bad aftereffects that present themselves. Flooding almost always leads to ruined crops, famine, and disease. Earthquakes lead to tsunamis and turn cities into infernos. A volcano can grill surrounding towns, but can also spew enough debris into the atmosphere to cause major drops in world temperature, leading to famine and disease. Nuclear and chemical disasters could go on killing for decades.

Another uncomfortable truth has become quite clear since the turn of the century: the potential size, complexity, and effects from technological disasters paint a picture of truly catastrophic future events. Early technological disasters like Bhopal, Chernobyl, and Hiroshima give us only a hint of ominous, similar events in the future. Add to that cyberterrorism, which is now considered the number one threat to national security and infrastructure. More than other forms of terrorism. More than war. More than pandemics. More than earthquakes or hurricanes.

The Reality about Disaster Planning

A comprehensive list of potential disasters would be larger than this book. If there's one convenient thing about disasters, it's that their effects have some things in common. This means that instead of preparing for each disaster, we prepare for them all based on their commonalities.

It's extremely rare that victims of disaster are satisfied with the response by government or aid groups. There's always blame, and the federal government will surely be the biggest scapegoat. People forget, or ignore, that preparedness starts with the individual. They also forget that outside response depends on a lot of factors: the complexity of the disaster, the location, the access, the budget, and most importantly, the preparation and response at the local level.

How much do you want to prepare and for how long? Traditional advice suggests that everyone should be prepared for a 72-hour disruption in access to services and supplies. That's pretty easy to accomplish. But as we saw in Katrina in 2005 and in the Boulder 100-Year Flood of 2013, even in affluent America, more complicated events may extend that disruption to a week or more.

Although Katrina was a catastrophe for those who perished or suffered in it, in the scale of disasters it was a fairly minor event. Imagine multiple complex disasters occurring at the same time . . . massive earthquakes during severe drought and a major pandemic, for example. Just for fun let's add to the mix that nuclear strike North Korea has been promising us. Huge numbers of people devastated and massive infrastructure collapses in multiple locations. An adequate response to a situation like this will take some time. If you truly want to be prepared for something like this, you're going to have to do a lot more than store a couple of MREs (Meals Ready to Eat) and a first aid kit.

How to Use This Book

It's a fact that most disaster prep books just sit on the shelf. It's amazing how many people are satisfied with the warm and fuzzy feeling of knowing they have a book, as though it will save them when the shit hits the fan.

If you are serious about preparing, here are the author's recommendations:

1. Familiarize yourself with this book, cover to cover. Read the chapter and section texts.

2. Collect as much information as you can without overwhelming yourself. This isn't the only book on disaster prep, and it doesn't hurt to have several.

3. Consult the worksheets and templates to determine the extent to which you wish to prepare and the steps you must take to get there.

4. Get your family involved. They may have other perspectives that will help you do it right.

5. Do some research to find out what disasters are most likely to happen in your area. The local disaster management (civil defense) office will have free information and suggestions.

6. Set aside an hour or two per week and assign a monthly budget that will allow you to accomplish the steps painlessly. Tackling it all at once will be expensive and you'll probably make mistakes.

7. Once you have accomplished your goals, plan to spend a couple of hours per month maintaining what you have put together.

8. Take some classes (more on this later).

9. Stay informed. There are only a few types of disasters that happen without warning. Most disasters develop over time and you can see them coming if you pay attention.

Chapter 1
Managing a Disaster

Let's first look at disaster management from the perspective of the emergency planners and responders whose jobs are to help us manage the mess. It will give you some ideas on how to manage disasters at a personal level.

1. The Phases of Emergency Management

Emergency planners and managers are concerned with four phases: mitigation, preparedness, response, families, and recovery

Mitigation consists of actions that prevent disasters from occurring, or actions that limit the damage done by disasters when they happen. Mitigation is done based on risk assessments. It may be related to physical structure or location, and very often includes insurance protection.

Preparedness is the phase in which action or response plans are developed, and resources identified and stockpiled. In the United States since the early 1980s, planning has traditionally been done using an All-Hazards approach, in which processes that are common to all incidents are defined, and experts responsible for those processes (e.g. communication, shelter, public health, etc.) are tasked to plan for those processes. This approach makes the general plan applicable to virtually any incident, and allows the specifics to be tweaked as needed for specific situations. It also eliminates the complex task of having to build large detailed plans around specific threats.

In the *response* phase, professional and volunteer emergency services teams and organizations mobilize and respond to actual events, providing search & rescue and humanitarian relief or assistance. Individuals and families might shelter in place or evacuate during this phase.

The *recovery* phase starts when the immediate threats to life have passed. The event may still be in progress, and the recovery may take weeks, months, or years. The recovery phase takes into consideration both the restoration of daily life to normal and the mitigation of future events. In other words, now that you know what needs to be done to survive the next event, do it.

2. Emergency & Disaster Professionals and Volunteers

Professional emergency managers come from diversified backgrounds and are responsible for government and community mitigation, preparedness, response, and recovery. Typically in the United States, emergency management positions were political in nature and a manager with real experience in response and management was the exception rather than the rule. The typical manager had a background in law enforcement or fire service, but little training or experience with disaster planning. Since 9/11 the trend has been to hire managers with specific emergency management training or to require managers to acquire specific training while in office. The result has been a significant increase in the competence of our emergency management politicians. There are now international, national, and state professional associations for emergency managers and planners. There are also serious professional certifications and extensive university degree programs.

At the front line of any disaster response are the actual first responders: the fire service, law enforcement, and emergency medical services (EMS).

Emergency Medical Services are the ground, boat, or air ambulances and the EMTs, paramedics, and sometimes nurses and doctors that staff them. In many cities these services are provided by the fire department, although many urban areas are served by commercial ambulance systems. In some countries these services are incorporated within a hospital's emergency department. These services are generally staffed with Emergency Medical Responders (EMR), Emergency Medical Technicians (EMT), or Paramedics. Because the skills and expertise differ enormously between levels, it's a good idea for you to understand what level of responder is used in your local EMS system. Emergency Medical Responders (formerly called First Responders) generally receive 60–80 hours of what is essentially advanced first aid training plus oxygen and automated defibrillator skills. They carry no drugs and perform no advanced-level procedures. A Basic EMT normally trains initially for 120 hours to acquire advanced assessment skills and carry a limited number of drugs (e.g. Epinephrine and injectable doxtrose). EMT-I (intermediate EMT) is a level that requires an additional 40–200 hours of training (depending on State requirements). Responders at this level can start intravenous (IV) lines, do advanced airways, and administer a larger inventory of drugs. The highest level of pre-hospital medicine comes from Paramedics. Paramedic training is an additional 1000–1200 hours and emphasizes advanced life support skills. Paramedics interpret EKGs, start advanced IV lines, administer electrical cardiac therapies, perform advanced airway skills, administer several dozen drugs, and perform a limited number of lifesaving invasive or surgical procedures. All of these pre-hospital medical responders operate under the direct medical control of a physician on an emergency room staff. In the event of an incident, medical control will commonly default to *standing orders*, which give responders greater direct control over treatment options.

New York, N.Y., September 29, 2001—NY Fire Dept. paramedics at the site of the World Trade Center. FEMA News Photo/Andrea Booher.

In addition to professional and volunteer law enforcement, fire, and EMS, there are what are sometimes referred to as *primary responders*. These include rapid-response specialty teams from local governments, such as the Health Department, and commercial infrastructure providers (e.g. utilities and roads).

Secondary responders may include professional and volunteer teams from relief agencies, such as the Red Cross, to provide first aid, supportive care, and basic needs assistance. Such NGO relief agencies will be discussed in a later chapter.

Federally supported community-based volunteer teams may also be put into action such as the Community Emergency Response Teams (CERT) and the regional Medical Reserve Corps (MRC). CERT is a Citizen Corps program focused on disaster preparedness and basic response. These volunteer teams are utilized to provide emergency support when events overwhelm the conventional emergency services. The MRC Program takes advantage of the skill and experience of medical professionals as well as concerned citizens interested in health issues, who volunteer to help their community during large-scale emergency situations.

This, of course, is not a complete list of the responders you'll find in your community. In the United States we are incredibly lucky to have an enormous skilled cadre of professional and volunteer organizations.

3. Incident Command and Control

All emergency response agencies that have been granted federal funds are required to use the Incident Command

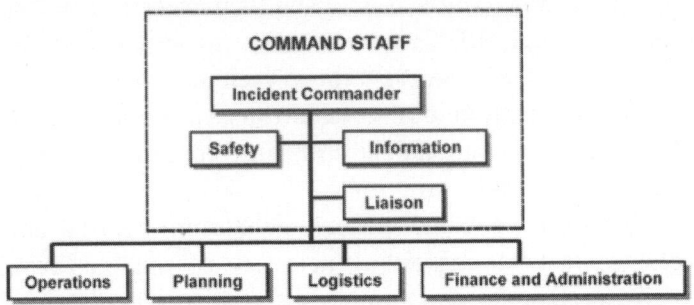

A typical ICS structure. Courtesy of the US Department of Labor.

System (ICS) as their management system for emergency operations. The ICS provides a common framework within which different responding agencies can work together by using common organizational structure and terminology. The ICS is designed to shrink or expand smoothly according to the situation, and it immediately answers the question of who's in charge: the Incident Commander (IC) or Unified Command (UC).

4. Some Notes on National Emergency Management in English-Speaking Countries

The United States

Under the Department of Homeland Security (DHS), the Federal Emergency Management Agency (FEMA) is the lead agency for emergency management. The US and its territories are all within one of ten FEMA regions. Tribal, state, county, and local governments develop emergency management programs and departments, which they operate hierarchically within each region. Emergencies are managed at the most local level possible, utilizing mutual aid agreements with adjacent jurisdictions as needed.

If the emergency is terrorism-related or if declared an "Incident of National Significance," the Secretary of Homeland Security will initiate the National Response Plan (NRP). Under this plan the involvement of Federal resources will be made possible, integrating with the local, county, state, or tribal entities. Management will continue to be handled at the lowest possible level utilizing the National Incident Management System (NIMS).

The **Federal Bureau of Investigation** is responsible for criminal investigation and assistance with lab testing in terrorism incidents.

The **Department of Health and Human Services** tracks and reports health data, conducts medical investigations, manages medical and pharmaceutical stockpiles, exercises powers to quarantine or isolate, and provides public health advice. Agencies within DHHS may also investigate or assist in the investigation of an event.

The **Environmental Protection Agency** tracks environmental contamination and helps manage major chemical incidents.

The Department of Energy provides radiological testing and response.

The **Citizen Corps** is an organization of volunteer service programs, administered locally and coordinated nationally by DHS, which seeks to mitigate disasters and prepare the population for emergency response through public education, training, and outreach. *Community Emergency Response Teams (CERT)*, *Fire Corps* teams, and *Medical Reserve Corps (MRC)* teams are Citizen Corps

CERT training in Puerto Rico.

programs focused on disaster preparedness and teaching basic disaster response skills. These volunteer teams are utilized to provide emergency support when disaster overwhelms the conventional emergency services.

Canada

Public Safety Canada, formerly known as Public Safety and Emergency Preparedness Canada (PSEPC), is Canada's equivalent of FEMA. Each province has an emergency management office and most local levels of government have emergency management offices (known as the EMO). PSC also coordinates and supports efforts of federal organizations ensuring national security and safety. It also works with other levels of government, first responders, community groups, the private sector (including operators of critical infrastructure), and other nations.

PSC's work is based on a wide range of policies and legislation. The Public Safety and Emergency Preparedness Act defines the powers, duties, and functions of PSC. Other acts are specific to fields such as corrections, emergency management, law enforcement, and national security.

United Kingdom

The Civil Contingencies Act 2004 (CCA) defines organizations as Category 1 and 2 Responders. These responders have responsibilities specified by the legislation regarding emergency preparedness and response. The CCA is managed by the Civil Contingencies Secretariat through Regional Resilience Forums and at the local authority level. The CCA works to identify and assess risks and ensures planning and preparations are in place at all levels of government. It also maintains readiness within the central government to respond and provide the support required by local governments, and it aspires to prepare society for, and to recover from, emergencies.

Australia

Emergency Management Australia (EMA) is a federal agency tasked with coordinating government responses to emergency incidents. EMA operates under the Federal Attorney General's Department to develop and implement plans, structures, and arrangements, which are established to bring together the efforts of government, volunteer, and private agencies in a comprehensive and coordinated way. They deal with the whole spectrum of emergency needs including prevention, preparedness, response, and recovery. Its purpose is to adopt a national resilience-based approach to disaster management.

The agency has four divisions: the Security Coordination Branch, Crisis Coordination Branch, Crisis Support Branch, and the Natural Disaster Recovery Program Branch.

The National Strategy for Disaster Resilience, adopted in 2011, was written to provide high-level guidance on disaster management to federal, state, territory and local governments, business and community leaders, and the not-for-profit sector. While the Strategy focuses on priority areas to build disaster resilient communities across Australia, it also recognizes that disaster resilience is a shared responsibility for individuals, households, businesses and communities, as well as for governments.

Australian state and territory authorities have a constitutional responsibility within their boundaries for coordinating and planning the response to disasters and civil emergencies. Under the Commonwealth Government Disaster Response Plan (COMDISPLAN), when the total resources (government, community, and commercial) of an affected state or territory cannot reasonably cope with the needs of the situation, the state or territory government can seek assistance from the Australian Government. Emergency Management Australia is designated as the agency responsible for planning and coordinating that physical assistance.

New Zealand

Disaster management is the responsibility of the Ministry of Civil Defense and Emergency Management (MCDEM). Local councils within each region are unified into regional Civil Defense Emergency Management Groups (CDEMG). Each CDEMG is responsible to ensure an appropriate local response to an incident. Once the local government is overwhelmed, mutual aid is mustered in, and when those resources are overwhelmed the Federal government has the authority to coordinate the national response through the National Crisis Management Center (NCMC) as regulated in the National Civil Defense Emergency Management Plan 2006.

5. International Organizations

United Nations

United Nations responsibility for disaster response rests with the resident coordinator in the effected country. The international response will be coordinated, if requested by the country's government, by the UN office for the Coordination of Human Affairs (UN-OCHA). It may send a UN Disaster Assessment and Coordination (UNDAC) Team.

World Bank

The World Bank has approved hundreds of international operations related to disaster management, amounting to tens of billions of dollars. These include post-disaster reconstruction projects, as well as projects with components aimed at preventing and mitigating disaster impacts.

Common areas of focus for prevention and mitigation projects include flood and fire prevention measures, such as early warning measures and education campaigns, early-warning systems for hurricanes, and earthquake-prone construction.

In June 2006, the World Bank established the Global Facility for Disaster Reduction and Recovery (GFDRR), a partnership of 41 countries and 8 international organizations committed to helping developing countries reduce their vulnerability to natural hazards.

Red Cross/ Red Crescent

National Red Cross and Red Crescent societies often have important roles in responding to disaster. Additionally, the International Federation of Red Cross and Red Crescent Societies (IFRC) may send assessment teams to an affected country.

Hazleton, Pa., September 17, 2011—The Southern Baptist Convention prepares meals for the Red Cross to serve to survivors of a tropical storm.

European Union

The following is taken directly from the EU's CMCP website:

"The main role of the Community Mechanism for Civil Protection is to facilitate cooperation in civil protection assistance interventions in the event of major emergencies which may require urgent response actions. This applies also to situations where there may be an imminent threat of such major emergencies. It is therefore a tool that enhances community cooperation in civil protection matters . . ."

"This may arise if the affected country's preparedness for a disaster is not sufficient to provide an adequate response in terms of available resources. By pooling the civil protection capabilities of the participating states, the Community Mechanism can ensure even better protection primarily of people, but also of the natural and cultural environment as well as property."

"The Community Mechanism for Civil Protection has a number of tools intended to facilitate both adequate preparedness as well as effective response to disasters at a community level.

The Monitoring and Information Centre (MIC) is the operational heart of the Mechanism. It is accessible 24 hours a day and gives countries access to a platform, to a one-stop-shop of civil protection means available amongst the all the participating states. Any country inside or outside the Union affected by a major disaster can make an appeal for assistance through the MIC. It acts as a communication hub at headquarters level between participating states, the affected country and dispatched field experts. It also provides useful and updated information on the actual status of an ongoing emergency. Last but not least, the MIC plays a co-ordination role by matching offers of assistance put forward by participating states to the needs of the disaster-stricken country."

6. Personal and Family Emergency Management

Disasters can happen suddenly, without warning, and the effects can linger for years. The immediate effects may include injury, homelessness, or loss of water, gas, and electrical services. Emergency services may be so overwhelmed that it may be days before they can respond to your situation. To ensure the safety and well-being of you and your family, most government agencies and non-government organizations (NGOs) recommend you stockpile a minimum of 72 hours of supplies to handle your basic needs. They also recommend that you make a simple plan, train with your family on an occasional basis, and make minor structural modifications to the home. A smaller version of the preparedness kit is recommended for the family car. We'll cover all this in a later chapter.

Obviously, in a long-term widespread disaster a 72-hour kit will not be enough. As water, food, shelter, and comfort items become harder to find, they may become precious commodities with a higher trade value than cash. In a worst-case scenario we could be bartering with these items, and those who have them will be in a far better position to survive than those who don't. When seen in that light, a one or two year supply makes incredibly good sense.

When it comes to stockpiling those supplies, how do we determine what it is we'll need to fill our basic needs? Although we all have our specialty and comfort items we think we can't live without, truly basic needs all fit under Maslow's Hierarchy. The lower level needs, those that are physiological, are the most primitive. Without satisfying them almost immediately and consistently, we cannot survive. The farther up we travel in the pyramid, the longer we can go without meeting the needs at that level. Apply this concept to your decisions on preparation. A 72-hour kit is just what it sounds like: a bare-bones survival package. Preparing for a months-long or years-long incident, on the other hand, means also preparing to meet the needs farther and farther up the triangle, but even then our primary focus

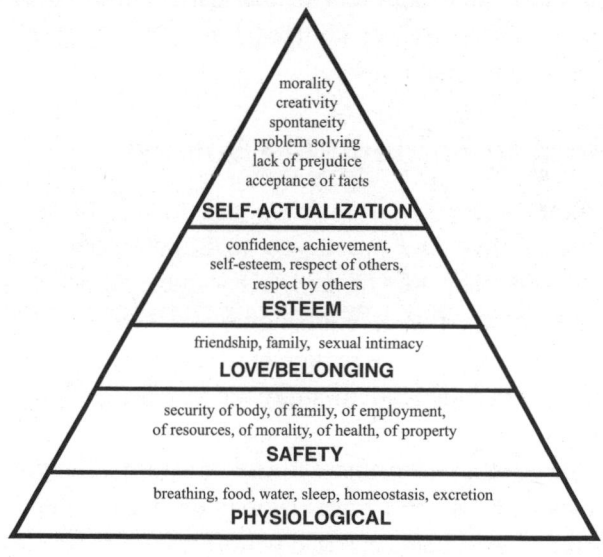

Maslow's hierarchy of needs.

should be on primitive physiological needs and safety. Survival first. Everything else is icing on the cake.

7. Business Emergency Management

Small businesses are the foundation of America's economy. According to Ready.gov, small businesses account for more than 99 percent of all companies with employees, employ more than 50 percent of all private sector workers, and provide nearly 45 percent of the nation's payroll. Businesses, large and small, must be ready to survive and recover to ensure personal, local, and national economies and to protect our business investments.

Doing nothing is not an option. Experience shows that even relatively short-term disruption can destroy a business. It also shows that disasters in one part of the world can shut down businesses in another. Some relatively simple planning can mitigate this.

8. Sorting Through the Bullshit

Governments are usually very open and truly want to share what they DO want you to know about disaster preparedness. The FEMA and CDC sites and Ready.gov, for example, are full of educational and media materials. FEMA's Emergency Management Institute is a master source of free, independent-study training accessible to the public.

On the other hand, there's a lot of information governments at all levels don't want you to know. Censorship is not dead, and governments can and will withhold whatever they want from the public under the rationalization that sensitive sources and national intelligence must be protected: ignorance is bliss and prevents panic, and censorship is good for national security. The underlying truth is much simpler: uncomfortable information is politically dangerous. Waste, corruption, and procrastination are an embarrassment. So where do we turn for comprehensive information? Unfortunately the answer is the internet and media. The internet is subject to fanaticism and exaggeration, and media to bias and sensationalism. All things considered, most people who want information now get it from the internet because it's easily available and it's available in bulk. Social networking makes it interactive and progressive. Smart phones and tablets put it at our fingertips 24/7. This is truly the age of information. Research, networking, and effective bullshit filtering skills are now as essential to survival as that 72-hour kit gathering dust on your shelf.

Chapter 2
Basic Personal Preparedness

A quick search on the internet will bring up hundreds of sites with excellent information on how to prepare yourself and your family for disasters. Each lists a number of steps to ensure adequate preparation. Although the steps may be in different order, they all have most of these components in common:

1. Getting information about **local hazards** and the emergencies that you and your family are most likely to encounter. While this may seem unimportant to you, knowledge like this reduces panic and confusion. For example, biologic warfare and pandemics are much less terrifying when you understand the walking dead zombie thing is a fairy tale, that you can avoid getting sick by using good hygiene, and perhaps earthquakes and hurricanes are bigger, more real threats you can actually prepare for.
2. Detailing **family communication strategies**.
3. Learning **how to shut off the utilities**.
4. Developing, rehearsing, and maintaining **an emergency plan**.
5. Assembling **disaster supplies kits**.
6. Gaining familiarity with **community warning systems and evacuation routes**.
7. Learning where to seek **shelter and how to shelter in place**.
8. Learning about **community, school, and workplace disaster plans**.

9. Obtaining adequate **insurance.**
10. Collecting and inventorying **vital records and documents.**

If you don't read any other chapter in this book, read this one. We'll go through the basic steps here and provide some simple ideas that will help you develop a reasonable plan and make other practical preparations. To make it even simpler, we'll then walk through the steps in flow-chart style by mapping out the concepts so you can see them all on one page. When you're ready to roll up your sleeves and get to work, find the appropriate section map and work out from the middle.

The Basics.

1. Knowing About Local Hazards

Go to the local emergency management (usually a county office in the US) and the local health department offices and pick up the prep materials they have available to you. **Visit their websites** for even more information. Contact the local Red Cross, the local responders (police, fire, emergency medical services) for additional information. Visit the Pacific Disaster Center worldwide Hazard Atlas on www. pdc.org. A particularly good source of hazard information and planning aids are some private utility offices (gas, electric, water). If you want more detail, get it on the internet by visiting the State disaster management site. These are usually under the State offices of Public Safety or Homeland Security. FEMA and the CDC websites also have specific hazard information, including the recent history of disaster declarations and health emergencies in each state. FEMA and EPA sites have hazard map databases. The FEMA map site moves like cold molasses and can be confusing, so be patient.

The purpose of this research is to establish what the prominent hazards are and what disaster-related emergencies are most likely to occur. As you learn about them, log them into your knowledge map:

2. Family Communications Plan

How many hours of the day are all members of your family at home, together, under one roof? Families may not be together when a disaster occurs, and events can easily pull families apart.

A critical part of communication is face-to-face contact. The family should designate a meeting place outside the

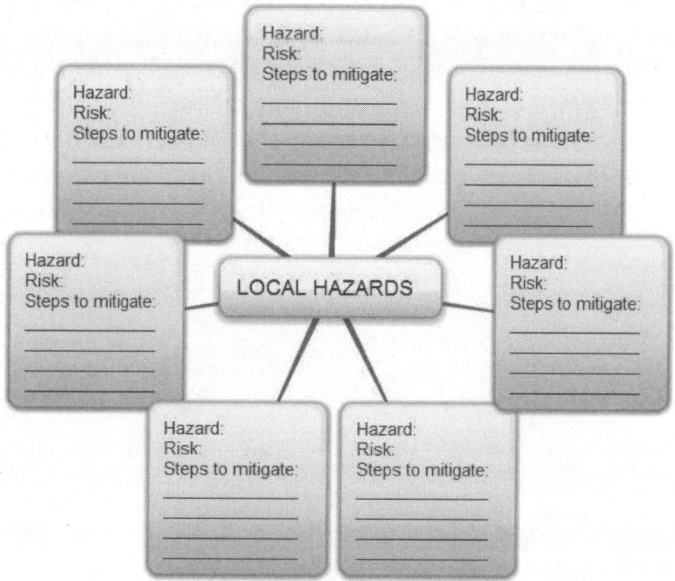

A hazard is an event with the potential to cause harm, for instance, an earthquake or flood. Level of risk is dependent on how often such events occur in your areas and how serious the harm (damages and injuries) can be. In this chart, list the local hazards and estimate the level of risk as low, medium, or high.

home for emergencies and local disasters, and another outside the neighborhood for more widespread problems.

All members of the family should know how to make contact with other family members and designated contacts outside the neighborhood and outside of the state. These are contacts your family members can notify that they are safe and where they are located. Establish phone and cell numbers as well as email addresses for these contacts and numbers for emergency services (poison control, 911, etc.).

It's easy to put all these numbers on a contact card or even a photocopy of the communications worksheet (see below) that can be given to each family member to be kept in their purse or wallet. Keep a copy by each house phone and save it on your smart phones as well. On the bottom of the worksheet, write clear directions to your home that can be read over the phone when calling for help. Send a copy to

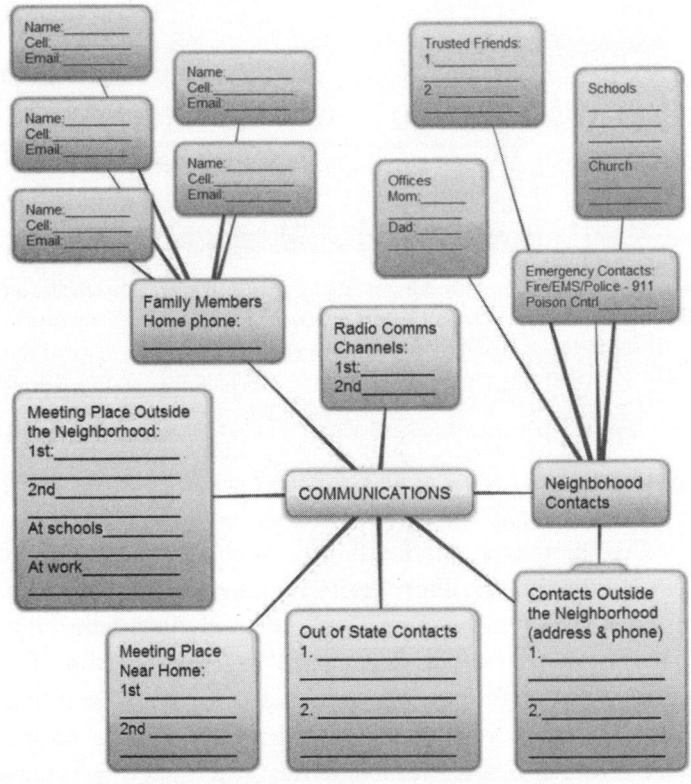

Communications worksheet.

school and one to your boss, and include a couple of copies in each disaster kit.

3. Shutting Off the Utilities

The reader might find it odd that shutting off the utilities is listed here, this early in the discussion. Not so odd, when you consider flood damage from broken water lines, explosions from damaged gas lines, and house fires from damaged electrical circuits. Potential loss of life can be prevented by turning off utilities immediately after an acute disaster such as a major earthquake. It's very possible your local authorities will plead with you to turn off utilities, and this can be very confusing if you haven't planned for this ahead of time.

4. Shutting Off Electricity

Electricity can electrocute someone or create sparks that can ignite a natural gas leak or spilled flammables. To shut off electricity:

1. Find the circuit boxes. There may be more than one. The box may be equipped with fuses or circuit breakers. For a fuse box, find a knife switch handle or a pullout fuse marked "MAIN." If it's a breaker panel or box, open the metal door. The main circuit should be clearly marked showing on and off positions.

2. Remove all the small fuses or turn off all the small breakers before shutting off the main breaker or pulling the main fuse.

3. If you have sub-panels adjacent to the main fuse or breaker panel, or in other parts of the house, shut them off before you shut off the main.

Not all circuit boxes look the same. This box has individual breakers above and below the "main" breaker.

5. Shutting Off the Gas

After the event, if you don't smell gas or you don't have severe damage to your home, you can probably skip turning off the gas, but do be aware that natural gas fires and explosions commonly occur in damaged structures and pipelines. Shutoff procedures may be different region to region and according to the metering device. Talk to the local gas company beforehand for advice.

If you do smell or hear leaking gas, get out immediately. Open a window on the way out if it's possible to do so

The box has individual breakers for areas in the house, but no "main" switch.

without wasting precious time. Turn off the gas main outside and inform the gas company about the leak.

The main gas shutoff is usually located outside on a pipe coming out of the ground into the gas meter. If the gas meter is located in a cabinet enclosure built into a building or located inside the building, the gas service shutoff valve will be outside on a section of gas service pipe next to the building near the gas meter, or in an underground box in the sidewalk. If you live in an apartment or dormitory, or rent an office in a large building, there may be multiple meters with individual shutoff valves near the gas meters, and a master valve for the entire building where the gas pipe comes out of the ground. Ask your landlord which is yours.

Turn the valve crosswise to the pipe using a 12- to 15-inch adjustable pipe or crescent wrench or other suitable tool.

All the pilot lights in your building will go out when you turn the valve off. You will need to have the gas company or other qualified individual (plumber, contractor, or trained house owner) relight every pilot when turning the gas back on. Not relighting all the pilot lights could result in a gas buildup and explosion in your home.

Clear the area around the main gas shutoff valve and mark the valve with fluorescent duct tape or paint for quick and easy access in case of emergency. A wrench should be left attached to the pipe next to the shutoff valve or in another accessible location nearby.

A main gas shutoff valve. When the holes are aligned, the valve can be padlocked closed.

6. Shutting Off Water Lines

Broken water lines can cause severe damage and spread disease. Precious water can be lost at a rate of 15 gallons or more per minute from a single house line.

To shut off the water you must find the shutoff valve where it enters the house or where it ties into the municipal water system. Once you find it, plainly label it (bright duct tape, paint, or flagging). If it's from a municipal supplier it will probably have a water meter and shutoff valve grouped together near the street in an underground access hatch. Inside the hatch you will find either a wheel, paddle, or valve with a straight metal flange across the top. Turn a wheel or paddle clockwise until it won't turn any more. Remember: "righty tighty, lefty loosy." If it's a metal flange, use a pipe wrench to operate it. It should close with a quarter turn. If a wrench is required, leave one near the valve for emergencies.

A corroded valve is a serious inconvenience when you need to turn off the water in a hurry, and may be difficult or impossible to close. Check yours *before* there's an emergency, and if it's starting to corrode, get it replaced; in the meantime stash a double-bagged and zip-locked vice-grip wrench near the hatch.

Most homes also have additional shutoff valves that control portion or sections of the house and yard water supply. You might find a hose bib and shutoff valve where the water main enters the house. In cold weather locations the shutoff may be in the basement or inside the house itself. This valve will typically shut off all the water inside the house but not outside.

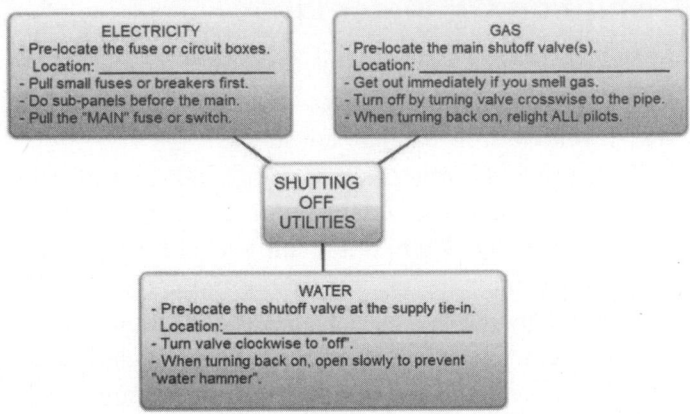

Utilities worksheet and shut-off instructions.

7. Developing an Emergency Plan

If you've gotten this far in the book and have been doing your worksheets faithfully, you've got a lot of your plan already completed. In fact, your plan is going to contain all 10 items of information we earlier described as the *basics for preparation.* This includes information on warning systems and signals, including the Emergency Alert system and NOAA Weather Radio, safety plans, communication plans, integration of community and school plans, awareness of workplace plans, insurance and vital records data, plans for special needs and pets, and the assembly and storage of disaster and supply kits. All of these will be covered in detail as you progress through this book.

8. Disaster Supply Kits

Survival after a disaster might require providing your own food and water for several days. Basic utilities could be cut

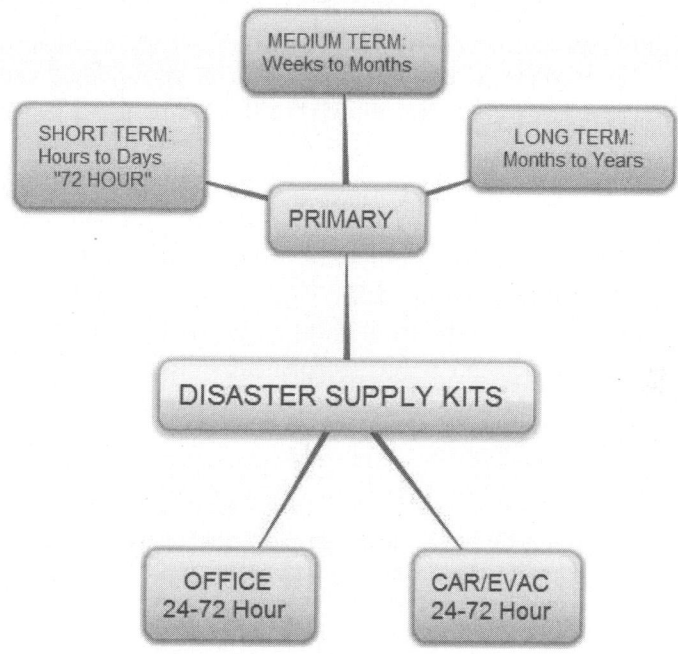

Disaster supply kits.

off for weeks. Evacuation means leaving the comforts of home behind. If there's any advanced warning, the store shelves will be empty well before the worst is over. If there's no warning, the shelves will be inaccessible by the time survivors are already in trouble.

It's smart to have different kits for home, work, and the car. The government would like you to build a home kit that has enough food, water, and essential supplies to see you and your family through at least three days. That and a one-day car kit are all we're going to work with in this chapter. Other experts recommend more extensive kits for longer periods. It's not unreasonable to put away enough supplies to see you through three weeks, three months, or even three years. In a worst case scenario, your supply can be bartered as well as consumed. We'll work on those larger kits in later chapters.

Your personal kit should contain at least a one-day supply of essentials: clothing, sturdy shoes, and outerwear for changing weather conditions. Keep it in a backpack, ready to grab when needed.

Everyone's 72-hour kit will be different. Customize it for your lifestyle and budget, and use the following checklist to guide you through the process. The components of your kit might include:

- Containers to pack it all in. Several small containers would be easier to move than one or two big ones. Large buckets and bins can be used for carrying water and as portable potties or wash basins.
- A three day supply of non-perishable food – three meals per person and pet per day
- Three day supply of water – one half to one gallon of drinking water per person and per pet per day
  - Consider packing a water filter.
- Portable battery or crank-powered radio or television and extra batteries. Replace batteries annually.
- LED flashlight or headlamp per person with extra batteries.
- First aid kit, with notes or small reference volumes
- Sanitation and hygiene items
  - moist towelettes
  - toilet paper
  - washcloth & towel
  - soap

- hand sanitizer
- razors
- contact lens solution
- feminine supplies
- sunscreen
- insect repellent
- small mirror
- toothbrush & toothpaste
- Matches and waterproof container, or a couple of disposable lighters.
- Whistle
- Multi-tool pocket knife.
- Extra clothing. One complete change per person, including socks, undies, shirt, and pants.
- Cold climate items:
  - Shell parka
  - Insulating coat (fleece) or sweater
  - Warm hat
  - Mittens or gloves
  - Sleeping bag or warm blankets
- Kitchen accessories and cooking utensils, including a can opener
- Photocopies of credit cards, identification cards, driver's license, passport, immunizations records, wills, deeds, stocks, bonds, contracts, bank numbers, and inventories
- Cash. Try for a minimum of $30 per person per day. Traveler's and personal checks are not a good choice. Pack your credit cards along.
- Specialty items:
  - Prescription medications
  - Eye glasses, contact lens kit with solution
  - Denture supplies
  - Small sewing kit

- Infant items: formula, diapers, bottles, pacifiers
- Small entertainment items (paperback books, playing cards, etc.)
- Extra house & car keys
- Paper goods and pens, pencils
- Local telephone directory
- Family contacts card
- Contractor-weight garbage bags (for garbage sacks, emergency shelters, emergency rain coats, potty bucket liners, etc.)
- Fire extinguisher
- Work gloves
- Camp shovel

The author's personal 72-hour kit for Hawaii includes ready-to-eat meals requiring no stove or kitchen utensils, and electronics (communications and lighting) that rely on disposable batteries and small solar chargers. A cold-climate kit would include cold-weather clothing, a sleeping bag and tent, and a stove and kitchen utensils for warm food and drinks.

Choose easy-carry containers like duffle bags, backpacks, and buckets for mobility.

The author's car kit for his Hawaii vehicle. It includes standard vehicle emergency items, tools, personal protective equipment, food, water, and electronics. It also includes a solar charger that can be used to charge phones, rechargeable batteries, and the vehicle battery.

- Cooking stove and fuel
- Cooking utensils
- Mess kit
- Dishwashing soap

A *car kit* is wise to have not only for disasters, but for simple mini-tragedies like getting stranded. It should contain the essentials for a day or two, also planning for wet and cold weather, as well as some road gear such as flares and jumper cables. Note that battery-operated safety flares with multiple flashing LEDs are available. You might also include a small tool kit, an inverter, a GPS and extra batteries, a roll of bright surveyor's tape, a tire repair kit and a can of tire sealant, an electric tire inflator, a tow line, and 5-pound bag of salt or sand.

A Warning on Gadgets

Don't confuse preparedness with paranoia. Somebody out there is making money off paranoia, selling us all kinds of gadgets we don't need. At best they're harmless. At worst they're dangerous. Before you spend the money on exotic or trendy items, ask yourself these questions:

- Do I really need it?
- Can I get a better price somewhere else?
- Can I improvise my own version of it?
- Does the sales associate have a clue what he's talking about?

Let's look, for instance, at gas masks. Real military-style gas masks are very pricey, and you have to know how to put them on and how to maintain them if they're going to do you any good. And are you seriously going to carry that thing around with you 24/7? Even if you just happen to have it with you when something happens, chances are you won't know until it's too late. Or you'll have the wrong filters, or not remember how to put it on and test the fit properly to get a seal.

There are lots of these gimmicks out there, from masks to skyscraper parachute escape kits. Very cool, but don't be fooled. Spend your money on things you'll actually need to survive.

9. Warning Systems and Evacuation

Ranging from the family dog to sophisticated gas and smoke detectors, most families have more than one personal alert system. These will be discussed in later chapters. Refer to them as you do the Warnings and Evacuation worksheet.

Locally, officials may provide warnings and information through the media, sirens, telephones, or loudspeakers. Check with your local agencies to learn pre-designated evacuation routes, especially if you live in flood or tsunami-prone areas.

Nationally, The Emergency Alert System is a method of alerting the public to disasters. Federal regulations require all TV and radio stations, both broadcast and cable, to participate in EAS tests and activations. EAS was designed to be a cooperative effort between government agencies and local broadcasters. EAS is the fastest and most reliable way to alert large areas or isolated locations to major emergencies.

The EAS consists of a network of broadcast stations across the nation with equipment designed to allow the

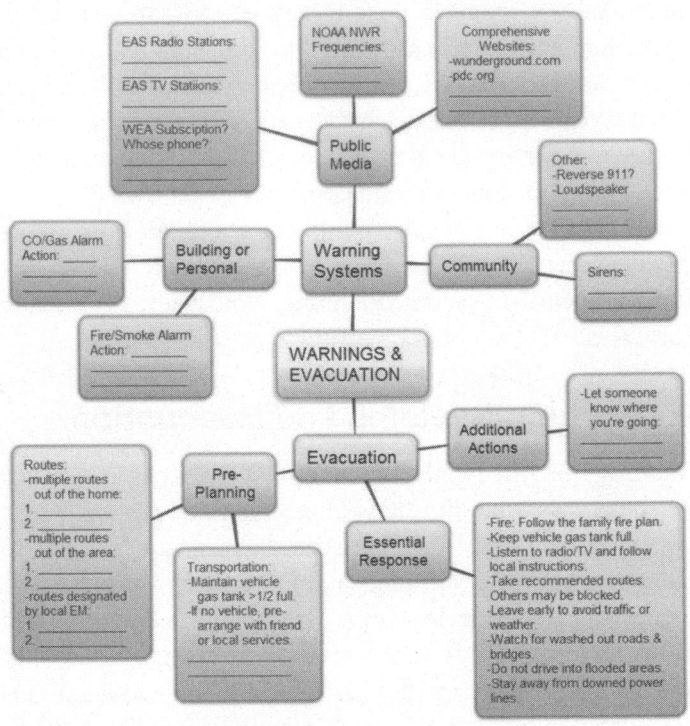

Warning & evacuation worksheet.

automatic transmission and broadcasting of emergency messages. Alerts pass from station to station and on to the air automatically, without human intervention. The state offices of Homeland Security and Emergency Management activate the EAS for state-level alerts.

The EAS incorporates coding that allows specific locations to be alerted. Only affected areas receive the alert, so as not to alarm locations not affected. The EAS allows alert information to be digitally coded, along with standard audio information, so that television stations can have a screen crawl that displays the text of the alert.

The National Oceanic and Atmospheric Administration (NOAA) Weather Radio (NWR) is a nationwide network of radio stations that broadcast continuous weather information to specifically configured radio receivers. Many Ham, GMRS, and FRS radio, and even smart phones and some weather websites, are also configured to receive NWR. NWR weather forecasts are regional, and not all regions are covered. To find out if your region is covered, go to nws.noaa.gov.

The National Weather Service (NWS) broadcasts warnings, watches, forecasts, and other non-weather related hazard information 24/7. The same information can be found on their website, www.weather.gov. During an emergency, NWS forecasters interrupt routine broadcasts and send a special tone activating local weather radios. Radios equipped with a special alarm tone feature sound an alert to give you immediate information about a life-threatening situation.

NWR broadcasts warning and post-event information for all types of local or regional hazards: weather (e.g. tornadoes, floods), natural emergencies, technological emergencies, and national emergencies of any type. Working with other federal agencies and the Federal Communications Commission's Emergency Alert System (EAS), NWR is an all-hazards radio and internet network, making it the most comprehensive weather and emergency information available to the public.

Wireless Emergency Alerts (WEA) are emergency messages sent by certain government agencies through your mobile carrier. These include local and state public safety agencies, FEMA, the FCC, the Department of Homeland

Security, and the National Weather Service. WEA alerts can be sent to your mobile device without having to download an app or subscribe to a service.

WEA alerts look like a text message and include a special tone and vibration, both repeated twice. The message shows the type and time of the alert, the action you should take, and the agency issuing the alert. When a message is received, get more details from your favorite TV or radio station, NOAA Weather Radio, news website, desktop application, mobile application, or other reliable source.

WEA is free and messages do not count towards texting limits on your wireless plan.

Regardless of whose information or decision it is that causes you to evacuate or be evacuated, there are some standard evacuation guidelines.

- Maintain your vehicle with at least a half tank of fuel. Keep a full tank if evacuation seems likely.
- If you have no vehicle, pre-plan transportation with a neighbor or friend, or with the local government.
- Bring along your disaster kits and important documents, including medical histories.
- Plan multiple routes out of each area: home, local, regional. Write them down in the appropriate blanks of the worksheet.
- Listen to your portable radio. Know and listen to local TV and radio stations, and tune in for information and instructions. Local emergency management may issue specific information and designate evacuation routes. Follow their instructions.
- Wear sturdy clothes and shoes that provide protection.

- Unplug electrical equipment. Leave refrigerators and freezers plugged in and turned on unless there's a risk of flooding.
- Close and lock doors and windows.
- Gather your family and go immediately if you are instructed to do so.
- Leave early enough to avoid being trapped by traffic or severe weather.
- Follow recommended evacuation routes. Do not take shortcuts—they may be blocked.
- Watch for washed out roads and bridges. Do not drive into flooded areas.
- Stay away from downed power lines.

10. Sheltering

You may find yourself at a community shelter. You may find yourself sheltering at home, school, or the office. It's not inconceivable that someday you'll be sheltering in a tent or vehicle. If you've done your worksheets and put your plan together, you'll be able to endure the temporary misery of whatever shelter you've been able to find. Shelters are explained in detail in a later chapter. Please refer to that chapter as needed as you fill out your worksheets.

11. Community, School, and Workplace Plans

Ask the local emergency manager if there's a disaster plan for the community or county. They will always tell you yes, whether they have a recent one or not. Rural communities are notorious for keeping their plans "in the head" of the local sheriff or mayor. If your local official claims that a plan exists, ask them how to obtain a copy. For security reasons many communities are restricting their plans and will only show them on a "need to know" basis. Don't be offended if you don't get access. If you do manage to get the plan in your hands, take note of what it contains and what hazards it covers. Look for what pertains to you and your family. Check how often it's supposed to be updated. If it looks out of date, mention it to someone.

Again, ask the administrators of your children's schools or day care about their emergency plan. Get specific information about how the school will plan to communicate with families during an emergency, and how they plan to feed and care for the children when the school is locked down or sheltering in place. Also, inquire about evacuation and sheltering procedures.

In light of recent events, schools are under particular pressure to lock down the facility and maintain a strict accounting of each child in the event of a crisis. It's likely you'll not be able to get in to sign out or talk to your child until the lockdown is terminated. Emergency officials and the media will issue instructions.

If you have not already been given adequate information about your workplace emergency plan, ask your boss to show it to you or explain specifically what the plan is and how you fit into it.

12. Records and Property Inventory

Part of your planning should include collecting and inventorying vital records. These include:

- Internet usernames and passwords
- Insurance Policies
- Deeds and property records
- Contracts
- Important financial records not saved electronically
- Medical records for each member of the family, including name, allergies, medications, immunizations, and medical history or any problem that has been or could be a threat to life or limb.
- Birth certificates

Keep documents in a waterproof container or safety box.

13. Insurance

Insurance is a gamble that buys peace of mind. It's a transfer of risk, from us to the insurance company, and is supposed to protect us against financially damaging events. We are gambling that the insurance company will cover us when something bad happens. They are gambling that nothing bad will happen, or if it does, that we won't make a claim. It's risky business. Often the decision about whether to be insured isn't ours to make. It may be too expensive or the insurance company may simply refuse to cover us. Even if we do get insured, most of us don't understand exactly how we're covered or what we're covered for. Most unsuccessful claims are submitted in good faith by policy holders who really thought they were covered, and they are denied based on some obscure exclusion or exception in the policy that takes the customer by surprise. Even if your claim is successful, you could lose your policy or your rates could soar. Insurance companies determine their rates largely on location, structure, risk, and property value. Other factors for eligibility and rates are a little more surprising: credit scores, marital status, occupation, gender, level of education, and your history of filing insurance claims. It can be horribly unfair and downright unethical, but that's the nature of gambling.

For anyone thinking about disaster insurance, there are five major factors that will determine the availability of the policy and your own willingness to pay for it: finances, location, type and age of the structure, its dollar value, and your level of comfort. Your choice to purchase insurance should be based on those factors and backed up by a sound awareness of what your policy will and won't promise to do.

The first thing you should do is examine your current homeowners insurance policy to determine exactly what it will cover. Discuss any questions with your insurance agent, then find out where and how you can get more coverage. This, of course, will depend on the type of disaster you're trying to insure against. Most policies don't cover flooding or earthquakes. Your insurance might not cover other disasters that your location is particularly at risk for. In that case, you'll have to go hunting for coverage.

Keep in mind many insurance policies only cover structural damage to the home, and not damage to landscaping, outbuildings, or septic/sewer systems.

After looking around you may decide to purchase new insurance or modify your old policy. If you decide NOT to have insurance, make certain your reasons are sound. Often the reasons are one or more of the following: high prices (premiums), high deductibles that must be paid before the policy applies, inadequate coverage, no legal or mortgage requirement to insure, or dumb reliance on the government and relief agencies for help.

If you believe the government and relief agencies are going to pull your ass out of the financial fire, think again. There's no disaster Santa Claus, and here's why: The majority of "disasters" are not declared states of emergency by the President, which is a step required before FEMA and the Small Business Administration step in and offer financial assistance. Federal grants will not have to be paid back, but they are very limited and generally reserved for those who are uninsured. On the other hand, loans must be paid back and will add to the overall financial burden on the property. Also, loans are restricted to the amount your insurance doesn't cover. On top of all that, shortages of construction materials and contractors after a disaster tend to result in inflated repair costs. In the end, you are not likely to break even on your losses.

If you're thinking you might not purchase insurance, here are some considerations before making the final decision:

- *Are you downplaying the risk* in your area? Many, if not most, homeowners and builders are in denial about the risks the scientists and local emergency managers have warned them about. In the US, most of us live in active earthquake fault zones and don't even know it. Many live in hurricane zones and simply choose to ignore it.

- *Have you considered the potential effects on your financial future?* If your home is destroyed, are you prepared to walk away from your mortgage and ruin your credit?

- *Do you have access to substantial emergency money?* Consider getting a home equity line of credit before a disaster strikes. After the disaster, your home might be valueless.

- *What forms of affordable mitigation might minimize the effects of a disaster? Would the cost of special construction or modifications be less than the cost of an insurance policy?*

When you decide to buy insurance, consider your existing insurance coverage. Check on local insurance requirements, state hurricane and earthquake insurance pools, and flood insurance from FEMA's National Flood Insurance Program. Flood insurance may be required for your mortgage if you live in a designated Special Flood Hazard area.

Insurance for Specific Disasters

Hurricane, tornado, and wind damage. This varies by state. In many areas, your homeowner's policy already covers wind and hail damage, but coverage for hurricane-related flooding will probably not be automatic. There are some state and private windstorm insurance pools. Ask your insurance agent and the state office of emergency management.

Earthquake insurance is normally available at additional cost from your homeowner's insurance company. In some states where the risk is exceptionally high and private insurance may be prohibitively expensive, there may be a state earthquake insurance pool that offers a more reasonable rate. Again, check with the state office responsible for emergency management.

Flood insurance can be a real pain. If it's not available for your homeowner's policy, try FEMA's National Flood Insurance Program (NFIP). The NFIP works in cooperation with private insurance companies, and basically subsidizes their losses.

Many people assume their policies cover them for flooding, when in fact they are only covered for certain types of flood damage or for none at all. There may be a waiting period for coverage after you've purchased your policy. If your insurance company can exploit any sort of loophole or nebulous wording in your policy, it will deny your claim. Some insurance companies will blacklist you even if you just file a claim.

Insurance can certainly be a conundrum. Shop around for the best coverage at the best price. Pay attention to horror stories about certain insurance companies. Make your decisions based on sound research.

Keep current copies of policies with other important papers in a sturdy waterproof container.

14. Progress Check

Use this checklist to see if you've made substantial progress with personal and family preparedness:

- I have contacted the local emergency management office, utilities providers, and the American Red Cross to learn about:
  - Likely hazards and risks
  - How you'll be warned
  - How to prepare for specific types of disasters
- I have completed evacuation planning.
  - I have made an escape plan for escape from each room and from the building.
  - I have considered escape plans for anyone in my family with special needs.
  - I have explained the escape plan and evacuation plans to family or co-workers.

- I have involved my family.
  - We have discussed types of hazards in our community.
  - I have explained how to prepare and respond.
  - We have discussed what to do if told to evacuate.
  - We have rehearsed our escape and evacuation plans.
  - We have discussed our family emergency communications plan.
- I have devised a communications plan.
  - I have picked two meeting places:
    - ◆ A location a safe distance from the house if there's a fire
    - ◆ A location outside the area if the house can't be reached
  - I have picked an out-of-state friend to be a "check-in person" for everyone to call.
  - I have posted the contact list and emergency numbers by every telephone.
- I have prepared for a short-term disaster.
  - I have shown responsible family members where and how to shut off the utilities.
  - I have installed smoke detectors on each level of the home, especially near bedrooms. I test them monthly and will change the batteries every six months, when daylight savings time changes.
  - I have surfed the internet or checked with the local fire department to learn about home and wildland fire hazards in my community.
  - I have prepared a 72-hour disaster supply kit and packed it so it becomes my "bug-out kit" in case I need to evacuate.
  - I have prepared a 24-hour kit for the car.
  - I have taken a basic first aid course (>10 hours)

- I have met with my neighbors to:
  - Plan how the neighborhood can work together after a disaster.
  - Learn what talents and skills exist in your neighborhood (medical, technical, logistical, etc.).
  - Discuss how the neighborhood can cooperate to help neighbors with special needs (the elderly, disabled, non-English speaking, etc.).
  - Arrange for child care if parents can't get home during a disaster.

Chapter 3
Communications Technology

1. Accessing Public Information

There's an endless supply of free information available on disaster planning. The internet and your local disaster management office are good places to start your research. That said, immediately prior to and during a disaster, updated instructions and real-time information may be not be as easy to access. For most of the population, the best source of information will be radio and television. Listen to broadcast and cable radio and television stations for news and instructions, and follow the advice of local emergency officials.

As technology and planning improves, public access to warnings and real-time information is rapidly improving, and may consist of any or many of the following: outdoor sirens, NOAA Weather Radio, Reverse 911 Mass Call, internet and wireless notification by email and cell phone text alerting ("internet alerting"), radio scanners, and the Emergency Alert System on broadcast TV and radio stations. It's recommended you use multiple sources of information rather than putting your faith in a single source. If you filled out the worksheets in Chapter 3 you've already established what sources are best for you and your plan. If you haven't done that yet, for right now, here are some basic steps to take advantage of real-time information resources:

Now, before an incident:

- Purchase a battery or crank operated weather alert radio and store it with extra batteries.
- Learn your local siren system.
- Subscribe to a wireless email alerting system to receive alerts on your cell phone. Many smart phones are factory-loaded with emergency warning apps. WEA is free and does not require downloading an app. Adjunct apps are available free or for a small charge.

During an incident:

- Listen to broadcast radio, television, or your chosen information source.

2. Communications Systems

Telecommunications systems can be categorized as wired or wireless, and within that framework are a lot of variations.

Telephone Systems

Landlines

POTS (Plain Old Telephone Systems) are tied together through above or below ground hardwired systems. The POTS network is also called the *public switched telephone network (PSTN)*. These traditional systems are powered through the phone line and will work during a power outage if the lines and stations are functioning. In an emergency, local lines may be tied up, but long distance service might be available. Portable (not to be confused with cell) phones need a power source to function. Pay phones might work when other POTS lines don't. Only use POTS lines if absolutely necessary during a disaster. 911 will need all available lines.

Other wired telephone services include digital communications lines, such as ISDN and DSL. The main differences between POTS and non-POTS services are speed and bandwidth. POTS is generally restricted to about 52 Kbps (52,000 bits per second). Although POTS is overshadowed by the cell phone system, *POTS remains more reliable and is the medium for basic Enhanced 911.*

Cell Phones

Cell phones rely on radio waves between the phone and a cellular tower. The radio channels can be overloaded, so call only when necessary. Also, cell service can be affected by power outages at the local servers or by destruction of relay and cell towers.

Turn your cell off when not in use to conserve the battery. Cell phones can be charged in your car or with solar, crank, and emergency chargers.

Signal triangulation allows Enhanced 911 systems to determine a general location from where cell phone calls originate, and as GPS is integrated into cell phones, E-911 will have the capability to pinpoint your exact location to within 50 feet.

Satellite Phones

Satellite phones transmit through low-orbiting satellites. They do not work well indoors without an external antenna and, compared to cell phones, are heavy and expensive.

The old adage *any port in a storm* certainly applies to disaster prep and modern technology. Cell phones, many radios, and other electronic devices can be charged via USB ports on solar chargers, battery-powered emergency chargers, and 12V DC car plugs. Many devices that can be charged via USB can also be used to transfer that charge to another device via USB.

An interesting recent development in satellite communicator technology are the Satellite Early Notification Devices (SEND), which combine personal rescue-beacon GPS technology with send-and-receive text messaging. Most of these devices pair with your Smart phone via Bluetooth to access this feature. Unlike sat phones, SEND devices are as small as your Smart phone. Like sat phones, SEND devices are expensive. Both devices require a service subscription and message or minutes fees.

Function	Frequencies or Bands	Transmitting Power	License Requirements or Fees	Pros and Cons
CB Citizen's Band	40 channels within the 27 MHz frequency band	4 watts	No license requirement	Short range (4–6 miles). May be used for business or personal. Emergency organizations include REACT
FRS Family Radio Service	14 UHF channels with 38 privacy tones	0.5 watts	No license requirement. No fees.	Short range. Repeaters not legal. Mass marketed and very inexpensive.
GMRS General Mobile Radio Service	22 UHF channels when combined with FRS	1–5 watts	License required. Fee: $85 (2013) No exam.	Short range, but repeaters are legal. FRS and GMRS radios share channels 1–7 and are compatible. Channels 15–22 are for GMRS only. Mass marketed and very inexpensive.
MURS Multi-User Radio System	5 VHF channels	2 watts	No license required.	Short range. Repeaters not legal. Defined by FCC as a "private, two-way, short-distance voice or data communications service for personal or business activities of the general public."
Ham Amateur Radio	Extensive frequencies or multiple bands, HF, VHF, UHF, TV, and data technology	1500 Watts	License required through examination. Fee.	Long distance communications possible when other systems are out. Extensive repeater network. Emergency organization include ARES and RACES.

Radio Systems

In the United States, radio communications are regulated by the Federal Communications Commission, which assigns radio frequencies according to function. There are several functions available to the public and NGO's. Each function has its own frequencies and unique regulations.

Radio signals, like all electromagnetic radiation, tend to travel in straight lines. However, at low frequencies (LF, under 3 MHz) diffraction effects allow them to partially follow the Earth's curvature, thus allowing AM radio signals in low-noise environments to be heard well after the transmitting station has dropped below the horizon. Additionally, frequencies between 3 and 30 MHz (HF, or high frequency) can be reflected by the ionosphere, thus giving radio transmissions in this frequency range a potentially global reach.

At higher frequencies (very high frequencies, VHF, or ultra-high frequencies, UHF), neither of these effects apply, and any obstruction between the transmitting and receiving antenna will block the signal. The ability to visually sight a transmitting antenna roughly corresponds with the ability to receive a signal from it. This propagation characteristic of radio in the higher frequencies is called "line of sight."

In practice, the propagation characteristics of these radio bands vary substantially depending on the exact frequency and the strength of the transmitted signal—a function of both transmitter and antenna characteristics.

Low-powered transmitters (FRS, GMRS, MURS) can be blocked by a few trees, buildings, hills, or even heavy rain or snow. The presence of nearby objects not in the direct visual line of sight can also interfere with radio transmissions.

Reflected radiation from the ground plane also acts to cancel out the direct signal. This effect can be reduced by raising the antenna further from the ground. The reduction in signal loss is known as *height gain*, and it's the reason mobile and base antennas get better propagation than hand radios at the same wattage.

Getting Licensed

FRS, MURS, and CB do not require licensing. GMRS does require licensing, so if you're using a GMRS/FRS hybrid hand radio, you'll need a license to run on those GMRS frequencies. Although GMRS licensing requires filling out an application and paying a fee, it does not require an examination.

In all countries amateur radio (ham) licensing requires a passing score on a lengthy examination to prove knowledge of basic radio electronics and communications rules and regulations. In return, hams get more frequencies (larger "bands") and can use a wider variety of communications technologies at substantially higher power. In some countries an additional pre-test is required.

For ham licensing information in the US go to www.arl.org.

For all licensing and regulations information, go to www.fcc.gov/uls/licenses.html.

Setting Up

Hand radios (walkie-talkies) don't require much set-up. Take them out of the package, put in some batteries, and start communicating.

GMRS and FRS radios are available in any department store. Look for these features:

- Full 14 channel FRS and 15 channel GMRS
- Water resistant or waterproof construction
- 38 CTSS codes (for privacy on whatever frequency you choose)
- Key lock
- Selectable call tones
- Programmable channel scan
- Hands-free VOX (voice-operated transmitting)
- NOAA weather frequencies with alert
- Conventional battery sizes so you can use disposable or chargeable AA or AAA batteries if your radio charger is broken or unavailable.

Mobile stations and base stations take a bit more planning and preparation. Have your mobile radio installed in your vehicle by a professional. If you want to install your mobile as a base station, get some detailed advice or have it done professionally.

When installing a radio in your home or building, follow these steps for a comfortable and safe station:

- Give your radio its own desk. You will need access to the outside for the antenna and ground wires. Ground it as instructed in the installation manual.
- Give the radio proper clearance from walls for ventilation.
- Use earphones to minimize noise if you're sheltering with a group of people.

- Cover the radio when not in use to protect it from dust.

Making Contact

These are the standard guidelines for two-way radio communications:

- Monitor the frequency or channel before transmitting.
- Plan your message before transmitting.
- Press the PTT (push-to-talk) button and very briefly pause.
- Hold the microphone two to three inches from the mouth.
- Identify the person you are calling first, then identify yourself. (e.g. Butthead, this is Cowpie. Over)
- Acknowledge transmissions directed at you.
- Use plain English unless you need to encrypt your message for security purposes. Avoid using ten-codes or CB jargon.
- Do not use profanity. The FCC won't catch you, but it's just bad form.
- Reduce background noise as much as possible.

So why bother with radios when cell phones are so much more convenient? Because radios rely not on cell towers, but on their own frequencies and antennas, they are more reliable than cell phones in many situations. Cell towers are vulnerable to destruction, intentional or natural, and to total disruption. Your hand radio is not. In addition, radios can be used for free in areas where roaming charges and minutes limits make cell phone usage expensive. Radios can be used where cell phones are prohibited. Radios can scan for other users. Cell phones can't. Radios don't require dialing. Just turn it on and talk—a nice feature when you're busy dealing with chaos and tragedy. It makes good sense to have a simple backup means of communication rather than relying entirely on cell phones dependent on an intact infrastructure.

3. Data Transmission

Discussions of this topic can get wildly complicated and confusing, so for our purposes we'll simply define data as information, especially information in a form that can be used by a computer. It can include text, numbers, sounds, and pictures. A single piece of information is called datum.

Data transmission is the transfer of digital and analog data from point-to-point, often by way of an electromagnetic signal over a physical point-to-point or point-to-multipoint communication channel. Basically, we're talking about radio waves and telephone systems or complex combinations of both. Data transmission channels include copper wires, optical fibers, wireless communication channels, and storage media. Devices used to transmit data include fax machines and computers of all sizes, from Smart phones to tablets, and PDAs to desktops.

Most of us use email, a form of message data transmitted over landline and wireless systems. Email has limited but important use in emergency and disaster communications, especially in the planning and recovery phases. It is still relatively unreliable as a means of forecasting or warning due to the fact that it isn't checked on a continuous basis. This problem is shrinking as the public switches to Smart phones with email alert tones and texting. Unfortunately, email and the smart net are subject to failure of lower-tiered devices: power supply, landline or wireless system, server. Computer-accessed technology, data transmission, and computer networking or computer communication applications will not be available if power sources are knocked out or remote servers are damaged.

Think of a disaster as a non-voluntary Smart phone Zombie Rehab Program. *Smart phone Zombie.* It's a new term in our English language, and it applies to anyone who is constantly focused on his or her Smart phone, ignoring the environment and events around them, and ignoring other people. How many zombies are out there? Late in 2012 one research firm estimated there were one billion, and that by 2015 there would be 3 billion. This means the majority of people living in well developed nations are prisoners of these portable computer and communication devices. We make phone calls and text messages on them, use them for photography, and shop on them. We check email, Facebook, news & weather, and the stock market on them. We play games, music, and videos with them. Travelers and backcountry adventurers use them for navigation. We record our contacts and our schedules in them. We use them for research. They are our primary methods of communication and self-identity. We are Smart phone Zombies, whether we want to admit it or not.

When the shit hits the fan and service from cell phone towers and Wi-Fi sources is gone, we will lose this communication function: anything that must be sent or received, uploaded or downloaded, via those sources will not be available. Apps and functions that don't depend on ISP's will continue to work. We're going to want all those functions to survive, especially if there's an FM radio on your phone, and if all your contact information is stored in it. 72 hours of hell is certainly going to be a bit more cheerful with music and e-books.

So how do we keep our phones running for 72 hours if there's no AC to charge from? The author tested field charging devices, trying to keep several Smart phones turned on and charged for 72 hours using the normal AC chargers that came with the devices. He also had three crank-powered radio/flashlight combos that claim to be able to charge a cell phone or Smart phone, one of which also has a small solar cell to help charge the unit. Also available were two USB mini DC car charger units that plug into the cigarette lighter of any car, a solar mini-charger, and two different backpacker solar charging units.

Conclusion after 72 hours: Smart phones could only be kept going by finding a solid 12-volt source (car battery or one of the large backpack solar charger units) to plug in or wire the USB mini car charger units to, or by tapping the power from a battery-based solar charger, a battery-powered booster, or USB ports on other battery operated tools or devices. Hand-cranking proved nearly useless in spite of the claims made on the packaging of the radio/flashlight devices (there was no increase in battery charge even with ten minutes of serious cranking). A charge increase of 6% was accomplished by plugging into the radio battery pack that had been charging with its tiny solar cell for 12 hours. Fully charged battery-based backpacker solar chargers and battery operated lanterns with USB ports were able to charge a Smart phone to 80%–90% from 0%.

A couple of important points: By showing some power discipline (i.e., turning your phone off when you don't need to use it, or at least turning off all the non-essential apps), most of us could probably get through 72 hours before needing a charge. If and when we do need a charge, especially in extended incidents, an adequate solar charger or access to a renewable 12-volt system with a cigarette lighter plug and an inverter or USB mini DC charger is going to make things incredibly less complicated.

4. Being Proactive with a Community Backup Communication System

Some serious thought should be given to your continuity of communications. Smart phones are rapidly becoming the primary communication system in our nation. If your primary system—your cell phone—goes down, how will you communicate with emergency responders, family members, and neighbors?

Some research is being done that is leading to the day when communities of household Wi-Fi servers will be able to combine forces to create an improvised cell tower. The idea is already being experimented with for limited use by emergency responders. In the meantime, while we wait patiently for that kind of technology to work itself out, what can neighborhoods and communities do to establish a backup communications system?

With some coordination and planning, an efficient and reliable tiered backup communications system can be organized among members of your community or among neighboring friends and family. The lowest tier consists of individual community members with non-licensed, low power personal radios (e.g. FRS). Groups are assigned to a neighborhood radio operator using a compatible higher powered radio (GMRS)—the second tier. Several second tier operators are assigned in groups to a designated licensed ham with sophisticated powerful equipment that can then tie the community into the city, county, and the outside world.

Chapter 4
Conserving What You
Have When It Isn't Enough

The purpose of this brief chapter is to help you make preparations for utilities (gas, water, electric) failures by taking some actions that will drastically reduce your dependence on them.

1. Landscaping

Before the zombie apocalypse, start grooming your yard or property to grow food and to conserve energy and water. Learn how to use compost and mulch to improve soil, provide nutrients, retain moisture, and slow evaporation. Plant some shade trees in strategic locations to keep your home cooler when there's no power to run the AC.

2. Energy Efficient Appliances

When buying a new appliance, take the time to look at the yellow Energy Guide labels. These tell you the energy efficiency of the appliance, and will actually show you how much energy the appliance uses compared to similar models.

Why is all this important? Most of us will never be totally self-sufficient and off the grid. Our emergency power source may be a generator with limited wattage, or a couple of small solar arrays and battery banks with an inverter for an appliance or two. The generator or each inverter must be matched to the power start-up and running wattage of the appliance(s) it will run, and an array and battery bank must be matched up to the amount of power the appliance will require over the period of time it will be running. In both cases, the lower the wattage and more energy efficient the appliance, the longer it will run and the less complex and prone to breakdown the system will be.

3. Home Improvements

Add some insulation to your home. When things go bad it will take the edge off daily temperature swings.

An inexpensive solar-powered exhaust fan in the attic will help keep the house cool. Commercial reflective films can screen out heat without significantly reducing the light coming through or the view out the window. Add some exterior awnings over south-facing windows. Drapes and shades will buffer the home from heat and cold.

Paint your house an appropriate shade. Dark shades are better in cold environments, as they collect more heat. Light shades are best in warm climates, reflecting solar energy.

Storm windows and doors significantly reduce heat loss. Covering the window frame inside with clear plastic does the same job. Weatherize your home with caulk and weather stripping to block air leaks around doors, windows, and cracks in the walls.

4. Lighting

LED bulbs use a quarter of the electricity and last about ten times longer than incandescent bulbs. If you insist on using incandescent bulbs, get the "energy saver" variety. This will not seem trivial to you if you find yourself running lights on a battery bank or a generator that just barely runs the fridge.

5. Ambient Heating and Cooling

Unless you have a huge hybrid back-up power system, it's unlikely you'll be running a central heating/cooling system on your alternative power source when the Shit Hits the Fan. Odds are, most people will be struggling to burn fuel heaters or power a couple of portable room heaters in the winter, and a room air conditioner or a couple of fans in the summer. In winter, opening curtains and blinds on sun-facing windows will help heat a room, closing them will help keep the warmth inside. Close off rooms that don't need to cooled or heated.

Using fans efficiently can eliminate the need to have or use an air conditioner. Fans use a small fraction of the electricity required to run an air conditioner.

When it's hot, avoid doing anything that would increase the humidity, like cooking, showering, or washing clothes. Do those tasks in the early morning or late evening when it's cooler. Also, ovens and other heat-generating appliances should be used only in the early morning or late evening.

6. Refrigeration

This is one of your critical survival appliances. Get this figured out before a disaster causes you to lose $500 of food to spoilage. Even in the worst of times, most refrigerators have at least a couple of days' food in them. If you don't eat it first or keep the fridge running, you'll hate yourself when the food in that 72-hour kit runs out.

Keep the fridge or freezer out of hot rooms, out of the sun, and away from ovens and heaters.

A hand-operated mini-washing machine for those who just can't bring themselves to hand-wash. Sells for under $60.

Keep the freezer compartment full, but don't block the fan that circulates the cold air. **A full freezer takes less energy to keep things frozen. Fill empty spaces with water bottles. If the power goes out, they'll keep the freezer cold and you can transfer a few of them down to the refrigerator to keep it cold too.**

7. Laundry

Time to relearn the ancient arts of washing by hand and hanging clothes out to dry.

8. Water Heaters

Unless your backup power system is big enough to handle a water heater, most of your hot water will be coming from a stove.

9. Dishwashing

If you're only planning for a 72-hour incident, you can get away with paper plates and plastic forks and never having to do a single dish.

If it's a long term incident you're expecting, plan on doing some dishes. Once upon a time in a land far, far away, people did dishes by hand and let them air-dry.

This propane camp stove/oven combo sells for under $200 and solves the disaster cooking dilemma. Highly recommended.

10. Cooking

If you've got a backup power source that will handle it, use a microwave oven. It cooks faster than your electric oven, and the energy loss, the heat, is focused on the food. The whole process uses far less electricity than a regular electric oven.

When using a gas-fueled camp oven or a low voltage toaster oven (which actually is a *very* good idea) it helps to cook several dishes at the same time and therefore the same temperature. Don't open the door to see how things are going. Just opening the door will drop the temperature significantly and waste fuel or power.

11. Transportation

When the shit hits the fan it's doubtful that gasoline will disappear from the face of the planet. It will just be hard to find and extremely expensive. You probably won't be able to afford to keep your gas-guzzler car running. Hopefully you will have a vehicle that gets exceptional mileage, and it will be days or weeks before you need a fill-up. If you want to be prepared with alternative modes of transportation, consider maintaining a motorcycle, scooter, or even a bicycle.

Chapter 5
Power and Light

Storms and technological failures often take out our power. In a major disaster power could be lost for a week or more. The heater will stop blowing, the refrigerator will fail. The freezer will thaw. The ATM won't work, and neither will the pumps at the gas station. Pump-fed water supplies will cease to work. The chronically ill will face life-threatening crises waiting for life-saving gadgets to kick back on. But for most, the real crisis will be no TV and the inability to charge our Smart phones.

Avoid these problems by investing in an emergency backup power system. Since most of our appliances run on 120 volts AC, we basically have two options:

1. A fuel-powered generator, or
2. batteries, with or without inverters, charged by solar panels, wind power, or vehicle charging systems

The first step is to decide what you actually need and, then, what you can afford. If you want to power a few fluorescent or LED lights, a battery charger, an electric blanket and a smart phone, you can get away with an inverter or a direct charge from a 12V or 5V (USB) battery device. If you want to keep your refrigerator going, run an electric heater, watch TV or use a computer, and light up the night, you'll need a generator and a lot of fuel, or a battery bank with an alternative charging system such as solar panels or a wind turbine.

Electrical power is measured in watts. All appliances have an operating power. Devices that employ motors or other devices that need an electrical kick also have what's called a *surge wattage*, which means extra watts are required to start the motor or device.

Common appliances and their typical power requirements:

Air Conditioner, "1-ton" window	1,000–1,700 watts (2000-3400 watts surge)
Blow dryer	900–1,500 watts
CD/DVD player	35 watts
Clock Radio	30–100 watts
Common light bulb	40–100 watts
Fan, ceiling	25–90 watts (50–180 watts surge)
Fan, floor	75–150 watts (150–300 watts surge)
Color TV, 36–48"	
LED	65–95 watts
LCD	82–147 watts
Plasma	158–273 watts
Coffee maker	650–1,200 watts
Desktop computer system	400 watts (600 surge)
Laptop computer	45 watts
Dishwasher	1200–3600 watts
Electric blanket	80–100 watts
Electric heating pad	12–36 watts
Game Box	100 watts

Iron	1,000 watts
Microwave oven	600–1,100 watts (1200–2200 surge)
Oven	2,000 watts
Range burner	800 watts
Toaster	800–1,500 watts
Toaster Oven	1200–1,700 watts
Furnace fan	750 watts (1,500 watts surge)
Refrigerator	600–1,200 watts (1200–2400 surge)
Vacuum cleaner	300–1,100 watts (600–2200 watts surge)
Satellite receiver	30 watts
Space heater	200–1100 watts
Stereo	30–100 watts
Washing machine	950 watts
Water cooler	120 watts
Well pump	2,400 watts (4800 watts surge)
Electric water heater	4,500 watts
Whole-house AC or heat pump	15,000 watts (30,000 watts surge)

Please note: this list cannot be considered accurate for your own devices. Power consumption varies by size and model, and devices with multiple modes and functions will consume varying amounts of power.

Two other notes while you're trying to figure out your power needs: first, most devices are used for only very short periods—they do not run 24/7; second, some appliances are in standby mode whenever they remain plugged in, even when they're not turned on. Geeks refers to this as "vampire power." It can suck precious power from austere power systems.

1. Figuring Out Your Emergency Power Needs

Think frugally and plan within the spectrum of your prepping goal. How much power do you really need to survive 72 hours? First aid, sleeping bags, proper dress, tents, cold ready-to-eat meals, and stored water require no power. Power only becomes a survival issue in environmental extremes and when we start looking at the upper levels of Maslow's Hierarchy. For 72 hours, most of that, from communication to entertainment to light, can be handled with simple batteries and solar chargers. We live in the Smart phone age, and it takes very little to keep one charged.

For more extended periods of time, though, comfort and safety will dictate planning for more complex and comprehensive power needs beyond a cache of batteries and simple chargers. A few days of austerity is no problem, but a month or a year of cold meals and cold showers is unthinkable.

For extended scenarios, then, to decide what kind of backup power system you want, you'll need two figures:

1. The total wattage of all the devices or appliances. Add up the normal wattages for all the devices you might be *using at the same time.*

   Take the wattages from the list above or directly off the manufacturer's service tag on the device. If it doesn't give the wattage it will likely give the volts and amps. Multiply volts and amps to get watts. Once you've added up those wattages, add another 10% in case you forgot something.

2. The possible surge requirement. For that figure, find the highest wattage of any appliance or device on your list and multiply that by two.

To be safe, your backup system should handle the additional surge of the most power-hungry appliance *plus* the total running wattages of all appliances. For instance, if the total normal running wattage of all your devices (plus 10%) is 1,500 watts, but your refrigerator alone runs at 1,000 watts and requires a surge of 2,000 to turn on, your system needs to provide a minimum of 1,500 running watts and a surge capacity of of at least 2,500.

If your generator or other system cannot handle the surge, the start-up power will be unstable and can damage appliances, especially TV's and computers. Switching on big power devices can cause the power to falter or fail. Protect critical devices with a good surge protector and/or an uninterruptable power supply (UPS).

Plan to stagger usage as much as possible. If you can ensure your devices will not all be running at the same time, you can get along with a smaller, less expensive generator or inverter as long as the surge requirement is covered.

2. Generators: "The Gen"

Generators today are relatively inexpensive and are a very acceptable method to get backup power. For instance, a reliable Coleman generator that produces 2,500 running watts and 3,100 surge watts can be purchased for under $500 and will provide ten hours of power on a three-gallon tank of gasoline. Propane and diesel burning generators are also available. When the diesel fuel is gone, diesel generators can burn filtered vegetable oils or an oil and diesel mix, but it will eventually clog the fuel injectors.

Generators are a very simple answer to the complex question of backup power. However, generators do have some distinct disadvantages. They produce toxic fumes and must be run outside and away from windows and doors. They tend to break down frequently. They make a lot of noise (some are far better than others in that regard), and they require large quantities of fuel, which must be stored somewhere where it won't be a fire hazard. Gasoline has a short shelf-life, even with stabilizers added. If you plan to use a generator and store fuel, it's a good idea to rotate the fuel supply just as you do your food supply. Every three months or so use the gas in the lawn mower and the car, then replace it immediately.

Using a generator to keep your fridge running 24/7 for three days is only going to take 25 gallons or so of gasoline—five 5-gallon cans. If you're prepping for the long term, say for a month- or a year-long incident, that's just too much gasoline to store for the average family. You're going to have to come up with some alternative ideas, and perhaps use the generator as a backup or a component of a solar, wind, or hydro energy system. Welcome to the world of inverters and big battery banks.

Generator Safety

- Don't connect your generator to a regular household outlet. You can kill somebody outside your building and not even know it.
- Don't overload the generator. Add up the watts of your appliances and leave some room for surge voltages.

- Don't use a generator indoors or in an attached garage. Place it where carbon monoxide will not drift into your building. Operate it outdoors in a well-ventilated area away from windows and air vents, and protected from the weather.

- Use proper power cords that are heavy duty and rated for use outdoors. Cords are a trip hazard. Tape them in place, but do not put them under the carpet where they can overheat.

- Make certain your generator is properly grounded, according to the instructions in the operator's manual.

- Do not store fuel indoors.

- Do not refuel while the generator is still running or when it is still hot.

- All equipment powered by the generator should be turned off before shutting the generator down.

- The generator will get hot. Don't get burned.

- Keep children away from the generator.

3. Inverters

Briefly (there's a longer explanation in the next chapter), inverters are devices that change 12-volt battery power to 120-volt AC power, or "house current." True sine-wave inverters produce a power wave that is identical to or even slightly better than power from the power company. Modified-sine wave and square wave inverters are the most common types of power inverters on the market. Modified sine wave inverters produce a power wave that is sufficient for most devices.

If your total wattage requirements are low, say under 300 watts, you can probably get along with an inexpensive small inverter that costs under $50. These inverters can be plugged directly into a car's lighter socket or clamped to a car or marine battery. A charged car battery can probably give you 150 watts for an hour or so, and 20 watts for a full day. But don't use it that long before you start the car for a recharge. Run the engine often to recharge the battery, and of course, the inverter can be used continuously while the car is running, essentially becoming an enormous and very expensive generator.

To run a larger inverter (over 300 watts) on a car battery, you'll want to connect it directly to the battery with the provided cables, and run the car continuously.

A car's alternator can only supply about 700 watts maximum. Purchase an inverter that's well under that wattage if you don't want to start blowing car fuses. If more power is needed, it's feasible to run inverters of even 2,000 watts or more off multiple deep cycle batteries (not car batteries) in parallel. We talk about these systems in the next chapter. Or use a generator. Do the little stuff on the car battery, the big stuff on the Gen.

4. Hasty Backup Wiring for Your Home or Shelter

By far, the easiest way to improvise house wiring from a generator or inverter is to run extension cords. You can run cords in for individual appliances, or you can run in a cord with multiple outlets. The disadvantage to multiple outlets is that they must be closely policed so the group is not plugging in at the wrong time and overloading the system.

If you have super-high wattage requirements and you plan to use your generator for extended periods to run big items like a furnace blower or well pump, or you are dependent on 240-volts for major appliances, you're going to need a big generator and should consider having the generator wired into your circuit panel so all the outlets in the house have power.

- Do NOT try to wire the panel yourself unless you're an electrician.
- Be certain to have the generator grounded according to the instructions in the owner's manual.
- If the generator is wired into your circuit panel, always cut your house off from the power grid before starting the generator. Failure to do so could electrocute anyone working on the grid lines. A positive interlock system installed by an electrician ensures the house main breaker is cut off when the Gen is on.

5. Other Power Systems

Solar, hydro, and wind systems are discussed in detail in the next chapter.

6. In the Event of Blackout

- Before you set up and tap into your alternative power sources, turn off or unplug all devices to protect them from a damaging surge when the power comes back on.
- Maintain your refrigerator/freezer protocol.
- If appliances get wet, turn off the power main, unplug the appliances, and allow them to dry before plugging them in again.

7. The Basics about Small Batteries

- For convenience, all of your battery operated appliances and equipment should use the same battery size. Almost any type of small battery-operated appliance or device can be found powered by AA's.

- Replace stored batteries annually. No worries if you forget one year. If batteries are stored in a dry place at room temperature – not in a refrigerator or freezer – their shelf life can be as long as three years or even more.

- For a 72-hour kit, stick to disposable alkaline batteries. Keep a mega-pack of them in your kit. If you must use rechargeable batteries, stick with NiMH. Lithium batteries are expensive. Alkaline batteries are cheaper than lithium, but lithium batteries work better at colder temperatures. NiCad batteries have 2/3 the life of alkaline batteries and can be recharged 500 times or so. Rechargeable NiMH batteries have 4/5 the life of alkaline batteries. You can get rechargeable alkaline batteries, but they have only half the life of disposable alkalines and they can only be recharged about 25 times.

- Chargers can run off a generator, an inverter, a 12V port, a USB port, and some directly off solar panels.

- If you are not going to use your flashlight or other device, remove the batteries to prevent damage from leaking battery acid.

8. Alternative Light Sources

Gone are the days when emergency lighting meant candles or hazardous fuel-burning flame lamps. Far more efficient light-emitting diode (LED) and fluorescent lamp technology

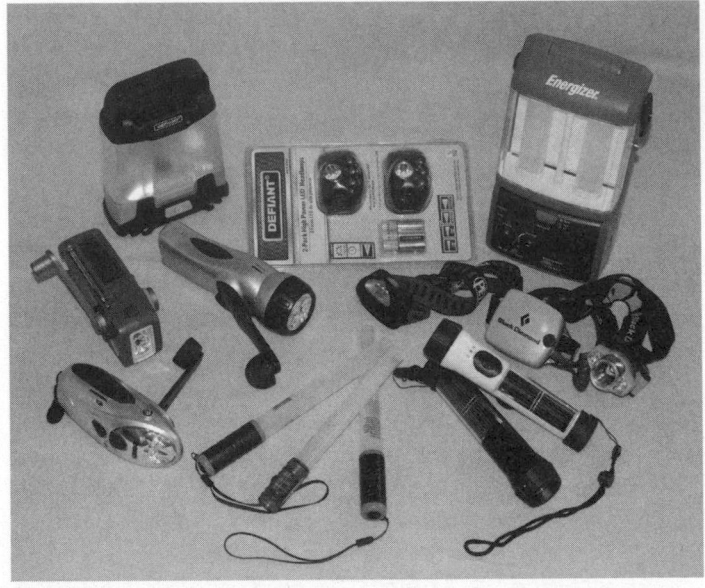

LED and fluorescent headlamps, flashlights, lanterns, and radio-lamps, powered by various combinations of cranks, batteries, and solar cells. With LED and fluorescent technology so advanced, there's no longer any excuse for burning down the house with emergency candles or fuel lamps.

has also replaced the normal iridescent electrical bulbs that were used in flashlights, lamps that wasted most energy as heat. LED bulbs last over 10,000 hours and are shock and cold resistant. Fluorescent bulbs last ten times longer than iridescent bulbs but are not as bright at cold temperatures. LED flashlights using clusters of bulbs will work many times as long and their equivalent iridescent bulbs on the same batteries. 1-watt LED bulbs combined with clusters of standard LED bulbs provides a wide array of operating modes and options. LED lights come in an enormous range of flashlights and hands-free headlamps, using batteries, crank, and solar power for charging.

Chapter 6
Alternative Energy &
Emergency Power

To make decisions about a suitable back-up power from alternative energy sources for disaster incidents, it helps to have a basic understanding of what power and energy are and where they come from.

The law of conservation of energy states that energy cannot be created or destroyed, but can change its form. When something happens and energy is used, it is converted into a different form. The final forms of most energy conversions are heat and light. Even these final forms are not destroyed, but are so spread out into the environment that they become difficult to use. The *energy chain* of a flashlight is a great example: chemical energy in the batteries is changed to electrical energy; electrical energy is changed to heat and light from the bulb, which is dispersed.

While much of our immediate needs are met by burning fuels, nearly all energy on earth comes directly or indirectly from the sun. Solar energy reaches the Earth in the form of electromagnetic energy, a form of energy that can travel across space. The sun warms the planet. Plants use the sun to make their food, and their food becomes ours. The sun's energy can also be used to generate electricity using a solar cell, or to heat water using a solar collector.

While solar is the renewable energy source that most often comes to mind for preppers, other sources to consider are hydro and wind. With hydro, moving water turns turbines that generate electricity. Wind generates electricity when the wind spins propellers that turn turbines.

Appliances and machines operate by taking one form of energy and changing it into another. An appliance is considered efficient if most of the energy used to operate it is changed into the energy that is needed. Fluorescent tube lights, for example, are more efficient than standard light bulbs because they change more energy (electricity) into light and less into heat.

1. Electricity

Electricity is a stream of negatively charged particles (electrons) flowing at the speed of light through a wire, similar to the way water flows through a pipe. Electrical forces exist between the charged objects, and the opposite charges attract (which simply means the electrons want to flow from the negatively charged object to the positively charged object in order to get the objects back to their neutrally charged states).

Substances through which a current of electrons can flow are called conductors. Substances through which an electric current cannot easily flow are called nonconductors or insulators.

So, electrical current is a flow of electrons from an area of high electric potential (too many electrons) to an area of low electrical potential (not enough electrons). It's this difference that makes the electricity flow, sort of like the flow of water from high pressure to low pressure. The potential difference is basically the electrical pressure, and is measured in volts (V).

You will often hear the terms *alternating current* (AC) and *direct current* (DC). DC is the flow of electricity in one direction. AC, on the other hand, intermittently reverses direction because of the way it's generated. Batteries and PV cells produce DC because the current always flows from a fixed negative point to a fixed positive point. AC comes from generators whose poles change 60 times per second, causing current to reverse directions. It's the type of current that enters your homes from the utility grid or from a generator. DC, such as that from a battery bank, can be converted to AC by passing it through an inverter. Inverters are available with high AC power outputs and with conversion efficiencies of 90 percent.

The amount of current flowing through a circuit depends on the strength of the potential difference (volts) and the resistance of the components in the circuit. Current is measured in amperes. All materials, even conductors, resist the current to a certain extent, reducing the amount of current that flows around the circuit. When a material resists electric current, it converts some of that energy into heat and light.

Resistance is measured in units called ohms. An ampere ("amp") is the current that will flow through one ohm of resistance with a "pressure" of 1 volt.

Components such as light bulbs in an electrical circuit convert electrical energy carried by current into other forms of energy (heat and light). The components in a circuit can be arranged in two ways: series or parallel.

What happens to voltages and current when they are stacked up in a series like the stack of batteries in a flashlight? In series, voltages add up, but the amps (current) don't. In parallel, the amps (current) add up, but the voltage doesn't. We'll explain this again later when we look at how battery banks and solar panels are wired.

Power is the energy used over a specified period of time. The amount of power (P) delivered by a given current (I) in amps, under pressure, or volts (E), is measured in watts. The formula is power equals voltage times amps, or P=EI. As you can see, watts (P), volts (E), amps (I), and ohms (R) are all interrelated and must be dealt with mathematically in order to understand electrical circuits and electrical systems.

For explanations of Ohm's Law, see the following websites:

http://www.hamuniverse.com/ohmslaw.html

http://www.youtube.com/watch?v=-4mUcnEr0d8

http://www.youtube.com/watch?v=-4mUcnEr0d8

Let's look a bit closer at watts. A watt is the amount of energy used per second and should be thought of as the rate or speed that energy is being used. The watt rating of an appliance is the rate or speed at which the appliance is using energy. For example, a 100-watt bulb uses 100 watts per second.

The unit of measure for electricity consumption is the kilowatt-hour (kWh). Check it out on your next power bill. Kilowatt hours are the amount of energy used, and are figured by multiplying the rate of usage in kilowatts by the time in hours that the device runs. Don't let the term confuse you about how much power your appliance uses. Again, wattage is the rate, kilowatt hours are the amount used.

A battery is a storage unit of chemical energy that is converted to electrical energy. The batteries familiar to most people are the AAA, AA, C, and D batteries in their portable appliances and flashlights. These are called dry cells, and contain electrolyte paste, a substance that conducts electric current. Chemical reactions make the charges separate and migrate to the appropriate terminal (positive or negative). When the necessary chemical properties of the electrolyte have been depleted (when the battery "runs out of juice"), the battery is dead.

Accumulators are batteries that can be recharged, like a car battery or like rechargeable flashlight batteries. Car batteries have a dilute sulfuric acid as the electrolyte that facilitates the potential difference between electrodes made of zinc and zinc oxide.

Household electricity is 110V (actually 110, 120, or 125V) or 240V, depending on what country you live in). Parallel circuits carry the electricity around the house. Appliances are often protected by fuses. The thin wire in a fuse melts under excessive current and breaks the circuit, stopping the flow of electricity.

Each parallel circuit in modern buildings contains three wires called the live (hot), neutral, and ground (or "earth") wires. The current is supplied by the live wires (usually black), and the neutral wires (usually white) carry the current back. The ground wire (usually green or bare copper) is a safety device that provides a path to the ground (earth) through which current can escape if the neutral wire is somehow broken or interrupted. The electricity would otherwise take the shortest path to the ground, which could be you.

A current flowing through a wire produces a magnetic field. A wire wrapped around an iron bar behaves like a bar magnet when current is passed through it. The wire and bar are called an electromagnet. If moving current can produce electromagnetism, it stands to reason that moving magnetism could produce electric current. A generator is a machine that converts the energy of magnetic movement into energy.

In a power generation, electricity is created by turbines spun by motors, wind, or moving water. The turbines then spin the shaft of a generator that has coils of wire (the armature) turning between two magnets. Turning the coil between two magnets induces a current that changes direction every half turn. This is called alternating current, or AC. The amount of voltage generated depends on the number of turns in the coil, the strength of the magnetic field, and the speed at which the coil or magnetic field rotates.

In smaller generation systems (e.g. micro-hydro or small wind systems) we sometimes see the terms AC generator (also called an alternator) and DC generator. DC generators use a bridge rectifier to convert AC to DC to serve battery banks. A rectifier is the opposite of an inverter. It changes AC to DC in a process called rectification. Rectifiers and inverters are known collectively as power supplies. A power supply is a device that converts one form of electricity into another and distributes it to the rest of the system.

Electronics is the use of devices or components to control how electricity flows through a circuit. Components include anything within the circuit that alters the path or intensity of the electrical energy: resistors, LED lamps, diodes, speakers, capacitors, antenna, and transistors.

2. Wiring

For most people this is the confusing part, and it's where most do-it-yourselfers get screwed up.

Those who want to put together a backup power source—whether it's solar, hydroelectric, or wind turbine—are likely to be working with powerful battery banks, charge controllers, and inverters. They'll be doing most of the maintenance themselves, and they'll need to know how and why the system works and how it's wired.

The simple solution for backup wiring: a multiport extension cord from your generator or power center, with plug-ins every 8 feet.

3. Photovoltaic Cells

Within a solar panel, a cell is the smallest structural unit capable of independent production of electricity. A cell is made up of a sandwich of semiconductor materials, the same materials that are used in transistors. The first layer is made of phosphorous (an N-type, or negative semi-conductor). The middle layer is the absorber (P-N junction). It's made of purified silicon. The third layer is made of boron (a P-type, or positive semiconductor). Each boron atom has one too many electrons. The energy of sunlight knocks some of the free phosphorous electrons off the layer, and current wants to flow as the extra electrons try to fill boron's deficit of electrons. In order to make this happen, the three layers are sandwiched between two electrical contact layers that form a pathway for electron flow.

The cells are encased within a transparent material, like tempered glass, on the front and a protective material on the back. Most panels are waterproofed, but there are some on the market that require the buyer to waterproof the panel with silicone around the edges of the frame, plugs, wire entries, and connections.

Each cell produces about half a volt. In a solar panel cells are wired in series to make panels with higher voltages. A typical 18-watt solar panel is made up of 36 individual 0.5 amp cells. The total voltage and total amount of current produced is determined by the intensity of sunlight and the configuration (series versus parallel) of multiple solar panels called an *array*. The output of a solar panel in watts is determined by the rated voltage times the rated amperage. Today 12-, 24-, and 36-volt solar charging systems are the industry norm. For needs under 2kWh, 12V is enough.

A panel that is rated for a 12V system probably has an effective voltage of up to 17 volts. Panels from different manufacturers can be added to the system if the voltage rate is comparable (within a volt or two).

There are basically four methods of producing solar cells:

Single crystalline is the traditional method of production and the most efficient of the four types of cells. It's also the most expensive process. The crystal is cut from a fat rod of silicon and is doped on the outside with phosphorous and the other side with boron.

Polycrystalline is also cut from a fat rod of a type of silicon that does not undergo the same cooling control or require the same purity of single crystalline silicon. The result is a matrix of many crystals. It's cheaper to produce, but since crystal boundaries tend to impede the flow of electrons, these cells are only 90% as efficient as single crystalline cells.

String ribbon cells are made by drawing string through liquid silicon to produce thin sheets which are then doped. These cells are cheap to produce but are only about 75% as efficient as single crystalline.

Amorphous thin film cells are produced by vaporizing a silicone material and painting it on non-tempered glass or flexible stainless steel. These cells are somewhat less efficient than other cells and are easy to shatter. These are the cells you see on small RV and boat systems, and small panels are often sold at truck stops to trickle charge automotive batteries (keeps them perky).

Solar cells have no storage capacity of their own. Neither do wind or water turbines. So if that's how you plan to back up your power, you'll be storing that electricity in a 12V battery bank. Fortunately, setting up a PV system is relatively simple. The panels themselves have no moving parts and require very little maintenance.

The total amount of radiation energy available is expressed in hours of full sunlight per square meter, or peak sun hours. This amount, also known as insolation value, is the average amount of sun available per day throughout the year. At "peak sun," 1,000 watts per square meter reaches the earth's surface. One full hour of peak sunlight provides 1000 watts, or 1 kW per square meter. To view a map that will help you determine the insolation value at your location, type "insolation map" into your search engine and choose from hundreds.

The performance of solar modules is rated on the percentage of solar energy they capture at sea level on a clear day. Weather, temperature, air pollution, altitude, season, dust, and anything covering the panel (snow, ice, raindrops, mud, dust, Plexiglass) all reduce the amount of solar energy a cell will receive. Cells are most efficient at higher altitudes, but at the average altitude of the earth's surface (about 2250 feet), clean cells will receive about eighty-five percent. Single crystalline and polycrystalline cells only manage to convert about ten percent of that to electrical energy, and amorphous and string ribbon cells are even less efficient.

The life span of a solar cell is decades. It takes two to four years for a single crystalline or polycrystalline cell to lose one percent of its efficiency.

Maintenance of solar panels is easy. Since there are no moving parts, you simply protect them from shattering and keep them clean.

It is possible to overcharge a battery and damage it. When a battery is fully charged, the current from the charging device (be it wind, solar, or hydro) should be turned off or used to charge or run another battery bank or appliance. A *charge controller* should be placed between the charging device and the battery bank to prevent overcharging. The controller opens the circuit to stop the flow of electricity. When the battery's charge starts to drop again, the controller closes the circuit to allow current from the charging device to serve the battery bank again. The controller must be compatible with both the voltage of the battery bank and the amperage of the panel system.

Controllers can be simple or extremely complex. They're rated by the amps they process from a solar array. Advanced controllers use pulse-width modulation (PWM), a process that ensures efficient charging and long battery life and maximum power point tracking (MPPT), a process that maximizes the amps into the battery. Some controllers have low voltage disconnect (LVD) which limits damage to the batteries, and battery temperature compensation (BTC), which adjusts the charge rate based on temperature (batteries are temperature sensitive).

It is possible to lose some of the battery charge at night and on cloudy days through a process called *reverse current*. Some older solar panels come with a diode that blocks reverse current. External diodes can be added to panels that do not have their own.

As you shop for solar panels, notice the wattage ratings. Most manufacturers list the best-case rating, based on full sun and perfect conditions of altitude, temperature, and clear skies. Don't be fooled by this. Your panel will rarely function at that level for a number of reasons. First, full sun is tough to find. Even in the rural Southwest there is often enough haze in the sky on a windy but cloudless day to reduce the sunshine reaching your array. Cells get more sun at higher altitudes and in remote areas not affected by pollution.

Temperature is also a factor. Cells lose efficiency in a hot environment. If it's too warm outside for your comfort, it's probably too warm to get maximum efficiency from your array. The best defense against this is to mount your array in such a way that the backs of the panels are well ventilated and where the full array is not enclosed in a natural or artificial amphitheater that acts like a solar heater. Considering these factors, it should be obvious that solar electrical systems are going to be more successful in rural or remote, dry, high-altitude locations, which tend to be cooler, less cloudy, and less hazy.

The most important factor is shading and shadows. Anything placed between the cell and the sun will create a shadow and diminish the output of the panel. A small shadow has a cascading negative effect. Think of the array as a bucket, and the sunshine as a stream of water from a faucet. Your goal is to fill the bucket so full of water that it overflows. That's essentially what your array does. It fills with electricity and sends the "overflow" to the battery bank. Now . . . think about the bucket again. If there's a big hole in the side of the bucket near the top, water leaks out. Sure, there's some water in the bucket, but it just doesn't fill quite enough to overflow. That's what shadows and shade do to your array. With crystalline cells, a shadow the size of a basketball could shut down your entire array. There are two morals to this story: First, mount your array where it will get the best sun and the least shade—that is, perpendicular to the sun at solar noon (more on this later). Second: Keep your panels clean.

Solar arrays do their best when they're set up to face at a right angle (90°, or perpendicular) to the sun. That's 90° to solar noon, at an angle equal to your latitude, give or take a few degrees for winter or summer. This is easy with a clinometer (a device that measures angles of inclination) or a swing-arm protractor.

Mounting systems secure the panels in their proper position, preventing wind damage and allowing ventilation with cool air circulation behind them. No part of the mount should cast a shadow on the panel. There are several types of mounts available commercially, including ground or roof mounts, pole mounts, and flush mounts. Homemade mounts can be built using anodized aluminum or galvanized steel for corrosion resistance. Wood is fine but won't last as long. Slotted steel angle stock is readily available and easy to work with. Portable arrays can often be mounted on guyed wide-base A-frame ladders or stepladders.

Adjustable tilt is nice for seasonal angle adjustments, but tracking systems that follow the sun across the sky are expensive and barely effective. The money would be better spent buying more panels and batteries.

Finally, solar power works very nicely for most appliances except large ones that use a large electric heating element (water heater, clothes dryer, electric stove, electric heater, etc.). To minimize the size of the of the PV system needed, consider using propane, natural gas, or another alternative to power these appliances.

4. Wind Systems

Wind turbines come in two common flavors: horizontal-axis turbines, which look like a propeller with two or

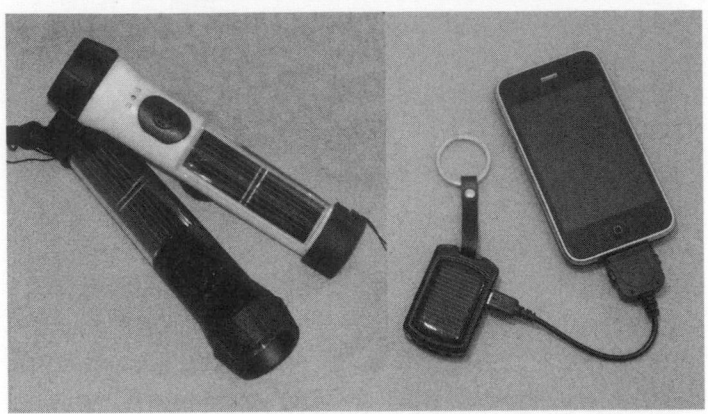

On the small end, built-in mini cells and key chain solar chargers are highly convenient power sources for continuous passive charging of small appliances like flashlights, radios, and phones.

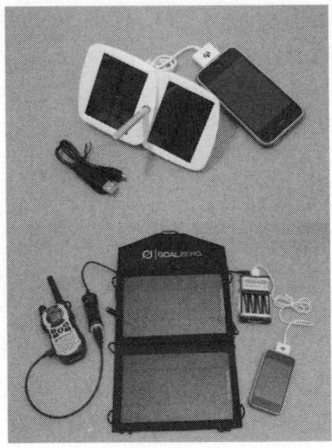

These small but powerful solar chargers fit easily in a backpack, bucket, or duffle. The panels and the internal or factory attached battery can be used to power battery chargers, and small rechargeable appliances, and could easily be the only source of backup power needed for a 72-hour emergency.

three blades (rotors), and vertical axis turbines that are often described as "egg-beater" turbines. Turbines are also described as being upwind or downwind. Upwind turbines, like most three-blade horizontal axis turbines, are operated with the blades facing toward the wind.

Horizontal-axis turbines with larger rotor diameters catch more wind and generate more electricity than those with small rotor diameters. An average to large size home will probably need a turbine with a rotor radius of at least 5 feet (a total wingspan of ten feet) to generate enough electricity to completely run an average household. Smaller turbines, called mini-turbines, have rotor radii of between 2.5 and 5 feet, and are suitable for smaller homes and vacation cabins. Transient and recreational venues (boats, RVs) can use micro-turbines, which have rotor radii of 1.5 to 2.5 feet.

Both wind and water systems are most often used as an adjunct for a PV system, often as a booster for power production in bad weather. These combination systems are referred to as hybrids.

A site that gets at least 8 mph of wind on a frequent basis can be a good site for a wind turbine. The turbines are mounted on towers because wind increases with height. The drag at the wind-ground contact is eliminated. The difference at 100 feet may be as much as 60 percent.

Hybrid wind/PV systems include a control and regulation center with charge controller, monitor, regulator, battery bank, inverter, and disconnects. Hybrid systems often incorporate a small backup generator to reduce the number of batteries needed.

Turbines use permanent magnet alternators or coil induction generators. Whatever is used, the important factor will be its performance at the low wind speeds common to your location. That will largely be determined by the rotor diameter (also known as the swept area) rather than the claims of the manufacturer.

Where will you mount the turbine? On a tower at least 30 feet tall and at least 200 feet away from wind obstacles would be ideal.

Turbines are heavy and require a hefty tower that is well-guyed. The tower, turbine, and guys are assembled on the ground and then raised. Some towers for small turbines are tubular steel masts. Others for larger turbines are complex framed structures. Many towers are hinged at the base for easy access. Others are constructed with crane-like devices. Obviously, wind and hydro systems are not the emergency power source of choice for "bugging out."

The electrical system should be protected from lightning by grounding. All the grounds in the wind and household systems are connected, giving the current a path outside your system. Also, consider a lightning arrestor, a device which directs excessive currents into the ground.

5. Water Systems

The nice thing about electricity produced from a stream is that it can work 24/7.

A simple micro-hydro system consists of a pipeline (penstock) that delivers the water to the turbine, which changes the water flow to rotational energy. The alternator or generator changes rotational energy into electricity. A regulator controls the generator or diverts excess energy.

Home and farm hydroelectric systems work like this: Water flow is collected into a pipeline. At the end of the pipe the water squirts out and strikes a wheel, which spins a generator, which makes electricity, which is then transmitted somewhere else by wire. The key piece to this is the head of the system—the distance the water falls from the collector to the turbine. The head determines the water pressure at the outlet of the pipe (pounds per square inch, or psi). The pressure and the flow rate (gallons per minute) determine the amount of electricity the generator will produce. Energy can be collected from large volumes falling over small distances (low-head systems), or small volumes falling over large distances (high-head systems). Obviously the most effective sites are going to be in the watercourses of the mountains. Any site which could support a pipeline that gives 10 psi— or at least 20 to 30 feet of head delivering at least 2 gallons per minute—can produce substantial electricity.

DC generators are typically used for smaller residential systems. High-flow, low-head sites and AC generators are complicated and expensive.

An impulse turbine functions by using the impact spray of water from a nozzle or jet, also at the end of the pipeline. It sprays onto little cups on the turbine wheel. Kinetic energy from the water spins the wheel (runner).

Sites with at least 150 feet of head are best served by a Pelton wheel impulse turbine. The Pelton is a wheel on an axis that's perpendicular to the flow of the current. Cups attached to the wheel catch the spurting water and cause the wheel to spin, which spins the turbine. Axial flow turbines are like propellers, with the rotors spinning on an axis that's parallel to the flow of water. Pelton wheels are the best choice for high pressure, low-volume systems (in other words, the typical mountain trickle). A Pelton system like this can be put in place for as little as $1,200.

The low voltage generated by micro-hydro systems is difficult to transmit in large quantities or over long distances. The battery bank should be as close as possible to the turbine. Extreme distances will require larger-wire and specialized technical expertise.

Micro-hydro systems require special charge controllers or regulators. Their controllers divert excess power to a secondary load, usually a water or space heater. These diversion controllers can be used with PV cells or wind turbines, but solar controllers cannot be used with micro-hydro or wind systems.

To get started setting up a micro-hydro system, a few measurements are needed. First, the head; this is the difference in altitude between the collection point and the turbine. The easiest ways to measure this are with a topographic map (7.5-minute series) or with GPS, or both. DO not rely on cursor points on web-based map services. When using a GPS for altitude, make certain the device has acquired at least three satellites to ensure accuracy. If the pipe has already been installed between the collection point and the turbine site, use a pressure gauge at the turbine site and multiply the reading by 2.31 feet (feet of head = psi x 2.31).

6. Sizing Your System

Advisory: Before you dive into the complexities of selecting, purchasing, installing, and wiring a complex system with all its components, take a close look at the simplicity displayed in the photos below. For the average individual, household, or small business, all-in-one units are an excellent way to get what you need without delving into

the madness of putting together larger complex systems on your own.

If you choose to ignore the advisory and photos below and decide to build your own utility dynasty, then prepare to have your brain scrambled like this morning's eggs. It's

All-in-one portable solar power generators like the one pictured above are the simplest solution and can be found for $1,000–$1,500. The systems consists of an internal battery, attached or portable solar panels, an internal charge controller, and an internal inverter powerful enough to run large appliances like a refrigerator or dishwasher. They include multiple AC, USB, and 12V plug-ins, and they can accommodate additional batteries and solar panels. The entire package is on wheels and can be placed almost anywhere for maximum sun exposure, and in a vehicle for total portability. For 90% of us, one of these plus a small gas-powered generator and extension cords would be the perfect medium or long term solution to emergency backup power.

About half the price of the commercial solar power generator shown above, this portable DIY emergency 12V system carries two batteries in parallel and two 18 watt panels in parallel, making a 12V, 36W system. A small charge controller and a two-receptacle-plus-USB inverter are mounted on top of the upper battery box with 12V receptacle. In this parallel PV panel array, all the red wires (+) are connected to the red controller wire, and all black (-) wires are connected to the black controller wire. The battery terminals in such a system would be connected with cables or jumper bars, and the red terminals are all connected to each other, the black terminals to each other, and the positive (red) and negative (black) outputs are taken from terminals on the opposite ends of the bank. Pulling the output from the opposite corners of the bank ensures that all the batteries in the bank are charged and discharged equally. Everything is mounted on a dolly for portability. Such systems are available as kits, without the dolly, batteries, or battery boxes for $300.

complicated and complex, so start researching and talk to some experts.

To figure out how big a system needs to be, you must first determine how many watts you'll be using and the amount of time those watts are used (watt-hours). You can then compare those figures to the amount of energy resources (the potential power produced by sun, wind, water available at your geographic location). There are formulas we won't discuss here to help through this. They factor in variables such as the AC and DC loads (appliances) in the system, the hours they will be used (to get watt-hours), and the efficiency of the inverter. The watt-hour totals are then divided by the system voltage to calculate the amp hours of electricity needed for the specified time (usually a day or week). This information is used to determine the size and number of components you'll need to provide the amount of power you require: batteries that will provide the required amp-hours of power to the appliances, and solar panels or other energy collectors that can supply the required charge to the batteries. To simplify, you'll need enough amp-hours stored in your batteries to last you through nights and unplanned cloudy days, and your power generating system must be capable of collecting and storing that amount.

Finally, let's repeat the obvious: the size of your system can be drastically reduced by taking a few conservation measures. Use energy-efficient lighting and appliances, and consider non-electric alternatives. Consider putting together a simple backup system, and plan your needs around its capacity rather than planning your system's capacity around your inflated needs.

7. Batteries

Batteries, or battery banks, are required by all stand-alone and utility systems. The two most common rechargeable battery types are nickel-cadmium (NiCad) and lead-acid (L-A) batteries. Lead-acid batteries have plates of lead submerged in sulfuric acid. NiCad batteries have plates of nickel and cadmium in a potassium hydroxide solution.

Lead-acid batteries are cheapest, and readily available. They come in several sizes and designs, but the most important thing to look for is the depth of the charging cycle.

Shallow-cycle batteries (car batteries) give high currents for short periods. They do not tolerate repeated deep discharging (below twenty percent), so are not suitable for PV systems.

Deep-cycle batteries are made to be repeatedly discharged by as much as eighty percent. Even so, these batteries will have a longer life if they're cycled shallow. Try to stay above fifty percent capacity. All L-A batteries fail early if they're not recharged after each cycle. A long-discharged L-A battery is subject to sulfation of the positive plate and permanent loss of capacity. An electronic de-sulfater can be added to extend battery life.

Nickel-cadmium batteries are expensive, but can last many times longer than L-A batteries. NiCads can be one hundred percent discharged and can stay discharged without damaging their capacity. Also, their capacity does not decrease in cold temperatures and they are not damaged by freezing. The voltage is stable from full charge to discharge. Because of these factors, smaller batteries can be used.

NiCad charging efficiency is the same as L-A batteries, and their shelf-discharge rate is very slow. They require a higher voltage (16 to 17 volts for a 12V battery) than L-A batteries to bring them to a full charge. Many AC battery chargers cannot provide the higher voltage, but some solar panels do. Note that some 12V inverters may shut down temporarily with a battery at that voltage.

Additional NiCads can be added at any time to the bank. L-A banks will "dumb-sown" to match the least-efficient or weakest battery in the bank, so the L-A's are best purchased together and replaced together.

Nickel-iron batteries have charge and discharge voltage, life, and cold-temperature performance similar to NiCad batteries. However, they don't deliver the high amperage that NiCads do, so a larger battery will be needed for the same power. One advantage of these batteries is that they are made without lead or cadmium.

A typical L-A battery contains liquid acid in cells that are not sealed. They can leak. Gel-cell, AGM, and sealed lead-acid are terms for batteries that are alternative choices in place of the traditional L-A battery.

A gel cell uses acid in a semisolid gel form and is therefore less likely to leak. The disadvantage is that a coating can develop on the battery plates, which reduces performance.

Absorbent glass mat (AGM) batteries use internal glass mats to soak up the acid. There's a slightly higher chance of leakage from cracks with AGM than with gel-cell, but AGM's deliver a more consistent performance.

A sealed lead-acid battery can be any battery that uses lead-acid for electrolytes and is sealed. This includes both gel-cell and AGM batteries. The obvious advantage of sealed batteries is that the battery fluid is less likely to leak and does not have to be replaced. They are virtually maintenance-free.

The size of a battery bank is determined by the storage capacity required, the maximum discharge rate, and the minimum temperature at the bank site (for L-A batteries). At 40°F, L-A batteries will only function at 75% of capacity, and at 0°F, at 50%.

Storage capacity is expressed in amp-hours. The battery bank should have enough amp-hours capacity to supply needed power during a long period of cloudy weather. Add another 20% for L-A batteries. If there's a back-up source of power, such as a generator and battery charger, the battery bank can be smaller.

8. Charge Controllers

Let's summarize what we've already discussed about charge controllers: When a battery is fully charged, the current from the charging device should be turned off or used to charge or run another battery bank or appliance. A charge controller should be placed between the charging device and the battery bank to prevent overcharging. The controller opens the circuit to stop the flow of electricity. When the battery's charge starts to drop again, the controller closes the circuit to allow current from the charging device to serve the battery bank again. The controller must be compatible with both the voltage of the battery bank and the amperage of the charging device system.

Controllers are rated by the amps they can process from a charging device (PV array, etc.). Advanced controllers use pulse-width modulation (PWM) to ensure efficient charging, maximum power point tracking (MPPT) to maximize the amps into the battery, low voltage disconnect (LVD) to automatically disconnect loads, and battery temperature compensation (BTM) to adjust the charge rate based on temperature.

"Monitor" or "regulator" units are charge controllers with additional bells and whistles. Typically they will include an ammeter for current measurement, adjustable voltage set points, and LED lights to show charge status.

9. Inverters

Inverters convert DC in batteries to on-demand AC through a process of transforming, filtering, and stepping voltages (changing them from one level to another). The more processing that happens, the cleaner the output, but this comes at the expense of conversion efficiency. When you shop for an inverter, you'll choose based on the following factors:

- Maximum continuous load. Inverters are rated by maximum continuous watt output.
- Maximum surge load. Asking an inverter for more power than it can give will simply shut it down or cook it. If your inverter will be expected to run induction motors (e.g. washer and dryer, dishwasher, large power tools, etc.), you might need a surge capacity of three times that of the highest appliance wattage. For example, if your air conditioner runs at 1,500 watts, you'll need about 5,000 watts of surge capacity to get the motor started.
- Input battery voltage (12, 24, or 48V).
- The output voltage needed (120V versus 240 V).
- Purity of the AC waveform required.
- Optional features.

Inverters deliver current in one of three basic waveforms: square wave, modified square wave (modified sine wave), and pure sine wave (true sine wave). The closest waveform to grid waveform is pure sine wave.

Square wave inverters are inexpensive but also relatively inefficient. Modified square wave inverters allow greater power surge capacity to start motors, and also allow economic power for running small appliances and electronics. Most appliances will accept them. However, they may damage or fail to run some printers and copiers and some rechargeable tools. They also cause a buzz in audio equipment, fans, and fluorescent lights. Pure sine wave inverters are the choice for running equipment that is sensitive to waveforms.

Some inverters have special features: internal battery charger, automated transfer switching, battery temperature compensation, internal relays to control loads, and automatic remote generator start-stop.

Note that efficiency losses between the inverter and the source, wires, and batteries can be as high as 25%.

10. Power Centers

A power center is a panel into which the inverter, charge controller, safety disconnects, lightning arrestors, breakers, and system meters are mounted. For larger alternative energy systems, a power center is definitely advantageous.

11. Connections

The clear standard for today's home-sized solar arrays are the MC connectors. MC stands for multi-contact. The MC is a proprietary switch that has male and female ends and comes with various cable sizes. It provides clean, code-compliant, weather-tight connections. MC1 has been in common use, but the trend is toward the MC2 connector because it's considered a better connection and is now required by most building codes. There are adapter kits for going from MC1 to MC2.

The small panels you often find at truck stops, auto part stores, and boat shops often use what are called universal connectors, or SAE connectors.

12. Electrical Safety Devices

Two of the most important safety components are good enclosures and overcurrent protection. Enclosures have many uses including a wiring point for energy sources, weather protection for overcurrent devices, and load disconnection. Overcurrent devices and switch gear provide safe means to disconnect power. Overcurrent devices include fuses, fuse blocks, and circuit breakers. Consult an electrician about electrical safety devices for your system.

13. Wiring the System

You will want to connect the components of your system using correct wire sizes to prevent loss of energy and overheating. A tutorial and chart showing the required wire size for wire lengths to connect the solar panels to the charge controller in a 12 volt system can be found here:

http://www.freesunpower.com/wires_cables.php

Make sure the batteries are matched to the voltage capabilities of the controller and the inverter (12V, 24V,

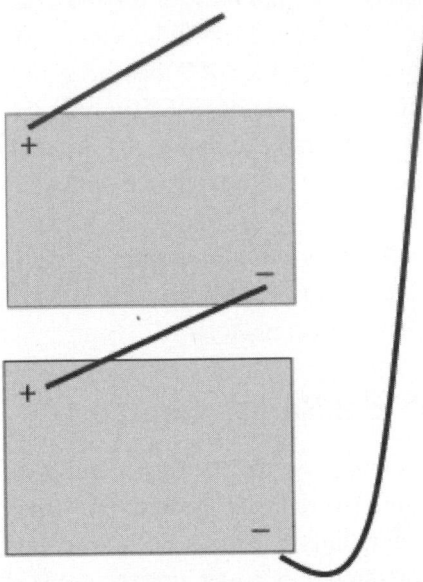

Batteries or solar panels wired in series. The amperage stays the same, but the voltages add up. These two 12V 120-amp batteries wired in series produce 24V at 120 amps.

48V). Batteries and panels are similarly wired in series to achieve the correct voltage, and in parallel to achieve the correct current (amps).

Series connections are made by connecting a pair of opposite poles or terminals of different batteries or PV panels (negative to positive). This increases the total voltage. The voltages are added together, while the amp capacity remains the same as just one of the batteries or panels.

Parallel connections are made by connecting the same poles or terminals (positive to positive and negative to negative) of multiple panels or batteries. The amperages are added together, but voltage stays the same as one of the

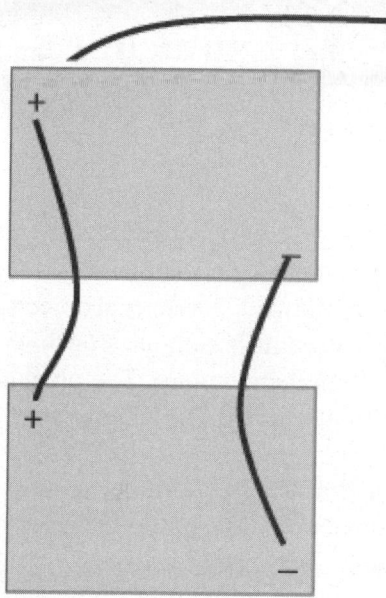

Batteries or solar panels wired in parallel. The voltage stays the same. The amps are added. These two 12V, 120-amp batteries wired in parallel produce 12 volts at 240 amps. Note that in parallel systems, the main cables must come from opposite corners to ensure that batteries arc charged and discharges equally.

batteries or panels, or as one of the parallel battery or panel strings in a bank or an array.

Battery banks often have batteries connected in both series and parallel.

Batteries are easy to wire when they're set in neat rows on long shelves. Make sure there's enough room above the battery to be able to access the caps to check and add water. Batteries can also be placed and oriented in different directions to fit tight or odd-shaped areas. However they are arranged, make certain the jumper cables or jumper bars don't obstruct the caps or threaten to contact the wrong terminal.

Chapter 7
Emergency Heating and Cooling

1. Heat

Heat is a form of energy, and understanding it will help you make decisions about producing and conserving or dispersing it.

Heat flows from warm objects to cold objects, changing the internal energy of both. It continues to flow until both objects are at the same temperature. The objects that lose heat also lose internal energy. The objects that gain heat, gain internal energy.

Heat flow, or heat transfer, can occur by conduction, convection, or radiation.

In conduction, heat is transferred by molecular excitation within a material without any motion of the object itself. Energy is transferred as the excited particles collide with slower particles and transfer the energy to them.

In convection, heat is transferred by the motion of a fluid or gas. The heated gas or fluid expands and becomes less dense, becoming more buoyant than the gas or fluid surrounding it. It rises, moving away from the source of heat and carrying energy with it. Cooler gas or fluid sinks and a circuit of circulation called a convection current is formed.

Radiation occurs when heat is transferred by electro-magnetic waves that carry energy away from the source.

Temperature is a measure of how hot a material is. Materials have different specific heat properties (thermal capacities). Two equal masses of different materials will reach different temperatures when heated with the same amount of energy. It's the difference in heat capacity that causes land masses to heat up faster than bodies of water, leading to sea breezes. Air warmed by the more rapidly heated land mass rises, and cooler air blows in from the body of water. These concepts of thermal capacity and heat transfer are important to understand when trying to efficiently heat a structure, especially when energy resources are limited.

Temperature can be measured in several different scales. The most commonly used by those of us who are not scientists are the Fahrenheit scale (F) and the Celsius scale(C). The steam point and the ice point (the points at which steam and ice are produced) are the reference points on these scales. The ice point is 32°F and 0°C. The steam point is 212°F and 100°C. For most of the world Celsius is easier to use because one degree represents 1/100th of the difference between the steam and ice points

2. Emergency Heating

When the power goes out and the gas shuts off and you're faced with a heating crisis, all sorts of bad things can occur. The house pipes can freeze, causing exaggerated structural damage. Drinking water and food can freeze, leaving the survivor struggling to avoid dehydration. Some of the most sinister hazards, though, are those posed by alternative heating and cooling sources that are often employed to make up for the loss of AC or the home furnace. During a real disaster incident the potential for a catastrophe is increased because fire and emergency services are already overwhelmed and may not be able to respond. For this reason, safety must be your primary concern when determining alternative forms of heat. Not a lot of people have frozen to death in their homes, bit plenty have died from fires, smoke inhalation, and carbon monoxide.

Look at what you can do to your home to mitigate the problem: caulking and weather-stripping doors and windows, plugging holes and air conditioning vents, applying a layer of plastic or an extra pane over windows, and installing insulating curtains. Have your fireplace or wood stove checked by a professional and get your chimney swept. Install battery-operated smoke alarms on every level of the building and check them frequently. Consider installing a battery-operated carbon monoxide detector.

During a heating emergency your first step is to put on some warm clothes, then:

- Find or improvise a heat source.
- Obtain fuel.
- Select an area or a room to be heated.
- Set up and operate the emergency heater.
- Deal with related problems—appraise for safety and make immediate changes.

In the planning stages you'll need to define the scope of the problem. In other words, how cold can it get, and how much will you and your home be affected? Even if your furnace burns fuel, how will it distribute heat? Fuel injectors, igniters, circulator pumps, motorized stokers, and most thermostats require electricity. Most coal, oil, and water heating systems are dependent on getting power.

As you're making your family plan or business plan, discuss the topic of alternative heating sources with your family members or business associates. What and where are they? How do you use them? How will you keep pipes from freezing? Consider your options. Could you operate the normal heating system by making minor modifications or operating it manually? With the right parts from your local gas supplier, could your natural gas appliances be modified to run off bottled gas? If your oven burns fuel, could you just simply turn it on and open the oven door? Are there other heating devices on the location that can be used, e.g., fireplace, wood stove, gas stove or oven, oil stove, space heater, camp stove, portable electric heater? Make a list of the fuels at or near your location. Can they be used in any of the alternative devices you thought of? Potential alternative fuels might include newspapers and magazines rolled tightly into log-sized bundles, dried weeds, firewood and lumber scraps, coal, charcoal, oil, kerosene, gas, camp-stove fuel, starter fluid, alcohol, gasoline, motor oil, fat, and grease, and even wood furniture and fixtures. Finally, ask yourself how much heat the alternative sources can supply (enough for several rooms?, for a single room?), and for how long?

If you can't figure out a way to modify and operate your normal heating system or other devices you already have to produce adequate heat, it's time to purchase or make another device that can. It may be as simple as getting a generator to run your heat pump. Or you might choose to purchase electric, gas, or kerosene space heaters or a wood-burning stove. Just remember . . .

Any heater that burns fuel must be vented to the outside in order to eliminate smoke and toxic fumes and to obtain oxygen for combustion. Make modifications and preparations ahead of time by having a professional set up a stovepipe or vent and flue.

3. Conserving Heat

During an actual heating emergency, your first concern should be conserving body heat. Here are some points regarding heat conservation:

- Eat enough food and drink enough water. Dehydration and low blood sugar accelerate the onset and progress of both hypothermia and heat exhaustion.

- Wear winter clothing, preferably many insulating layers rather than one huge bulky layer. Layers can be added or removed to adjust to the temperature.

- Additional insulation can be provided by sleeping bags, tarps, blankets, curtains, rugs, big towels, cardboard, or newspapers.

- Consider personal heating devices that would have a small demand on inverters, generators, or batteries. These include electric blankets, heating pads, and personal heaters or trucker's 12-volt low-watt cab heaters.

Need to heat or cool a tiny room for that 72-hours event, but you're limited to power from one of those DIY solar kits and a couple of batteries? Consider a small low-voltage space heater like the RoadPro 300-watt 12V Direct Hook-Up Ceramic Heater/Fan.

This 200 watt personal space heater goes for under $20 and could make
tip the balance towards a good night's sleep and non-frozen water bottles
and pipes.

- Huddle together, everyone in the same room. Consider huddling with your neighbors for additional heat.

- In your home, bed will be the warmest place. You can share body heat there with other family members and pile the bed high with whatever insulation you find.

- Sleeping in a tent pitched indoors will conserve body heat at night. If you have no indoors, a tent might be all you have, and you will be glad you have it.

- If you have no shelter, find some. A community emergency shelter will be heated.

- The smaller the space you heat, the easier it will be to heat and maintain heat. Choose one or two rooms. If you have a fuel-burning stove or a fireplace, the choice has been made for you. If you're going to use a portable heater, choose a room on the warmer side of the building, ideally away from prevailing winds but exposed to the sun. Choose a well-insulated room with few windows over a poorly insulated room with big windows. Interior bathrooms are well-suited for this. In some conditions, a basement may actually be warmer than the rest of the house because it may conduct heat from the ground. Insulate windows and openings, and partition with cardboard, curtains, or plywood if necessary. Close the door and block other openings to prevent unwanted drafts, but remember that if you're using a fuel-burning stove or heater, you'll need a chimney vent or flue or you'll need to provide a cross-draft for ventilation.

- Bring your stored water into that same room to keep it from freezing, or run a heating pad into the storage area from your inverter or generator. If it's already frozen, bring it in to passively thaw. Actively melting ice or snow for water in a waste of precious fuel.

- If your house has no heater and you have a trailer or camper with a heater, move into it.

- As a last resort, get into your car and use the heater. This is risky, and you should carefully ventilate the cab to prevent carbon monoxide poisoning.

4. Safety

- The very, very last resort is using improvised heaters like charcoal grills and gas ovens. These are very risky. Charcoal will produce copious carbon monoxide so efficient that in many countries it's a very common tool for suicide. Gas ovens are an asphyxiation hazard. If you use them be prepared to provide plenty of ventilation to outside air. Better to be cold than dead.

- **If you're using a catalytic heater, a fuel-burning heater that provides heat with no flame, or any unvented fuel-burning heater, provide adequate ventilation. Keep a nearby window open at least one inch whenever the heater is used. Even better, provide cross-ventilation by opening a window one inch on each side of the room, but close it when the heater is not being used to prevent heat loss.**

- Turn fuel-burning space heaters off before you go to bed. **Never sleep in a fuel-heated room with no ventilation.** Having an extra battery-operated carbon monoxide or CO/smoke combination detector for the sleeping room is a good idea.

Sensors are now being produced which work remotely with Bluetooth to warn of the presence on carbon monoxide, smoke, gas, and other toxic or hazardous substances.

- If you plan to use unvented gas or kerosene heaters, the following applies:
  - Read the manufacturer's instructions carefully.
  - Use space heaters that are certified to meet safety standards by the Underwriter's Laboratories (UL) or the American Gas Association laboratories.

- Use space heaters that have an oxygen depletion valve so it shuts off if there's a lack of good air or there's excessive carbon monoxide.
- Have the heater inspected before you store it. If you use it, have it inspected annually.
- Use only the fuel for which the appliance was designed.
- In a kerosene heater, use only clear white water-free IK kerosene.
- Refuel heaters outside with the fuel valve closed and after the device has cooled. Never attempt to refuel while the stove is still lit. Fill only as directed in the owner's manual.

- Keep flammable materials away from vents and stovepipes. Keep portable heaters several feet away from furniture and other flammables.

- If you're using wood or coal burning stoves, be careful with the ashes. Empty them in a covered metal container and store them outside away from combustibles. Do NOT attempt to vacuum up dry ashes.

- Assign someone to fire watch whenever open-flame cooking and heating are in progress.

- Set up your firefighting items near your heating and cooking devices. If you don't have a dry-powder extinguisher, keep a bucket of sand, salt, baking soda, or water to smother and cool the fire (the water will not work on liquid fuels and may actually spread a fuel fire). A heavy blanket can be used to smother a small fire. Make sure the family or group understands the evacuation plan and at least two ways out of the building.

- If you have neighbors with special needs, do a courtesy check to ensure they are safe.

5. Storing Emergency Fuel

Store enough for several days. If your kit is a three-day (72-hour) kit, store enough for three days. If it's a two week kit, store enough for two weeks. Do some thinking. You don't need 24/7 power to your big appliances. Run your fridge or furnace in one- or two-hour spurts with equal periods without power in between. You won't need lights during daylight or sleeping hours, or heaters during the day. For a conservative, small household most mid-size generators can do the work with 2–4 gallons per day. To be safe, figure it out by multiplying the generator's gallons-per-hour by the number of hours you think you'll need to run it.

Let's assume your backup power source is a generator. Contrary to what the Prepper sites endeavor to tell you, it IS possible to store your generator with a full tank of gas. The key is to shut off the fuel supply valve and run the engine until it's dry of fuel (it will stop running at that point). That gives you a full tank of fuel in your generator without having to screw around in the dark, and without having to get the fuel from that nasty 5-gallon storage can through the little nozzle and into the invisible tank cap!

Based on what we've said here, 20–25 gallons in total would be a very generous supply of fuel for a 72-hour incident, with extra just in case you need it for the car or truck. Easy to do: fill the generator and store the rest in four five-gallon cans. In addition, a full 1-gallon container with an easy-to-use spout is a real convenience to get started with.

Don't let your fuel-powered devices sit without running them. Run them a couple of times per year for a few minutes to keep them humming and intercept problems.

Make things easy by storing fuel in their traditionally colored containers: red for gasoline, blue for kerosene, yellow for diesel. Sticking to the color codes will keep you from pouring the wrong fuel into the wrong apparatus.

Fuel should be stored airtight in a safe, cool, dry place away from the house or residence, such as a garage or shed.

For various reasons, fuels like gasoline, kerosene, and diesel lose their potency with time, and if stored for long periods (usually many months, not weeks) without a fuel stabilizer they can be rendered useless. The additives commonly used to prevent this deterioration are STA-BIL and PRI-G or D (Gas or Diesel). Other additives are available, and Preppers are often very zealously attached to one product or another. Go with PRI or *Sea Foam* and the *Sta Bil*-izers might stop inviting you to coffee.

Rotate fuel by occasionally using it to fill your car or to fuel a campout, but always replace it immediately.

During the emergency, store fuel where it's easily accessible, but do NOT store flammable or highly combustible fuels like gas and kerosene in or near the residence or the heated area.

Find out if there are community stockpiles of emergency fuel, and where community plans have designated emergency shelters.

6. Dealing with Frozen Pipes

Drain pipes and containers that will not be getting heat pose a problem. This includes anything in any room where the temperature drops below 35°F: house plumbing, toilet tanks and bowls, bathtubs, dish and clothes washers and their hoses, the hot water heater tank, and the furnace boiler.

Cover un-drained pipes with whatever insulation you can spare. Consider heating vulnerable pipes with a heating pad (only 12 to 36 watts each) powered by your inverter or generator. If the water supply is intact and the main valve is open, try running a trickle of water from a faucet or two to keep water circulating, which helps prevent it from freezing.

To flush toilets, use a bucket of water that is not fit for drinking or cooking. Flush only as often as it's necessary in order to prevent the system from clogging or freezing.

7. Emergency Cooling

When the power goes off during a heat wave and you're faced with a cooling crisis, all sorts of bad things can occur as a result. The fans and air conditioners will stop. Ice melts, food rots. Everyone becomes dehydrated and cranky or truly sick. Like heating emergencies, cooling emergencies can be a real threat. Heat is especially hard on the very young or very old, and anyone with chronic health problems.

There are plenty of things to do to limit the effects of heat:

- Be prepared. In the evening open the windows and turn on the fans for cross-ventilation. That will cool the house down. When the sun comes up in the morning, shut all the windows and doors, close the curtains, and leave them shut and closed all day until the cooler evening. Then open things up again.

- Drink plenty of water, even if you're not thirsty, and even if it's humid. Dehydration will speed the effects of heat illness. Alcohol will dehydrate you, and caffeinated, carbonated, and heavily sugared drinks like lemonade are not efficient hydrators. If it's real hot, drink the coolest water you can find. Be aware that it IS possible to overhydrate. On a hot day with moderate physical activity an adult will go through about a gallon. Too much more than that can cause a condition called hyponatremia, with symptoms similar to those of heat injuries.

- Sports drinks can be beneficial in replacing electrolytes you have sweated off. Avoid salt tablets unless a doctor tells you otherwise.

- Avoid strenuous activity, and work during the coolest parts of the day (early morning).

- Stay inside, or at least avoid direct sunlight and stay in shaded areas. Outside, wear lightweight, loose-fitting, long-sleeved clothing. A hat with a large brim helps protect against the sun.

- If possible, keep the air moving. Put a fan in an upstairs window to blow off the heat in the upper levels. A fan in a lower window will help create a heat reducing cross-draft.

- Turn off any sources of heat, including lights and computers. Keep the stove off. Eat foods that don't require cooking.

- Eat frequent small meals and avoid high-protein foods.

- Move to the lowest level of the building (probably the basement). Cold air is more dense and sinks to lower levels. Also, lower levels might stay cooler because of the colder ground it conducts from.

- Wet your wrists frequently with cold ice or water.

- If you're sweating, use it to your advantage. Stand in a breeze or in front of a fan. When water evaporates, it absorbs heat, drawing it away from the body.

- Get in a tub of water or take a shower if it doesn't deplete precious water supplies. Sit with your hands or feet in a basin of cold water.

- Fill a glass with ice and blow into it and let your face catch the cool air that comes out.

- Take off your shoes and hats. The head and feet have a big role in regulating body temperature.

- If you can't keep up with the heat, go to a community shelter where it's likely to be cooled.

- Turn yourself into a human swamp cooler. If you live in a dry climate, one of these techniques can cool you off considerably.

  - Use a squirt bottle to saturate the sleeves of your shirt or the legs of your pants. Evaporation will cool the arms and legs.

  - Put on a dripping wet t-shirt.

- Put a wet towel on the back of the neck or the top of the head.
- Consider wearing a "gutra," the large white scarf made of thin breathable material and worn by Arabian men. Make your own out of whatever material you can find. Soak it with water and plant yourself in a breeze. Reap the benefits. The author actually tested the cooling efficiency of wet gutras while doing remote backcountry projects in Arabia. The temperature difference between unshaded air outside the gutra and air around the face beneath the gutra was significant—as much as 40°F on hot, dry days.

Is your refrigerator sucking up so much juice you can't run the AC? The improvised AC unit seen here uses one tenth the power your window AC does, and consists of a cooler with a couple of PVC elbows to direct the airflow. A fan on low speed blows air through a hole and across frozen plastic water bottles stacked inside the cooler.

- Run a fan over an ice chest. It will melt precious ice, but it can provide localized relief for a couple of hours.

- Consider purchasing an inexpensive portable single-room air conditioner, with the understanding that running it will require about 700 watts or more to cool about 300 square feet. That means you'll need a generator if the power's off.

- Portable air coolers (swamp coolers) can be found for less than $100 and can run on less than 100 watts from an inverter. Unfortunately they are only substantially effective in dryer climates.

The bottom line is that with some knowledge and preparation you can survive a disastrous heat wave. Sufficient water is the key for both hydration and body-cooling.

Chapter 8
Water

The importance of proper hydration can't be over-emphasized. Emergency responders and emergency medical personnel are acutely aware that when the body is subjected to physical stressors such as heat, cold, injury, and infection, hydration is an essential key to prevention, and to limiting the damage and promoting recovery.

Active adults need a couple of liters of water or equivalent fluid hydration per day, and even more in extreme conditions. Within just a few days dehydration can easily become life-threatening. In a major disaster you can expect to lose your normal sources of water due to the loss of power to pumps, infrastructure collapse, structural damage, and contamination. Keep adequate water in storage, and stay ahead of the game. If you think there's a chance your water sources will be cut off, fill the tub and other clean containers as soon as possible and then shut off the main supply to protect the water that remains in the house.

Here are the basic rules of thumb for water in disaster situations:

- Store a minimum of three days of water, at a gallon per person per day. Add more if you have children, nursing mothers, chronically ill family members, a highly active group, or if your area experiences excessively hot or cold weather.
- Drink only the water you know is safe. NEVER drink untreated floodwater.

- Potentially contaminated water can be used after it has been purified or treated properly as long as there's no lingering chemical contamination.

- Reduce your water and food requirements by keeping physical activity to a minimum.

- Don't ration water unless told to do so by the authorities.

- Caffeine, alcohol, and dehydrated and freeze-dried foods do not contribute to hydration. Use these drinks and foods cautiously in moderation and not as a substitute for water or other fluids.

The primary sources of water for consumption will be commercially bottled water or tap water that's been stored beforehand with your disaster kit.

Commercially bottled water should be kept sealed until it is used. Try to comply with use-by dates but don't just toss it out if it's past its date.

Tap water can be stored in food-grade water storage containers that can be purchased at preparedness and outdoor sports stores, or in sanitized two-liter or gallon soda or water bottles. Don't use milk or juice bottles because the odor and taste can carry over, and unless they're thoroughly sanitized, they can culture bacteria. Use plastic, food-grade containers instead of glass to avoid getting your water containers shattered. On the bottom of the container will be a triangle with a number in it. Generally the safer choices for food and water storage have a triangle with number 1,2,4, or 5. Supposedly these plastics react least with the contents and should off-gas less than other plastics. Also, consider mobility. If you need to evacuate your home, a 20-gallon container is going to weigh 160 pounds and won't fit in your backpack. Smaller containers can be divided among the group and will be easier to handle.

To clean and sanitize containers for water storage, here are the steps:

1. Clean the container with a dash of dishwashing soap and lots of hot water, then rinse thoroughly several times.

2. Drop a teaspoon (5ml) per quart of unscented liquid bleach (3–6% sodium hypochlorite) into the container. Replace the lid loosely. Shake the container to completely cover all surfaces, then hold the bottle upside down to make sure the remaining bleach coats the neck of the bottle and the inside of the screw cap. Rinse with water that has been purified and treated.

3. Fill the bottle with water to the top. If the water is treated already (e.g. tap water from an uncontaminated water line, or water purified and treated by you), then screw on the cap tightly and store the container in a cool, dark place. If the water is untreated, before putting it in the bottle perform the purification or treatment processes discussed later in this chapter.

4. Replace stored water every six months.

Of course it's all much simpler to just go to the local discount store and purchase bottled water. Pint bottles are convenient, but one- to three-gallon jugs are easier and less bulky for storage. It's cheap and easily replaced.

Once you've lost your main source of water and you resort to using your stored supply, you should be searching for alternative sources for future use. How do you determine which sources are safe?

Large commercial water containers are available from stores handling emergency preparedness supplies. Above: a 7 gallon container that integrates a water filter in the spigot and a hand-operated water filter.

First, make it perfectly clear to your group that the stored water is only for consumption, not for flushing toilets and washing clothes. Use other questionable water sources for those purposes.

The following sources can be considered safe for drinking and cooking if no contamination has occurred prior to shutting off the main water valve:

- Remaining pipe water.
- Toilet tank water, if not treated with cleaning or deodorizing chemicals. A few drops of bleach will make skeptics more comfortable.
- Water from undamaged hot-water heater tanks.

The following sources can be used if properly purified or treated:

- Water from wells and cisterns
- Rainwater and water from streams, rivers, ponds, and natural springs
- Salt water

These sources should be considered unsafe and should be used for flushing toilets and washing clothes:

- Radiators
- Hot tubs
- Swimming pools

To use water remaining in house pipes, open the highest faucet in the house or building and get the water from the lowest faucets. To get the water out of the main hot water heating tank, shut off the electricity and gas, close the cold water intake valve, and drain the water from the hot water valve. Refill the tank before turning the electricity or gas back on.

1. Water Harvesting

If you're not lucky enough to have property with a well or spring, eventually you will be required to undertake water harvesting. In any case, the key to water sustainability is conservation and the art of catchment. Catchment systems work where wells can't be dug, groundwater is contaminated, springs can't be found, and other sources are scarce. Even in the desert, a short rain can deliver enough water to keep the household going until the next storm.

The easiest form of storm harvesting is any variation of the basic rain barrel. Simply placing a single wide-top bin out for catchment could easily double your supply.

The next step up is to feed the rain barrel via the downspout of the rain gutters or the edges of the building. Yes, the water will certainly be dirty, but can be filtered and treated. Metal or clay tile roofs seem to be cleaner than shingles roofs. If a water catchment is already a part of your household routine, you may be using commercial rain barrels with perks like roof-cleaner diverters and pre-barrel filters.

Water from a barrel is not pressurized, except by gravity, but that gives it just enough pressure to water as garden or run a simple shower using a hose from the barrel drain. Elevating the barrel, using cinder blocks, increases the pressure, but it won't support a plumbing system of any kind without a pump. Large storm harvesting systems intended to provide water for drinking, cooking, and bathing will need pumping, filtration, and disinfection systems.

Some preppers will have gone to great lengths to build extensive harvesting systems, with small systems draining into larger above-ground tanks, underground cisterns, or dammed reservoirs. Some commercial versions also have roof-cleaning diverters.

Aside from roofs, melt- and rainwater can be captured from gullies and washes, but the obvious problem is sediment (mud) buildup and the control of raging floodwaters. Large systems like this can become hazards to anything downstream.

Some old-school harvesting methods are more labor-intensive but work well. Excavate the available land area so impermeable surfaces (cement, pavement, etc.) are minimized and the ground is morphed in a way that it catches the rain and funnels it in the direction you want it to go as irrigation or catchwater. Terracing is a simple method of keeping rain- and met-water from running away. Directing the water into a mulch basin is another effective variation. Mulch basins are pits or trenches planted with high crops (large plants or trees) and covered with mulch. A mulch basin is also a good place to send gray water if the basin has been planted with alkaline tolerant plants.

A cistern is a tank made of concrete, steel, fiberglass, or plastic and can sit either above or below ground. If the cistern or water tank is aboveground and higher than the building's internal plumbing, the weight of the water in the cistern may provide adequate pressure. Otherwise a pump is needed to send water from the catchment to the house. Again, filtering and disinfection will be needed before using the water for drinking, cooking, or bathing. A rain barrel or any other aboveground storage device requires steps to keep it from freezing.

Water harvesting can come to a standstill in very cold conditions. Melting ice or snow can consume enormous amounts of precious fuel or power, and without a means of melting ice and snow, a survivor will be helpless. A black plastic tarp or large black garbage bag laid out in the sun can be used to harness solar energy to melt snow for water. In seriously frigid temperatures, this may require careful aiming of the tarp toward the sun and standing by to frequently spread snow thinly over the black surface. Collect the trickle by funneling it into a container. Knowing how to do this may make the difference between life and a rim death from dehydration and starvation.

In sub-freezing environments water will freeze overnight, if not kept warm, and will be useless by morning. Insulate bottles and store them with you in bed or under your coat to keep them fluid.

2. Contamination

Disasters can contaminate local water resources. Water can be contaminated with industrial pollutants (chemicals), but the most common contamination is by disease-producing microorganisms (bacteria, viruses, protozoa, and helminthes) from sewage, leading to diseases such as cholera, typhoid, dysentery, and hepatitis. Once many of these diseases have started, they are rapidly spread through bad water consumption and oral-fecal contamination (for example, the germs from scratching your butt getting left on the doorknobs or tools you handle).

Simple hygiene—washing the hands and cleaning utensils—can prevent gastrointestinal diseases. Use warm soapy water for cleaning hands, especially after urination and defecation. Alcohol-based hand sanitizers are good to have around, but are only effective when there is no visible dirt on your hands. So wash with soap and water anyway.

Used correctly, alcohol-based hand sanitizers kill most bacteria and fungi, and some viruses. Rub it thoroughly on hands and wrists for 30 seconds until it's dry. Pay attention to fingernails and between fingers. Follow this procedure before and after preparing food, eating, treating wounds or giving medicine, touching a sick or injured person, using the toilet, changing a diaper, touching an animal or animal toys, leashes or waste, blowing your nose, coughing or sneezing into your hands, handling garbage or possibly contaminated items (e.g. bedclothes, dirty laundry).

Keep cooking and eating utensils clean and as sanitized as possible. Do not use contaminated, untreated water to wash or rinse utensils. The rumor that all germs will die when the dishes dry is completely false. Consider storing paper plates, disposable cups, and disposable utensils in your kit. Do not re-use them. This will conserve water and help prevent diseases.

3. Purification and Treatment

Gastrointestinal illness from bad water is a major cause of death from hypovolemia and diarrhea during disasters. The goal of purifying and treating water is to reduce the pathogens ("germs") so there's an acceptably low risk of illness. Important: Judging water by taste, appearance, smell, and source is not reliable.

The most common ways of treating and purifying water are simple:

- Distillation
- Boiling for a few minutes (longer at higher altitudes where the boiling point is lower than at sea level.
- Chemical treatment from chemical purification tablets or household liquid chlorine (3–6% unscented

sodium hypochlorite) at four to eight drops per quart.
Shake and stir, then let sit for 30 minutes.

- Water filters, which vary greatly in their effectiveness.
- Ultraviolet (UV) purifiers.
- Solar disinfection (SODIS).

If you're serious about getting the best water possible under
austere conditions, the purification and treatment process is a

4. Steps in Water Purification

---

1. Screening

Screening removes the largest contaminants.

Fill a container by dripping or pouring water through a cloth,
bandana, handkerchief, coffee filter, t-shirt, or fine strainer.

2. Standing

Allow the water to remain completely still for an hour. Clean off
the floaters and then pour off the water into another container to
leave the sediment behind.

3. Flocculating

This is an optional process that removes fine suspended particles.

Add a pinch of alum or baking powder per gallon. Stir gently for
five minutes. This promotes agglomeration of small particles to
form a precipitate. Let it stand for a few minutes, then pour off the
clean water or filter through a coffee filter.

4. Disinfection

This step is accomplished by using one or more of the following
methods:

Heat

Most GI pathogens are easily destroyed by heat. The effectiveness
of heat depends on the temperature and the exposure time. Lower
temperatures can be effective at longer exposure times.

(cont'd.)

Steps in water purification

It's risky to estimate temperatures, so use the boiling point as the target temperature. At that temperature disisnfection has already occurred by the time the water boils. At altitudes over 6,500 feet (2,000 meters) the CDC recommends boiling for three minutes. Disadvantages: Boiling is fuel-intensive and requires waiting for water to cool

Filters

Pump filters screen out bacteria, protozoa, helminthes and their cysts and eggs if they filter down to the 0.2 micron range. Most filters are not reliable against viruses less than 0.1 micron in size. Filters clog over time, and operating a clogged filter can actually force pathogens through. Where viruses are a problem choose a filter with iodine resin or upgrade to a purifier. Filters impregnated with iodine or bactericidal crystals are of questionable efficiency. When unclear about the efficiency of a filter system, use other methods of disinfection as a final step.

For families or big groups, gravity filters are quick and filter out everything pump models do, but handle larger volumes of water.

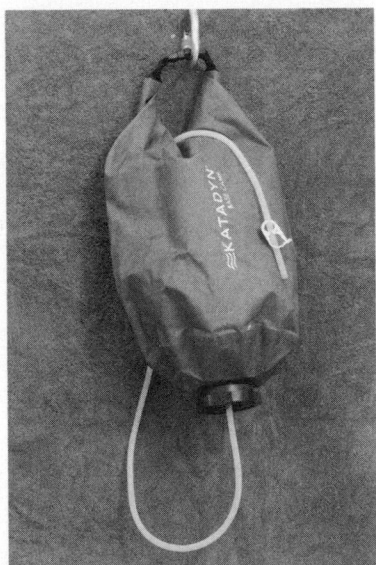

A group-size gravity filter.

(cont'd.)

Steps in water purification

Chemicals

Halogenation uses chemicals like iodine and chlorine to purify water. These chemicals are effective against viruses and bacteria, but their efficiency against helminthes and protozoa and their eggs varies. *Cryptosporidium*, a parasite commonly found in lakes and rivers, especially when the water is contaminated with sewage and animal waste, is resistant to halogenation.

The efficiency of halogen depends on the concentration, the length of exposure, the temperature of the water, pH, and the presence of contaminants. Chlorine bleach is the most sensitive to these factors and is less suited for cold water. In these conditions halogens require increased time and increased concentration. Be sure to strain the water first. Particulates deactivate halogen.

That said, bleach is the cheapest, most convenient method of disinfecting water. How long can you store bleach? Bleach loses its potency over time. Whether or not the container has been opened, temperature is the determining factor. Assuming the bleach is stored around 70°F, you have about six months from the date of manufacture, or about 3-5 months from the date of purchase where the bleach is at the effectiveness level stated on its label. At 90°F you'll have about three months from the date of purchase. That doesn't mean the bleach is bad when it's six months old. It just means you'll want to add an extra drop or two to each liter. Store bleach in a cool place, and replace it at least once per year.

Chlorine dioxide comes in liquid and tablet options. It reacts less with pollutants than chlorine bleach and is effective within a wider range of pH. It also has a less offensive taste than other halogens, and is effective against cryptosporidium.

Chlorine dioxide tablets weigh almost nothing (less than an ounce for 30). They're easy to use—just pop one tablet into your bottle—but they take 30 minutes to kill Giardia and up to four hours for cryptosporidium. Iodine tablets are also lightweight and cheap, but they won't kill crypto and leave an unpleasant taste.

UV

Ultraviolet disinfection using special lamps is effective against even stubborn cysts. UV may not actually kill pathogens. Rather, UV light renders them harmless by scrambling their DNA with radiation. The organisms become unable to reproduce and no

(cont'd.)

Steps in water purification

longer capable of infecting a host (i.e., a human body) when consumed. In the past UV lamps required a lot of energy. Another problem with UV is that particulates shield the pathogens. To work, the UV light must reach the organism in the water. Anything that blocks the light may lessen its effectiveness. Therefore, particles should be filtered from the water before it's exposed to the UV treatment device. In a worst case scenario it would be possible to achieve adequate disinfection by using a process called SODIS (solar disinfection). Sodis is performed by simply filling a one- or two-liter plastic water bottle with screened or filtered water and laying it on its side outside on a light colored reflective surface like cement, tile, or metal. If the sun's out, the UV radiation will disinfect the water within six hours. If it's cloudy, leave the bottle out for at least two days. Any clear plastic or glass bottle can be used, but the best plastic bottles are those that have a faint blue tinge.

Steps in water purification

A battery-powered ultraviolet light purifier like this SteriPen (steripen.com) works in less than a minute and doesn't leave a chemical aftertaste. Carry extra batteries.

detailed, multi-step procedure involving screening, standing, flocculation (optional), and disinfection.

5. Distillation

Distillation is a slow process that is gadget-intensive, but it will remove microbes that resist other methods. It will also remove heavy metals, salts, and most other chemicals. This is the ONLY way you'll be able to prepare saltwater for consumption. It involves boiling water and then collecting the vapor that condenses back to water. Distilled water is popular, and countertop distillers are available for under a hundred dollars. The problem is they require electricity, which you might not have unless you have an alternative power source. There are some camp stove distillers on the market. Their drawback is the excessive fuel requirement.

An astoundingly simple distilling set-up: a ¾ x ½-inch tubing in an old liquor bottle. Water is boiled in the bottle and collected in a cup or glass. Two cups of seawater yield one half cup of fresh water from an hour of boiling.

To distill without one of these devices, a Red Cross site recommends the following method: Fill a pot halfway with water. Tie a cup to the handle on the pot's lid so the cup will hang right-side up when the lid is upside down (make sure the cup is not dangling into the water) and boil the water for 20 minutes. The water that drips from the lid into the cup is distilled.

Chapter 9
Food and Nutrition

In physically stressful times it's important to eat enough to maintain your strength and alertness. When we get hypoglycemic one of the first symptoms is a decrease in mental capacity. As long as you eat at least one large well-balanced meal each day, or several small meals, it's okay to ration food if you think the event will be prolonged. It's *not okay* to ration water. The body can function adequately for extended periods with reduced food, but skimping on water or fluids will quickly lead to debilitating dehydration. Drink a minimum of two quarts per day just to ensure you're getting enough, and take in enough calories to enable you to do any necessary work. If you don't have the food to keep up with the work, reduce the workload first, then reduce food consumption if necessary. Include vitamin, mineral, and protein supplements in your food storage.

The ideal food supply for a disaster situation will be relatively compact and light weight for portability. It will require no refrigeration and minimum cooking. Cooking requires bulky pots and pans, a stove, electricity or fuel, and dishwashing puts a strain on your water supply.

But let's back up and take a look at these two basic technological bits: refrigeration and cooking. In a major disaster our electricity will be cut off and gas lines will be shut off. It could be days or weeks before it's restored. Obviously you'll want to keep the perishables good as long as possible, and you'll need need to eat the perishables first. That's going to take some cooking. Steps can be taken to keep those perishables good as long as possible, and there are some things you can do to provide yourself with alternative means of cooking.

1. Emergency Refrigeration

After the power fails, avoid opening the refrigerator or freezer. An unopened fridge will remain adequately cold for about two hours. Insulating the fridge or freezer with blankets will retard the escape of cold, but be careful not to block vents.

Additional time can be gained by transferring blocks of ice from the freezer to the refrigerator, and by putting dry ice in the freezer. The transfer should take seconds, not minutes, or the benefits will be lost. Open the appliance doors only as long as it takes to quickly move the ice.

The amount of dead air space in a fridge or freezer affects the time it will maintain acceptable temperature. Fuller is better. Solid ice blocks and cold water bottles replace harmful warm air. The cold of a fridge full of ice blocks or ice water will last must longer than the cold of a fridge that is half full.

If the power is still on, or if you have a warning period before an event, turn the temperature to maximum cold in both fridge and freezer and start making ice blocks.

If coolers are used, put ice in the cooler first to pre-cool it then quickly transfer the food. Dead air in a cooler has the same effect as in the fridge. Use a smaller cooler to avoid dead air. Store the cooler in a cool shaded location and insulate it with a blanket. In winter and extreme very high altitude environments, refrigeration can be managed quite well by keeping coolers in the shade. Don't drain the melt water unless absolutely necessary. Cold water stays colder longer than cold air.

Dry ice is frozen carbon dioxide. It has several times the cooling energy of water ice per equivalent volume. It's so cold that it can actually burn the skin. It sublimes instead of freezing: five pounds will sublime within a day in a cooler. Dry ice can be used to extend the life of regular ice. Unfortunately, dry ice will be in extremely short supply after a disaster. If you're going to need it, you'd better make arrangements with your supplier (usually a large supermarket) beforehand.

Once the power has gone off, you'll need to start "triaging" your food supply. Eat perishable items from the fridge first. Eat or toss out meat, poultry, seafood, dairy, and all cooked foods if they've been in a closed fridge without power, with a temperature greater than 40°F, longer than four hours. A thermometer for the fridge is a good idea but do NOT open the fridge to check the temperature. Plan to check the temperature only when the fridge is opened to obtain food. If you have your refrigerator packed with ice blocks, the food should be good until the ice blocks are melted as long as the interior temperature stays below 40°F. Do NOT rely on odor or appearance.

After you've eaten the foods from the refrigerator, eat perishables from the freezer. Foods from the freezer should only be eaten if they still have ice crystals in their interior or if the temperature in the freezer has not gone above 40°F.

Immediately throw away any food that may have come into contact with flood or storm water, and any food in containers with screw caps, crimped or twisted caps, snap lids, and snap open tops if they have been in contact with flood water.

Any of the following foods should be eaten before they sit unrefrigerated for more than two hours. Otherwise, toss them out:

- Raw meat, poultry, seafood
- Casseroles, stew soups
- Milk, cream, yogurt, soft cheese
- Cooked pasta, pasta salads
- Fresh eggs, egg substitutes
- Mayonnaise and tartar sauce
- Cream-filled pastries

These foods are okay for several days at room temperature:

- Fresh fruits and vegetables
- Butter and margarine
- Opened jars of salad dressing, peanut butter, jelly, relish, mustard, ketchup, olives, pickles
- Hard and processed cheeses
- Fruit juices
- Fruit pies, bread, rolls, cakes, muffins

Shelf life of common food items:

- The following items should be eaten within 6 months: boxed powdered milk, dried fruit, dry crisp crackers, potatoes
- These items should be consumed within a year: canned meat and veggie soups, canned fruits and veggies, peanut butter and jelly, hard candy, canned nuts, vitamins

- The following items keep indefinitely as long as they are packaged properly and stored in the right conditions: wheat, soybeans, white rice, dry pasta, bouillon, vegetable oils, baking powder, salt, instant coffee, cocoa, tea, powdered milk, and powdered soft drinks.

2. Emergency Cooking

When the utilities go down, both the gas and the electricity are gone, and so is the cooking. An emergency stove and the fuel to run it are prudent items to pack in the emergency storage. The size, weight, and complexity of the stove a person packs away will, again, depend on the duration he or she hopes to be prepared for. For most people that will be three full days (72 hours). A three-day stove does not need to be complex, heavy, or bulky, and can be fueled most easily by one tiny compressed gas cartridge, a handful of fuel tablets, or a couple of cans of Sterno. On the other hand, those preparing for the long haul (months to years) are going to want something more substantial. That includes a stove rig with multiple burners and perhaps an oven.

Emergency stoves fall under four basic categories:

- **Unpressurized liquid fuel stoves** include simple alcohol and jellied fuel stoves. They're container stoves. Open the factory-filled can or pour the fuel into the container and light it. Burn it until the fuel's gone or smother the flames by covering the container with its cap. Simple. No moving parts. Advantages: cheap, fast, quiet. Disadvantages: Slower boiling time than with compressed gas stoves, and sluggish to light in extremely cold temperatures.

A folding stove for canned fuel or solidified alcohol fuel. When the normal fuel runs out, these stoves can be used to burn natural fuels.

- **Solid fuel stoves** include two subtypes:
  - **Chemical Fuel tablet** stoves using hexamine or trioxine tablets
  - **Natural fuel** stoves using wood or other natural products (including charcoal). Natural fuels may be difficult to light and tend to produce a sooty smoke, but they have some very obvious advantages: they're free and easy to find, so there's little need to carry or store it. Even better—there's no spill or explosion hazard.

    Natural fuel stoves commonly have a base plate, legs, pot supports, and air holes (ventilation) top and bottom. Versions improvised from tin cans and soda pop cans are referred to as "hobo stoves" or "penny stoves."

- **Pressurized liquid fuel** stoves include those that use liquid fuel (white gas, gasoline, kerosene) heat-pressurized within the burner, and stoves that use compressed gas cartridges (butane or propane). These stoves are efficient, but in some cases liquid fuels require priming, and compressed gases burn slightly colder.

- A **solar oven** uses the energy of the sun to heat food or liquids. Solar ovens are generally bulky, fragile, low tech devices. They use no fuel, which is great, but commercial stoves are expensive, and improvised stoves are rarely effective enough to be considered for survival when there are easier solid-fuel alternatives. The simplest solar oven is a two-quart wide-mouth glass jar on the dark dashboard of a car with the windows rolled up: Heats a can of ravioli or an MRE in an hour.

A cast iron two-burner propane stove, a camp heater/stove combo, and a backpacker stove.

Whatever type of stove you use, wind screens improve the performance of the stove by blocking wind and reflecting heat onto the cooking pot or pan.

For a wonderful fountain of information on improvising survival stoves, go to youtube.com.

3. Food for Disaster Kits and Food Storage

In a crisis you'll need to maintain your strength, and that requires eating nutritiously. Don't fill your kit with "junk food." Of course, what constitutes "junk food" varies from person to person. Trust me on this one—when you're starving, there's not a lot of food that qualifies as "junk." Here are some standard tips on reasonable food.

- Plan the meals so you know what and how much you'll need to stock for the period of time you're preparing for.
- Include a good variety of foods.
- Eat at least one well-balanced meal per day.
- Consume enough liquid (two quarts per day) to avoid dehydration and to allow your body to process your food.
- Consume the calories you'll need
- Take vitamin, mineral, and protein supplements if necessary to ensure good nutrition.
- When choosing foods, consider how you will prepare them. The easiest meals require little or no cooking or water for preparation.
- If any of your food has to be heated, don't forget to put a stove and plenty of fuel in your disaster kit. Also, make certain you have the can openers and

knives or scissors you'll need to get into the food containers.

- Compact and lightweight foods are easier to manage and move around.

- Make a list of dates when food items need to be rotated (used and replaced). Better yet, use and renew your storage twice per year on the same days each year. For instance, the author replaces his storage on the winter and summer solstices.

- Use what you have on hand in your home cupboard and fridge to supplement and extend your disaster food supply. Remember to eat your perishables first. If you must leave your home and you have time to do so, fill a cooler with ice and whatever food you can take from the fridge and freezer, and fill a duffle with the food from the cupboard. Most households could easily make their 72-hour kit last a week or two by supplementing it with what's on hand.

To help you decide what to store for emergencies, look over the following chart:

What Category Of Food Prepper Are You?

Study the chart above and compare the information to your vision of personal preparation. You'll see disaster food storage can be easily categorized. As a rule of thumb, you'll be happier and better prepared if you store about 70% of your food from the category that fits you best, and 30% from the other three categories.

Category 1: The Pessimist: This Category best fits the devout Survivalist or the mega-Prepper stocking up for an Armageddon-style event. (> 1 month)

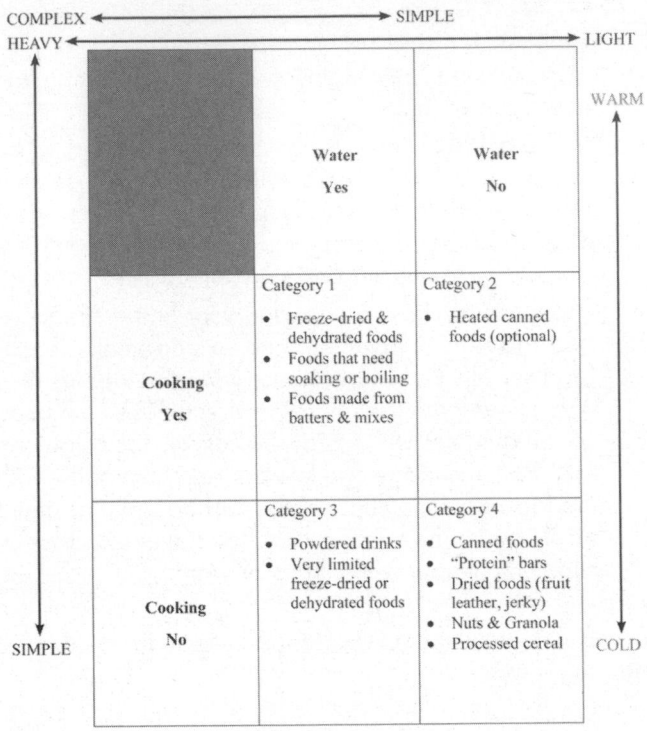

Category 2: The Minimalist: For the short to medium term, for the person who wants his meals easy and hot.

Category 3: The Optimist. Short-term only (1–3 days). Survival on vitamin-laced lemonade is a tough row to hoe.

Category 4: The Realist: For short to medium term survival with maximum variety and instant availability of meals without being tied to a kitchen ritual. (> 3 days)

A reasonable disaster stash for a few bad months . . . heavy on the ready to eat food with a healthy portion of staples and mixes.

Food for the 72-hour Kit

A typical 72-hour kit should contain a selection of the following foods:

- Ready to eat canned meats, fruits, and vegetables
- Canned juices, milk, soup
- Sugar, salt, pepper
- High-energy foods – peanut butter, jelly, crackers, granola bars, trail mix
- Foods for anyone with special needs – infants, elderly, or those requiring special diets
- Dry and/or foil-sealed pet food
- Comfort and stress foods like cookies, hard candy, sweetened cereals, suckers
- Instant coffee, hot chocolate, tea bags

- Vitamin supplements
- One half to one gallon of clean water per person or pet per day
- Disposable plates, cups, utensils for at least nine meals per person

This could all be taken care of easily by tossing nine or more military-issue MRE's per person into your storage. But if that's what you plan to do, you're going to need a very, very large bag for it all.

THE LOWDOWN ON MRE'S

MRE means Meal, Ready to Eat. MRE's require little or no preparation, otherwise they wouldn't be "Ready to Eat." MRE's run the gamut from genuine military MRE's to a can of Spaghetti-O's. Most of us, though, think of the military MRE, and that's where the buyer really needs to be aware. If you've been in the military, you know what a military issue MRE should contain and how it's packaged. With a military issue MRE you are assured of a big selection and lots of amenities. It's a far cry from the wimpy commercial copycat "MRE" being sold in some stores. Military issue or commercial copycat, you'll end up paying just about the same, probably about $10 per meal. True, military issue MRE's have a great shelf-life, but unless you have access to fresh military issue MRE's, stay away from them and concentrate on making your own ready-to-eat meals from what you can get inexpensively at your local supermarket.

In recent years the markets have been flooded with an enormous variety of power drinks, rehydration drinks, and electrolyte sports drinks. Power drinks, whose main active ingredients are caffeine and taurine, are designed to give a burst of energy. Power drinks are great to have on hand when you need a boost. Putting a couple in your storage won't significantly increase the bulk or weight. Coffee drinks are also available canned and are nice for a morning boost. Some power drinks come in small two ounce bottles, and a few power drinks come in powders.

Food for the Long Term

If you're making a kit or planning food storage for an extended event, say a month or more, you need to approach the task differently. Pay closer attention to long-term nutritional needs rather than focusing on short-term survival, energy, and hydration. Part of that supply is the normal food you keep on your shelves. One strategy is to just increase how much of it you put on your shelves and rotate through it in your normal fashion. Another is to set aside a separate area for disaster food and water storage. However you decide to do it, here again are the standard pointers. Go heavy on food that's ready to eat or simple to prepare. In addition to the items listed above consider:

- Shelf stable boxes of juice and milk
- Crackers
- Jerky
- Instant oatmeal
- Dry milk
- Powdered drink mixes

- Instant pudding
- Dried soups
- Bouillon cubes or powder
- Instant rice or potatoes

The discount membership super-stores like Costco and Sam's Club are now carrying a wonderful array of foods for long-term storage. Go to their websites and check it out. For example, at the time of this writing one of Costco's popular food-storage combos includes 280 servings of various freeze-dried meats for $200. They're packed in gallon size cans and have a shelf life (sealed) of 25+ years. Served as an entrée alongside a couple of canned vegetables, that's dinner for a family of three for over three months. It doesn't get much cheaper and easier than that.

If you're stocking up for the worst-case scenario (years of misery and deprivation), consider storing bulk staples and an even larger inventory of canned goods. Wheat, corn, beans, and salt can be purchased in bulk inexpensively and have a long shelf life. They're best purchased in nitrogen-packed cans. Because of advances in food preservation and storage technology, storing bulk staples seems a bit outdated. But there will always be that fringe that insists on storing bulk staples because it's extremely economical or perhaps because it seems more "natural." If you fall into that category, remember to store the additional items you'll need to turn that bulk into palatable meals. Such a list would include things like cooking oils, salt, baking soda, baking powder, vinegar, sugar, and enough kitchen supplies, water, and fuel to carry on this cooking-intensive form of meal preparation. Also, you'll want to add a few of the yummy items from the other lists because meals from staples can get boring very quickly.

Finally, unless you have backup power to run a fridge, avoid buying giant cans of foods that will need refrigeration after they're open.

4. Storing Dried Foods

Keep dry foods in airtight, moisture-proof containers away from direct light and in a cool location. Store-bought packages of staples should be stored in their original packages in airtight plastic containers so you'll have the containers for storing leftovers when the package is opened. Stock a supply of Ziploc® food storage and freezer bags to store leftovers from opened containers of dry food.

5. Food Dates

Sell by and *expires on* dates tell the store how long to display the item for sale. With proper refrigeration (including during transportation) meats will last a day or two beyond the sell by date, other products as much as four days. If you buy eggs before the expiration date and you refrigerate them properly, they should be good for three weeks after the date you purchase them.

Best if used by and *best if used before* is are the dates to use the products at their best quality of flavor. They're NOT final safety dates or final sale dates.

Use by is the last date you should use or eat the product. Toss it out after that date. Better yet, if there's a dog in your group, use it to extend its food supply.

FYI dogs can eat meat that has just gone bad and not get sick. Their saliva and stomach enzymes kill bacteria, and their short digestive tracts pass it all along so quickly that there's little chance for food poisoning to develop.

Chapter 10
Shelter

Your shelter is wherever you decide to hunker down and wait out the emergency. It may consist of sheltering in place, at your home or work, or even in your car. Hardcore preppers will have their "survival retreats" in place. Or you might evacuate and find outside shelter at the home of a friend or relative, or at a community mass care facility.

The decision to stay or go might be made for you by local authorities. When a disaster is imminent or has just happened, listen to the TV and radio and check the Internet to find out if instructions are being given. It may take some time for local authorities to make their initial assessments and decide what they want the public to do, and it will take even more time to get that on the air or online. If you are aware of a large-scale emergency that has the potential to affect you, and you're unable to find out what's happening or what to do, your decisions might then be based on your gut instinct. In any case, you'll be making your decisions based on the perception of the hazard, then you'll be choosing on-site sheltering or evacuation and off-site sheltering. The safest places will vary by hazard.

Wherever you decide to shelter, stay there until local authorities say it's safe to leave. Manage food and water as indicated in previous chapters. Assign shifts for 24-hour communications and safety watch so no important information or safety issues go unnoticed. Have at hand or take with you your disaster supplies kit.

1. Mass Care Shelters

Make no mistake about it, crowded mass care facilities can be unpleasant, but it beats the alternatives. Mass care shelters will probably have free water, food, first aid supplies, medicine, first aid and medical providers, heating and air-cooling, basic sanitary facilities, blankets and cots.

If you go to a mass care facility, take your disaster kit with you to ensure you have what you need for yourself and for bartering. Do NOT take alcohol or firearms to the shelter unless you are told specifically by the shelter manager and local authorities to do so. Also be aware that smoking probably will not be allowed inside the shelter.

2. Sheltering in Place

Sheltering in place basically means staying at home or the office, and often means moving into a small interior room with few or no windows. This type of sheltering is likely to be used when hazardous materials, including chemical/biological/radiological contaminants, are released into the environment. It could also be the result of weather emergencies, civil unrest, and many other causes. The recommendation to shelter to shelter in place will probably be given over radio, TV, or the internet. Local authorities may pass the word by telephone and loudspeaker. It's likely the information will be repeated often on EBS and NOAA. It may happen that local authorities cannot respond and make those decisions before it's necessary for you to make a sheltering decision. In that case, if there's a large amount of debris in the air or the probability that the air is badly contaminated, your decision will probably be to shelter in place.

If infrastructure is still in place and you have an adequate food supply, sheltering in place may seem confining but in actuality will be little more than a simple vacation from work and school. Here's a rather standard list of steps to take for sheltering in place at home:

Before the Event

- Bolt the walls of the structure securely to the foundation.
- Attach wall studs to roof rafters with metal hurricane clips.
- Secure large appliances (especially the water heater) with flexible cable or metal stripping.

During the Event

- Close and lock all windows and exterior doors. Locking pulls the door tighter for a better seal.
- If there's a possibility of explosions, close window shades, blinds, and curtains.
- Turn off all fans, air conditioning, and heating systems.
- Close fireplace and stove dampers.
- Choose an interior room without windows or with as few windows as possible. In many homes this will be an interior bathroom. The room should be above ground level where gases and vapors heavier than air won't collect. Basements are not recommended for sheltering in place during hazardous materials emergencies because chemicals can seep in even if the windows are closed.
- Get your disaster supplies kit. Make sure the radio and lights work, and move the kit into the room.

- Move into the room. Bring the pets, too, and make certain there's enough food and water for them.

- If necessary, use the battery operated LED or fluorescent lights in your disaster kit to light the room. One standard LED bulb will run for days on a single fully-charged battery. Do not burn anything for heat or light because of the limited oxygen in your shelter space and the possibility of toxic combustion products (smoke, carbon monoxide). No candles.

- A POTS (Plain Old Telephone System) line to the room is nice to have, but nowadays very rare. If you have a cell phone, make certain you bring it with you. Call your emergency contact and let them know where you are and what phone or radio you'll be using. Keep the cell phone turned off, or at least turn off running apps and set settings (e.g. background light, volume, etc.) as low as possible for minimum battery consumption.

- If your emergency involves an imminent known or suspected airborne hazmat threat, put on your N95 face mask. Use duct tape and plastic sheeting to seal cracks around the door and any vents into the room. Alternatively, use pre-cut N95 air filter strips to fill the bigger cracks under the door and any vents (much safer than sealing the room entirely with tape and plastic).

- Establish a 24-hour communications/information and safety watch, monitoring radio or television and providing security.

- Stay there until local authorities give you the all clear, call for an evacuation, or tell you to seek medical help.

Studies indicate that sealing a room with plastic and duct tape will allow enough air for a few hours. Of course, the more folks in the shelter, the less air time you'll have, and staying in the room too long can lead to death by suffocation. Increased number of occupants, increased carbon dioxide emission rates, or increased activity resulting in oxygen depletion will seriously cut down on your air time. For the best protection for everyone, occupants should enter the shelter before contamination, and leave the shelter after exposure. Contaminated occupants will bring the contamination in with them and nullify the protection. Contaminated occupants should do a quick "dry-decontamination" (strip down) before entering the shelter. If you've done your disaster supplies right, there should be a set of clothes waiting for you in the shelter.

If there's a heavy chemical exposure, after two or three hours the shelter is likely to be compromised by contaminants leaking slowly into the room. Authorities by that time will probably recommend evacuation. Keep listening to the radio and follow their instructions completely.

When the emergency is over, ventilate the shelter to remove the contaminated air.

Safe Rooms

A safe room is the modern version of what we used to call a *storm cellar.* Safe rooms are made using wood and steel or reinforced concrete, welded steel, or other strong materials. Safe rooms are usually built in a basement, on a slab-grade foundation, garage floor, or in an interior room on the lower floor. The room is anchored securely to resist overturning. When building a safe room make certain the walls, ceiling, doors, and all connections are built to withstand extremely high winds and windborne debris. If the room is built below ground level, it must be flood-proof. FEMA has detailed plans for safe rooms on their website (www.fema.gov).

Shelter in Place at Work

Your business or workplace should use a means of alerting employees to shelter in place that is distinct from the alert to evacuate. Employees should be trained in SIP (shelter in place) procedures and their roles during an emergency.

When the decision to shelter in place has been made, here are some additional recommended steps:

- Close the business.
- Ask customers to stay.
- Tell employees and customers to call their emergency contacts to tell them where they are and that they are safe.
- Turn on call forwarding or alternative answering systems. Change the recorded message to say the business is closed and the staff and clients are sheltering there until authorities advise them to leave.
- Write down the names of everyone in the room.

Shelter in Place in Schools

In addition to basic steps already discussed:

- Bring students and staff indoors. Ask visitors to stay.
- Close the school and activate the school's emergency plan.
- A phone with the school's listed number should be available in the shelter room, and a person should be assigned to answer calls.

- If multiple rooms are used, there should be a way to communicate between rooms (intercom, radio, etc.). Make announcements through the public address system.
- Change the voicemail recording to say the school is closed and the students are safe.
- Write down the names of everyone in the shelter and call the school's emergency contact or local authorities to report who is there.

Lockdown

Lockdown is used to protect people inside a building from external danger. In a partial lockdown, no one goes in or out of the lockdown area. In a full lockdown, those inside the lockdown site are confined to their assigned rooms or spaces.

Community Containment vs. Shelter in Place

Community containment is a group of measures taken to control potential exposure to patients with contagious diseases. These steps include *isolation* and *quarantine*. Local, state, and federal health authorities are all empowered with the authority to order and enforce these measures. These agencies have what are referred to as "police powers" to "detain, medically examine, quarantine persons suspected of carrying communicable diseases" (42 CFR Parts 70 and 71). Isolation and quarantine may be voluntary or enforced. When enforced, failure to comply can result in arrest and criminal prosecution.

Isolation is the separation of person known to have an illness from those who are healthy. The separation may be for focused delivery of health care (TB, for example).

Quarantine is separation or restriction of movement of persons or things that may have been exposed but may or may not become ill. Quarantine can apply to people, vehicles, buildings, cargo, animals, or anything else thought to be exposed. Isolation and quarantine are public health's best weapons against mass infection.

If you are placed in isolation or quarantined at home, take the following steps to protect your family and others:

- Stay at home, and when at home stay at least three feet away from other people. If possible, stay in a separate room with the door closed.

- Do not have visitors. Arrange to have deliveries placed outside your door, then you can bring them into the house.

- Cover your mouth and nose with a clean tissue when coughing or sneezing. Consider wearing a surgical mask.

- Everyone in the home should wash their hands frequently. Have some waterless hand sanitizer handy.

- Wash hard surfaces and anything handled by the isolated patient with a 1:10 solution of bleach and water (1½ cups of bleach to a gallon of water).

- Do not share dirty eating or drinking utensils.

- Wash clothes in hot or warm water and detergent.

- Household members living with an isolated patient should consider themselves on quarantine unless directed otherwise by the enforcing health department.

3. Emergency Shelters

If you're forced out of your home and your neighborhood, and you can't get to a community shelter or to the safety of an unaffected friend's or relative's home, where do you go? It's not a problem if you have actually done your preparation homework.

The Car

Sheltering in a car is not as uncommon as one would think. In areas where storms or hazmat incidents are in progress, the motoring public is often told to stay in the car. In a long-term incident there are lots of reasons you might find yourself sheltering in a car:

- You may already have plans for the car to be your evacuation vehicle.
- There are nearly as many cars as there are people in the US and Canada. That's nearly one potential emergency shelter per person.
- Living in a car does not expose you to the structural instability of a severely damaged building.
- Cars provide warmth, passive solar heating, ventilated shade, storage space, a signaling device (horn), and relative privacy.
- Cars have mirrors, tools, a battery bank, a generator, an air conditioner, a radio, a heater, and even a hotplate (the manifold) until the fuel runs out and the batteries die.

Here are some tips for using a car for shelter:

- Along with your emergency car kit, stash a car cover and a silver-reflective windshield sunshade.

- The sunshade will help keep the car cool during the day. The car cover will keep it warm at night and in winter. Be sure to tie the cover to the bumpers and doors or it may blow away).

- Overnight leave the windows cracked slightly open to improve ventilation and reduce condensation (from breathing) inside the car.

- Be hygienic. Establish a place to poop and pee well away from the vehicle. Use sanitizer to keep your hands clean, or wash them with soap and water frequently. Store trash away from the vehicle. Take daily spit-showers or wipe down with baby wipes. Keep dirty clothes in a plastic bag in the trunk or outside.

Improvised Shelters

We're talking tarp lean-to, snow cave, etc. This is survival information. It's been re-worked and repeated endlessly in survival books, survival websites, and YouTube. We do not need to get into it here, because when you prep, you're already going to have shelter of some kind in your kit (maybe a tent, perhaps just a huge plastic garbage bag). Two suggestions:

- Get on your browser and type in "improvised shelters" and spend some time practicing the ones that make the most sense for you.

- If at any time you find yourself making shelters in or from damaged debris, it is critical to ensure that you do so where it's structurally sound, and the shelter you build will not collapse or be crushed by something falling onto it.

The Bivouac

A bivouac is a temporary encampment, often in a harsh, unsheltered area. Bivouacs will be those places you crash in as the sun goes down and you grow weary of looking for a better place to be. Some bivouacs are more comfortable than others. If you're unprepared, your bivouac may consist of crawling into a hole and covering yourself with dead vegetation to stay warm. Or if you are minimally prepared, you might pull your mega-sized garbage bag(s) from your kit and crawl in. A sleeping bag helps, and something underneath to insulate you from the ground makes it even better. The bottom line is everyone should pack some bivouac equipment into their 72-hour kit. Your decision about what to pack will depend on several things: how comfortable you want to be if you must bivouac, the range of weather conditions in your region, how mobile you wish to be, etc. The more you pack, the more comfortable you'll be, but the lighter you pack, the faster you can move. A couple of points to help you with this:

- Don't plan on getting any shelter from a space tarp or space blanket, unless it's the heavy-duty kind and you use it as a lean-to or A-frame tent. If you simply pull a blanket over you, it will be worthless as soon as the wind starts blowing. They'll flap uselessly and dump any heat they're supposed to retain, and flimsy versions will shred mercilessly. You're better off with large heavy-duty plastic garbage bags. Pack several in your kit. If you look around you can find "space" bags, or just spend the money and buy a nylon bivouac sack from the camping store. Add a heavy duty fleece liner or light sleeping bag, and a second if it's a cold environment, and stick it all on a layer of something that will insulate you from the cold ground (camping mattress, closed cell foam pad, or whatever you can improvise), and voila! You've got a comfy, relatively water- and wind-proof "bivi."

- Two or more individuals snuggling in a bivi are warmer than one!

Tents

Even today tents are the mainstay of modern armies and of relief agencies providing temporary housing and storage for displaced masses. Tents are a key piece of gear for anyone venturing into the backcountry. Tents are economical, portable, and generally easy and quick to set up. In a truly massive event, one way or another you will eventually end up in a tent for shelter. Having your own may prevent you having to share shelter space with a crowd of people you don't know.

A small two-man tent is not an unreasonable item to pack in your 72-hour kit. It's a little bulky, but it beats a bivi bag hands down and provides some cooking space and a dry place for you to use your electronics or keep documents dry. Two-man tents that will easily survive a week's thrashing are available in the mega-stores routinely for under $40. If you want something that will last longer, plan on spending a few hundred on a high quality unit.

Tents are made from many materials, but nylon and cotton canvas are the most commonly used. Nylon is the material of choice due to its light weight and its inability to absorb significant moisture. Nylon materials are often coated with substances like silicon and polyurethane that make them almost completely waterproof. The disadvantage of nylon is its tendency to break down under UV radiation (sunlight). A tent may last through a season of hard use, but would be very lucky to last a year in the sunlight. If you're going to store a nylon tent in your two-year kit, store at least two tents.

Cotton canvas is heavy and it absorbs water easily (making it even heavier). When it absorbs water, the threads swell and become so tightly packed that the tent eventually becomes temporarily very water-resistant. Cotton tents are great in dry environments, but in humid environments they tend to stay wet and will rot or collect mold faster than nylon tents.

Tents come in all shapes and sizes. Most of the popular tents on the market are dome tents that are supported by external pole frames. Stress on the weak points of the tent will be reduced with poles and flies (rain covers) that are shock-corded to the main frame. Double wall construction increases the weight of the tent but also increases durability, weather resistance, and insulation value. Bug-screened windows and doors are nice. Dual zippered doors and windows are another plus.

Speaking of zippers . . . be forewarned that zippers on a cheap tent will be the first thing to fail and can only rarely be repaired, leaving you with a tent that has doors and windows that won't close. If you're buying a cheap tent, as soon as you get it home, make certain you check the zippers and trim away any loose threads or material that can get caught in the zipper.

The next thing to fail on your cheap tent will be the stake loops and the fabric channels that attach the tent to the frame. These fail because the material is of poor quality and the sewing is weak. Consider using a surge sewing machine to double- or triple-stitch any of the seams and channels that will be highly stressed. Stitching a patch to a weak point may help spread the stress over a wider area and prevent it from tearing.

So, what is a "cheap" tent? Let's just say that if you're paying less that $1 per square foot of floor space, it's a cheap tent. In fact, at that price it's probably a real lemon—a disaster in its own fashion. True, this isn't always the case, but "you get what you pay for" stands true for tents. Buy brand names you can trust.

When choosing a tent, look for

- Comfort
- Space, including floor space and head space or standing room
- Ease and simplicity to set up and take down
- Durability of construction
- Performance in non-ideal conditions (wind and rain).

Living area. You want plenty of room for yourself, your roommates, and your stuff. Take it from those of us who have been days and weeks imprisoned in tents, space is crucial. For a long-term event, sixty square feet of floor space per person is about the minimum you'll need to keep from getting claustrophobic. Add some additional space for a few other amenities (i.e. tables and chairs), and if you want to be able to fit a guest in on occasion, better add another 60. Unless you're cooking outside or in a separate tent, add another 40 square feet for a kitchen. How are we doing?

Family of three X 60 + 60 + 40 = 280 square feet.

Do they even make tents that size? Glance through the online catalogs of your favorite budget mega-stores, you'll see tents with 600, even 800 square feet. That's as big as a small house.

Ceiling height is important if you're actually going to turn a tent into a home for the long term. It sucks to not be able to stand up at home.

Durability. A tent should have hefty, strong poles that will not allow the tent to collapse or lie down in a stiff wind or under a moderate load of snow. Seams should be double-sewn and sealed, and the windows and doors should have heavy-duty zippers. A *three-season tent* is designed for mild climates or for use in spring, summer, and fall. They perform well in windy conditions as long as the poles are sturdy and correctly attached, the tent is staked per instructions, all the guy lines are staked, and the fly and guy lines are tensioned correctly. Three-season tents have fewer poles, lighter material, and less aerodynamic designs than what are called *four-season tents* or *expedition tents*. These tents are more aerodynamic and stoutly constructed, and their frame and guy systems are built to withstand the rigors of severe winter storms and intense monsoon activity. A good four-season tent is worth the extra expense.

Protection from water. Many poorly made or poorly designed tents come without a rain fly, relying solely on waterproof material to keep the rain out. Avoid these. Condensation from breathing and cooking will collect on waterproof ceilings and run onto the floor or rain on the occupants. On the other hand, some very expensive tents are made from breathable, vapor-barrier materials and manage to shed rain and minimize condensation. To be on the safe side, get a tent with a rain fly. Tents that incorporate a rain fly are called "double walled tents." The fly should cover most of the tent and certainly any windows or skylights that cannot be zippered shut. Look for a tent whose fly has tension adjustments and is shock-corded (the tie-downs or stake loops are elasticized). A vestibule is a floorless extension of the tent. The sleeping area of the tent can be sealed off completely from the vestibule. This makes vestibules ideal for changing out of dirty clothes and shoes before going into the main tent.

Protection from bugs. All openings, including vents, doors, and windows, should have bug screening. If you're in an area that has a continuous problem with particularly nasty invaders (like scorpions or centipedes), use duct tape to seal any holes that are not screened (i.e. the utility port).

Go into a serious climbing or outdoor adventure store and almost everything will be very acceptable, highly durable quality. It will also be unavoidably very expensive. Buying a $1,500 tent, just to keep in a closet with your dust-covered 72-hour kit and other forgotten treasures, is a waste of money. Some very good, durable tents in a moderate price range can be had from companies like Kelty and Eureka. If you're like average preppers, though, you'll be heading straight for Costco, Walmart, or Kmart to check out the big tent sales. Let the buyer beware. In research for this book, the author found that statistically, three low-budget tent lines lead the pack in customer satisfaction. From 480 tent models by 23 companies, the highest marks most consistently went to Coleman, with Ozark Trail in second place, and Texsport right behind. I won't say which companies were at the bottom. Let's just say a tent from one of these three companies is less likely to be a lemon than from any of the other budget tent makers.

Trailers, Campers, and RV's

Truck Camper: Any shelter or living unit carried in the bed of a pickup truck (aka *slide-in* or *cab-over*). Campers range from a simple single-walled shell with no amenities, to an enormous mini-home with kitchen, bedroom, shower, and dining facilities. At some point, a truck camper unit basically becomes an RV.

RV, or Recreational Vehicle: Also known as a *motor home*, an RV is an enclosed motorized platform dually used as a vehicle and a dwelling. As an emergency shelter they offer greater mobility, comfort, and protection than a tent. RV's decked out specifically for emergency travel, evacuation, and mobile shelter are often referred to by survivalists as a "BOV"—a bug-out vehicle.

Again, as with tents, there are some bargains out there, especially for a used camper or RV, but you generally get what you pay for.

At a minimum an RV will contain at least one bed, a table, and food preparation and storage areas. Large, more expensive units will have their own bathroom, plumbing, a refrigerator, and may include a living room and master bedroom.

Onboard appliances run off the 12-volt system of the vehicle but may also have a *converter,* which changes the AC current from a grid source or generator to the DC power needed to run most of the onboard appliances. Many RV's will have what are called two-way or three-way appliances. Two-way appliances can run on either 110V (grid current) or 12V (battery current). Three-way appliances can also run on LP gas. For an emergency shelter or BOV, multi-way appliances are a big plus.

Fancier RV units will have satellite TV, satellite internet, slide-out sections (some slide out on both sides of the unit to make a huge living room), and awnings.

Who wouldn't want to have one of these in a disaster? Realistically, though, an RV is a big target. If the house and neighborhood has been obliterated, what makes anyone think a huge unprotected RV will fare any better? In addition, the convenience of the vehicle and all its appliances and electronics seems less important when you consider how much fuel it's going to take to run it all. Outfitting the RV with solar panels and/or a wind turbine and an adequate battery bank makes this mobile paradise seem more practical, but again it's likely to be destroyed, and if the disaster hasn't flattened the RV, chances are the house is also intact enough to provide shelter, and you won't have needed the RV in the first place. The real advantage of the RV is as an evacuation vehicle.

Trailers: *Travel trailers* and "*5th Wheelers*" are towed behind a road vehicle to provide living quarters. A *mobile home* is a prefabricated home, built in a factory, with a chassis and wheels. It is pulled behind a tractor-trailer to its permanent or semi-permanent site. The general public often refers to all of these as "trailers."

One way or another, trailers often become shelters during and after large-scale disaster events. In the US, FEMA has a fleet of thousands of travel trailers and small mobile homes for those who qualify to receive them.

4. Survival Retreats

In simple terms, the difference between a survival retreat and emergency shelter is this: emergency shelter is where you will lay your head at night, find rest and sanctuary, carry on basic life functions, and where you will get out of the elements during any serious disruption of normal life. Emergency shelters, by definition, are temporary in nature. A survival retreat, on the other hand, is essentially a household or community fortress prepared to function in that capacity for the duration of lengthy widespread apocalyptic, cataclysmic disasters that result in societal and economic collapse and the breakdown of normal community protection systems, culminating in widespread pandemonium and chaos. A retreat is protective living-space with the added components of aggressive self-defense and fundamental survival measures to counter anarchy and lawless bedlam.

This book is not about building a survival retreat. For that there are a multitude of books, including one in this author's survival series (*Survival Retreats: A Practical Guide to Creating a Sustainable, Defendable Refuge*, Skyhorse Publishing 2011) and endless information on the internet.

Chapter 11
Evacuation and "Bugging Out"

If authorities have issued an evacuation order or recommendation, do so immediately. Take minutes, not hours. During an evacuation you'll be responsible for your own food, water, fuel, and supplies . . . and, again, that's what your 72-hour kit is all about.

1. In-Advance Preparation for Evacuation

- Know the evacuation plans for your building and community.
- Maintain a disaster supplies kit. Include copies of all your important documents, IDs, and some cash.
- Discuss possible evacuation procedures with your family and coworkers so they all know what to do.
- Choose a destination outside the area and keep a road map and directions.
- Establish a check-in contact outside the area, to whom all family members can report their status. Make certain they all have the same numbers.
- If an evacuation seems likely, keep a full tank of gas in the car. There will be no gas available during the evacuation.
- If you don't have a car, arrange for transportation with friends or neighbors, or contact the emergency management office and find out what plans are in place for busses or air evacuation.
- Make plans for your pets.
- Know how to shut off the utilities, and have the tools to do it.

2. Imminent Evacuation

- Let others know your destination. Leave a note or make some calls.
- Close and lock your doors and windows.
- Unplug appliances and electronics.
- Shut off water, gas, and electricity. If flooding is not likely and the gas is shut off, consider leaving the power on and the refrigerator plugged in.

3. Evacuation has been Ordered

- Put on some sturdy long-sleeved clothing and stout shoes if possible. Grab your 72-hour kit, and everything you can reasonably carry from your home emergency storage. Take along a bedroll for everyone: blankets or sleeping bags and ground insulation. Don't forget your medications.
- Follow the recommended routes. Others may be blocked.
- Keep away from downed power lines.
- In flood conditions, be careful crossing bridges and stay off washed-out roads.

4. Returning Home

- Listen to the media for instructions. Return when authorities say it's safe. Don't re-enter homes or buildings until authorities say it's safe.
- Be very cautious in buildings that have possible structural damage. Wear sturdy shoes or boots, heavy gloves, and safety goggles if available, to do initial assessment of the building or when sifting through any debris.
- If you smell gas, leave immediately and tell the gas company or fire department. Don't switch on lights.

- Use flame and spark-free lights when possible to avoid fires until the area is known to be safe from gas and flammables.
- If appliances are wet, switch off the power main and unplug the appliances. Give them plenty of time to dry out before you try to use them again.
- Inform your contacts that you and your family are safe.
- Watch for critters: bugs, snakes, spiders.
- Don't drink the local water until it's declared safe.

5. "Bugging Out"

This annoying term is often used by survivalist and some preppers to describe the act of leaving your shelter to escape from the chaos and survive in the wild. It evolved from older definitions of this slang term: to flee in panic, or to depart rapidly. Ultimately it has to do with escape and evasion from a hostile world. In the end, it's just joining the zombie horde, because at some point you'll need the support of all the other desperate survivalists hunkered down in the woods, unsuccessfully foraging for food and warmth.

Bugging out means leaving everything behind, including all the comforts of home and protective norms of society. The chances of actually having to do such a thing are next to zero. The world is not the same place it was even a hundred years ago. If we had a small frail infrastructure, wolves at the door, and no hope of outside support, bugging out might at some point be necessary. But the Western world and its economic partners are a tightly knit group. They know it pays to help your neighbor. So a drought in a cluster of farm counties doesn't cause the people of those counties to starve. The shelves are just filled with goods from somewhere else where there is no drought. An earthquake in one corner of the world brings relief aid almost immediately from countries that didn't have earthquakes. Even under the worst multiple-incident disaster, it would be highly unlikely for most of us to have to "bug out." Our nation is so vast, wealthy, heavily populated, so highly educated and trained, and so protected with such redundant infrastructure and geographic diversity that it would take layers of repeated massive ongoing disasters to cause the type of situation that would require you to "bug out." We're talking a large scale nuclear war on top of a lethal pandemic on top of the worst drought and crop failure in a millennium due to the catastrophic eruption of a massive super volcano situation. It's just not going to happen.

Having a few outdoor skills is a great idea. Fishing and hunting can certainly augment your food supply, as can knowing some local edible plants. But if you've got some kind of warped idea that when the shit hits the fan you'll run to the woods and survive off the land, think very hard about this. Unless you're already an expert farmer and the world's best hunter-gatherer, you've got some surprises coming. Survival off the land may seem romantic, but it's not. It's insecure, cold, filthy, bug-infested misery at its worst. Do a dress rehearsal. Go live in the woods for a month with nothing but what's in your little "bug-out kit." It's the author's guess you'll be home before the first weekend.

For an excellent opinion piece on this, see https://survivalacres.com/blog/blogindex.html

A 72-hour kit is NOT a bug-out bag. Don't stock it or treat it like one. It's there to augment what you have at home or in the temporary shelters you find yourself in when you've been evacuated or otherwise cut off from your home.

CHAPTER 12
First Aid

In a disaster situation you will have little to work with. You'll be limited to what you already know and what supplies you have stockpiled. Fortunately, you will also have your common sense and your hands, which are the primary tools of first aid.

This book is not a substitute for formal first aid or medical training. Take a course. In fact, take several. Do research. The more you know, the more comfortable you'll be giving medical assistance.

In a disaster we will be concerned with injuries and illnesses which threaten life or limb. Minor bumps and scrapes, tension headaches, bug bites, and the heartbreak of psoriasis will just have to wait.

In any situation, if there are life-or-limb-threatening injuries, call 911 or your local emergency services number immediately. In a major disaster, emergency crews will be swamped, and you may have to provide care yourself for an extended period of time.

1. The Patient Assessment System

The initial patients in most disasters are likely to be trauma and burn victims, so that's where we'll start. The three basic steps are Scene Survey, Primary Check, and Secondary Check.

Scene Survey

Assess and manage hazards. Don't play hero. A dead hero doesn't help anyone and just complicates matters. Ensure your own safety first, then the victim's safety from hazards like falling debris, rising water, etc.

Primary Check

This is a rapid check to find and correct life-threatening conditions, and is always done in this order: Responsiveness, Breathing, Severe Bleeding

Responsiveness: Tap and shout. If the victim can talk, he's responsive. If he doesn't respond, he's unresponsive.

Breathing: A responsive victim is breathing. Check for breathing problems. If the victim is unresponsive and not breathing normally, send someone to call 911 while you start CPR.

- Ideally for CPR provide 30 chest compressions and two rescue breaths, and continue until help arrives, you're relieved, or you're exhausted. In reality, multi-casualty situations may require the dead to be left dead so the rescuer can attend to others who can be saved.
- Fix any obvious deadly, traumatic chest injuries or obvious major breathing problems: plug a sucking chest wound; splint a major flail chest, treat anaphylaxis, etc.

Severe Bleeding: Check quickly for heavy bleeding and stop it with direct pressure.

Secondary Check

Check the victim from head to toe, looking for deformities, open wounds, tenderness, and swelling:

- *Head and neck. Do not move the head during this part of the check.*
- *Eyes. Changes in pupil size may be signs of a problem.*
- *Chest and Abdomen*
- *Extremities*
- *Back & spine*
- *History:*   S   *Signs/symptoms*
  - A   *Allergies*
  - M   *Medications*
  - P   *Past medical history*
  - L   *Last food and drink*
  - E   *Events leading to the injury or illness*

Treat all injured victims for shock:

- Treat life-threatening injuries
- Prevent heat loss with blankets
- Keep victims on their backs, except:
  - Head injury and stroke patients should have their head slightly raised (if there's no spine injury suspected).
  - Victims with difficulty breathing, heart attack, or chest injuries should be semi-sitting.
  - Unresponsive breathing victims should be placed on their side.

Shock, by the way, occurs when the components of the circulatory system (the fluid, the pump, and the pipes) are somehow inadequate and cannot maintain enough pressure to push oxygenated blood through the tissues of the body. Signs and symptoms of shock include pale, clammy skin, rapid pulse, changes in the level of consciousness, and a mechanism of injury.

> ### What are normal adult vital signs?
> *Level of Consciousness: Alert*
> *Pulse: 60 to 100 per minute, strong and regular*
> *Respirations: 12 to 20 regular and non-labored*
> *Skin color: pink, dry, warm. For dark-skinned patients look at places where the skin is pale.*
> *Systolic Blood Pressure: 80 plus age (plus 10 for males).*

At this point you should make a list of what's wrong—a problems list—and fix the problems you can actually do something about.

2. Injuries

Bleeding & Wounds

Serious wound: Apply a dressing and apply direct pressure, then apply a pressure bandage. Stack on more dressings and apply more pressure as needed.

Minor wound: Wash with soap and water. Apply antibiotic ointment. Cover with sterile dressing and bandage.

High-risk wound: (bites, dirty wounds, punctures): Wash with soap and water. Apply sterile dressing. Clean the wound & seek medical care.

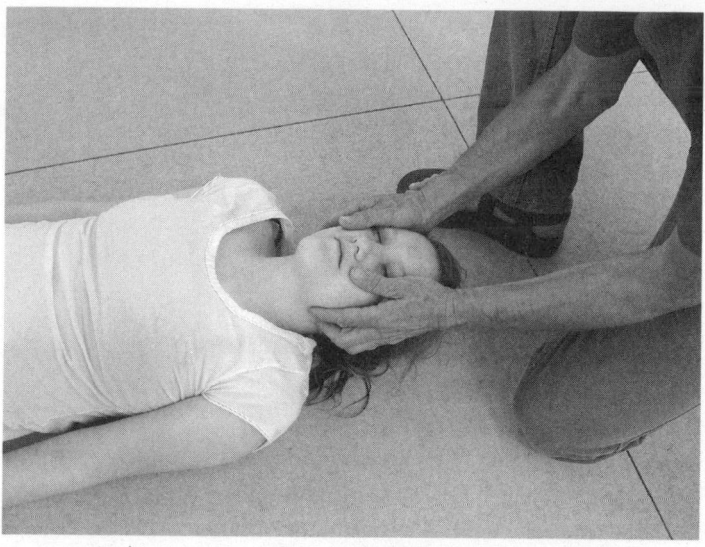

Jaw thrust and accompanying neck stabilization.

Coma position protects the airway of an unconscious patient from aspiration.

Notes: Do not remove an impaled object. For amputated parts, wrap in dry, sterile gauze, place in a plastic bag, and keep it dry and cool. Do not freeze.

Forget about closing wounds with sutures or other devices unless you're trained and you're certain medical assistance is more than three days out. Keep the wound clean. Consider irrigating it with clean water and dressing the wound. It will reduce infection and preserve the wound for later repair.

Head Injuries

Head wound: Control bleeding. Suspect spinal injury and skull fracture.

"Concussion" or brain injury: Suspect it when there's an appropriate mechanism of injury and any change in consciousness. Stabilize the head and neck with your hands or rigid materials alongside the head and neck. Control severe bleeding but don't stop blood or fluid flowing from the ears. Seek medical help. Don't give food or drink.

Eye Injuries

Impaled Object: Do not remove. Protect the eye with paper cup or cone, and cover both eyes to keep both eyes from tracking.

Impact to Eye: Apply a cold pack. Seek medical care if vision becomes blurry.

Eyelid cut: Bandage both eyes to minimize eye movement. Don't try to wash out a stuck object. Do not apply hard pressure.

Chemical burns: Irrigate with water for 15 minutes. Bandage both eyes. Seek medical care.

Foreign body: Blink. Pull the upper lid over the lower. Flush out with gentle rinsing. Examine the inner lid and remove the object with moist gauze.

Sun or light burns: Rest in darkness. Apply cold moist packs.

Nosebleeds

Stay seated, with head tilted slightly forward. Pinch together both nostrils for 15 minutes.

Dental Injuries

Objects between the teeth: Try dental floss.

Bit Tongue or Lip: Apply direct pressure with a clean cloth. Apply a cold pack for swelling.

Knocked-out tooth: Place the tooth in saline (saltwater), milk, or spit. Seek dental care immediately. If care will be delayed, rinse and replant the tooth in the socket and push so it looks even with adjacent teeth.

Broken tooth: Wash and swish with warm water. Apply cold pack, and seek dental care.

Chest Injuries

Rib Fracture: Splint by having the victim hold a pillow or other soft bulky material against the injury.

Sucking chest wound. Seal the hole immediately to prevent collapsed lungs. Tape some plastic wrap in place on three sides. The untapped side makes a flutter valve.

Abdominal Injuries

Severe blunt trauma: Place the patient on his side in the position of comfort. Protect his airway from vomit. Watch for shock.

Impaled object: Do not remove it. Instead, bandage around it to stabilize it and control bleeding.

Protruding organs: Do not attempt to reinsert. Cover with a moist sterile dressing.

Blisters

Hotspot only: Cover with adhesive bandage or duct tape.

Intact blister: Moleskin donuts or gauze pads with holes stacked over the blister and tapped over.

Painful blister, ready to pop: Puncture along the edge with a sterile needle. Don't remove the blister's top.

Burns

For all burns: Extinguish or remove the heat source. Remove smoldering clothes unless stuck or melted to the skin. Do not apply ointments or butter. Rinse burned eyes with cold water and cover with a clean dressing.

First-degree burns: Red and tender. Immerse burns in cold water. Ibuprofen. Apply aloe vera or commercial burn gels.

Second-degree burns: Blistered and painful. Immerse burns in cold water. Do not break blisters. Cover with a dressing. For large scale burns, treat as third-degree.

Third-degree burns: Grey or black charred. Seek medical care immediately. Treat for shock. Cover burns with sterile dressings. Elevate extremities to minimize swelling.

Chemical burns: After brushing off dry chemical, flush the skin with large amounts of low-pressure water. Discard contaminated clothing. Do not try to neutralize because the reaction can generate more heat. Write down the name of the chemical and seek medical help.

Electrical Injuries

Outside: Power lines must be turned off before approaching the victim. Do crowd control and avoid touching anything.

Inside: Don't touch the victim until the current has been killed at the breaker or fuse box. The do a primary check. Treat for shock. Look for and treat burns. Seek medical care.

Musculoskeletal Injuries

Fractures: Broken bone. An open fracture has an open wound, a closed fracture doesn't. Signs and symptoms include deformity, open wound, tenderness or pain, swelling and discoloration, and loss of use. Treat for shock and control bleeding before splinting. To splint, immobilize the joints above and below the fracture. Keep fingers and toes visible to check circulation. Common splinting materials include cardboard, newspapers pillow and blankets. Hopefully you'll have SAM splints in your kit. If all else fails, make a "buddy splint" by splinting the injured part to an uninjured part. Apply RICE (Rest, ice, compression, elevation) to minimize pain and swelling. Seek medical assistance.

Dislocations: A separated joint that stays apart. The signs and symptoms are like a fracture, and you should care for a dislocation as a fracture. Seek medical help.

Muscle Injuries: Do RICE. Rest, Ice (20–30 minutes), Compression (with an elastic bandage), Elevation.

Spinal Injuries

Suspect them with anyone who has suffered a high impact trauma. Spine injuries often accompany head injuries. There may be numbness, tingling, or paralysis in the extremities. Immobilize the victim to prevent movement of the head, neck, or body. Do not move the neck to reposition it, and only move the victim if there is immediate danger. Get some help and seek medical attention. Spine injury victims in the water should be gently floated toward shore and secured to a rigid board for removal.

3. Medical

Childbirth

Delivery is imminent when contractions are less than a minute apart, the mother feels she needs to push or poop, and the baby's head (normally) is visible. Send someone to get medical assistance and prepare a clean area for the

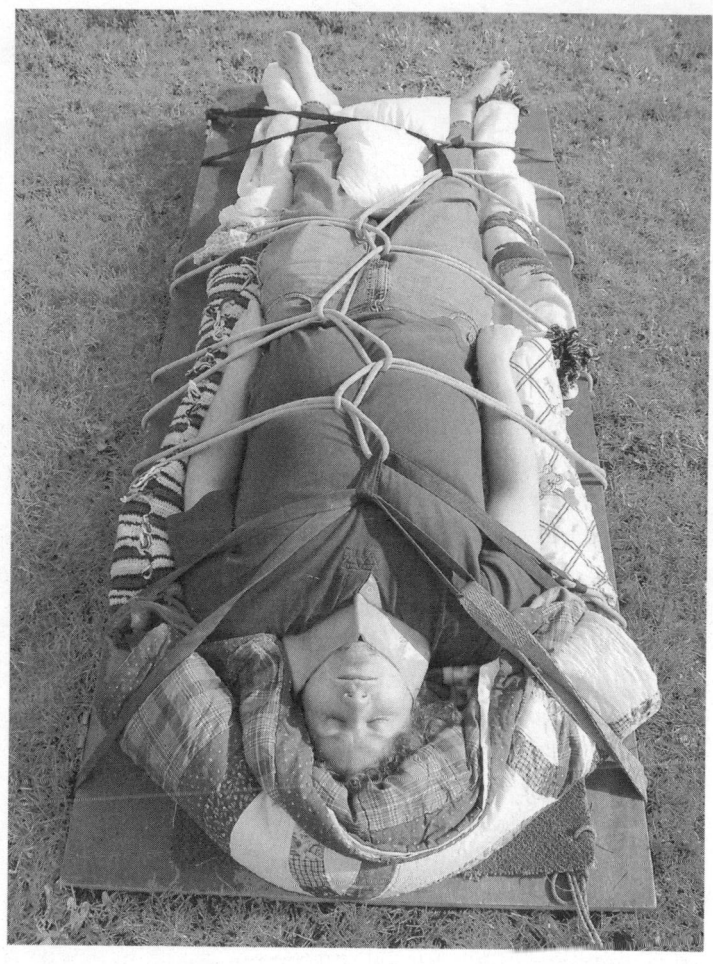

Total immobilization of the spine using a SAM splint and a door. Note how the patient is well padded to take up space and prevent movement of the head, neck, torso, and legs.

delivery, with lots of towels or sheets and pads to deal with the blood and fluid. Wear exam gloves and a mask, and do not touch the vaginal area or put anything into the vagina.

When the baby is on the way out, tell the Mom to stop pushing, and support the baby's head. You may have to prepare the way by tearing open the amniotic sac if it's still intact, or by untangling an umbilical cord looped around the baby's neck. If the baby is in breech presentation (any part other than the head comes out first), do not try to pull the baby out. Place Mom on her left side and send for help.

When the baby is out, hold its tilted head down to drain fluids from nose and mouth. If the baby is not breathing, tap or rub it. Be prepared to do CPR if breathing doesn't start.

Dry the baby off and wrap it warmly. Keep baby lower than Mom's tummy to keep blood going to the baby. Using wide material like shoelaces, tie the cord at 4 inches and 8 inches from the baby and cut the cord in between.

Let Mom hold the baby. Reduce the bleeding by massaging Mom's abdomen, and if it doesn't slow, treat her for shock. The afterbirth (placenta should make its way out within half an hour, and should be saved along with any other tissue and taken to the doctor with the mother.

Seizure

Prevent injuries to the victim, but do not hold him down or try to put anything between the teeth. Monitor the airway and roll him to the side if necessary. Most seizures last only a very few minutes and resolve with no additional problems.

A victim with no history of seizures should seek medical attention.

Diabetic Emergency

Sudden diabetic emergencies are almost always due to low sugar. If you have a diabetic acting strangely or you observe changes in the level of consciousness, give sugar. Too much sugar will not hurt them right away, but too little sugar will.

Stroke

Signs and symptoms may include a rapid onset of weakness or numbness on the face or extremities of one side of the body, difficulty speaking, loss of vision, pupil changes, dizziness and incoordination, and headache. Seek medical care immediately. Monitor responsiveness and breathing. Let the victim rest in a position of comfort, preferably on the back with shoulders and head elevated. Prepare to roll the victim onto the side if unresponsive and vomiting.

Heart Attack

Signs and symptoms can include heavy chest pressure, squeezing, or pain that may spread to the shoulder, neck, and jaw; weakness, cold clammy skin or sweating, shortness of breath, fatigue, and dizziness. Seek medical assistance immediately. Have the victim rest in a sitting position of comfort. If using nitroglycerin, assist him in taking it. Give one regular aspirin or 4 chewable baby aspirin. Monitor responsiveness and breathing.

Heat-related Emergencies

Heat Cramps: These are due to dehydration from sweating. Rest in a cool place. Drink water or sports drinks. Stretch and rub painful muscles.

Heat exhaustion: Usually marked by sweating (the body's response to mild hyperthermia), fast pulse, and weakness or headache. Stop heat gain by getting in a cool place and resting. Apply cold packs or cold wet towels, and fan the victim. Give water or sports drinks, Victim should improve rapidly.

Heat stroke: Victim is unresponsive and the victim has stopped sweating, although the skin may still be wet. Body temperature is high, pulse is rapid, and the victim is acting strange or unresponsive. Move to a cool place. Strip of all clothing. Cool by any means available. Apply icepacks to neck, armpits, and groin. Seek medical care.

Hypothermia

Low body core temperature. Shivering is the body's response to mild hypothermia. Stop heat loss by getting out of the cold and into dry clothes. Put insulation under and around the victim, and cover the head to prevent major heat loss there.

Frostbite

Frozen tissue, usually of the fingers, toes, nose, or ears. If medical care is severely delayed and if there's no chance of refreezing the part, consider rewarming. Remove clothing and restricting jewelry from the extremity. Immerse the extremity in warm water (102°F to 106°F) or pack the face or ears in warm, wet cloths until the tissue is soft (about half an hour). Painkillers help. Don't break blisters and do not rub frozen tissue.

Insect Sting & Anaphylaxis

Severe allergy to anything can cause a life-threatening problem we call *anaphylactic shock*. The most common culprits are insect stings.

The general treatment for stings is to scrape away the stinger and venom sac, then wash the site. An icepack will slow the spread of the venom and relieve pain. OTC pain meds (e.g. ibuprofen) and hydrocortisone cream may help.

Signs of an anaphylactic event are difficulty breathing, itchiness and swelling in the face, throat, tongue, or mouth.

Epinephrine is needed to treat anaphylaxis. It's a good idea to have a prefilled epinephrine syringe such as the EpiPen in your first aid kit. These pens, injected into the thigh, deliver one or two doses, which essentially reverse the allergic process. Diphenhydramine (the active ingredient in Benadryl) is an OTC oral antihistamine that works to block the allergic process. It's normally taken after an Epi injection.

Diphenhydramine is also used to relieve the symptoms of minor allergies, but epinephrine should only be used for severe allergic reactions.

Poisoning

Swallowed: Get information: who what, how, when, how much? If you have phone coverage, contact poison control

(800-222-1222). If victim is unresponsive, do primary check and seek medical care. Do not dilute or induce vomiting unless advised to do so by a doctor. Save the clues (pill bottles, vomit, etc.).

Injected, snake bite: For pit vipers (rattlers, copperheads, moccasins) and all venomous snakes, get away from the snake. Stay quiet & calm, avoid walking. Wash the site with soap and water. Don't cut, suck, or apply cold. Do not apply a tourniquet or use electric shock. For coral snake bites wrap the extremity in an elastic bandage. Seek medical help.

Injected, spider bite: Use your cell phone to photograph the spider, or keep the dead spider for later identification. Wash the bite site with soap and water or alcohol. Cool the site with an ice pack. Stay quiet and calm. Seek medical help.

Injected, scorpion sting: Observe the patient. Wash the site with soap and water or alcohol. Apply an ice pack to ease pain and burning.

Inhaled, carbon monoxide: Signs and symptoms include headache, difficulty breathing, dizziness and blurred vision, nausea, decreased consciousness. Remove victims into a fresh air environment. Perform a primary check and seek medical care.

Fainting

Treatment: Lay the victim down. Turn him on his side if vomiting. Loosen clothing. Don't slap, splash with water or use smelling salts. Don't give food or drink until full recovery.

Notes: Usually not serious if the victims recovers quickly.

We've only seen the tip of the first aid iceberg here. Not a word about diarrhea, abdominal, respiratory infection, infectious diseases.... my apologies, there's just too much to cover in a short volume like this.

The author highly recommends two comprehensive books that the average Joe or Jane without a medical background can read and understand:

Where There Is No Doctor, 2013 reprint & update, by Werner, Maxwell, and Thumen for the Hesperian Foundation (downloadable free)

Wilderness Medicine and Rescue, 6th Edition, by Isaac and Johnson; Jones & Bartlett Learning, LLC, and Wilderness Medical Associates International.

4. First Aid Kits

The best first aid kit is the one you know how to use. Putting in a lot of fancy medical gadgets and drugs you can't use or know nothing about makes no sense. The following is a typical kit for the family or office, adequate for that 72-hour-to-one-week disaster you've been planning against.

- First aid manual
- LED headlamp and batteries
- Surgical masks
- Sterile adhesive bandages ("Band-Aids")
- Exam gloves (lots of 'em), or dishwashing gloves that can be sanitized and re-used
- 2-inch sterile gauze pads (20)

- 4-inch sterile gauze pads (20)
- Triangular bandages (4)
- 2-inch sterile roller bandages (4)
- 3-inch sterile roller bandages (4)
- 3-inch Elastic bandages (6)
- 2-inch cloth first aid tape, or a roll of duct tape
- Scissors (trauma shears)
- Tweezers or forceps (2)
- Needles (various sizes)
- Chemical cold packs (3-6)
- Pocket CPR mask
- Tongue depressors (12)
- Antibacterial soap (1 bottle)
- Alcohol wipes (12)
- Provodine-iodine wipes (20)
- Antibiotic ointment (1 tube)
- Hydrogen peroxide (1 bottle)
- 50ml syringe for wound irrigation
- Thermometer (digital)
- Assorted safety pins (diaper pins are stronger and last longer).
- Petroleum jelly (1 tube)
- Hand sanitizer (1–2 bottles)
- Sunscreen (1 tube)
- DEET bug repellent (2 tubes)
- OTC anti-inflammatory pain reliever (ibuprofen, one bottle)
- OTC antidiarrheal tablets (1 bottle)
- OTC antihistamine (diphenhydramine; 1 bottle) for allergy, motion sickness, sleep
- Antacid (1 bottle)

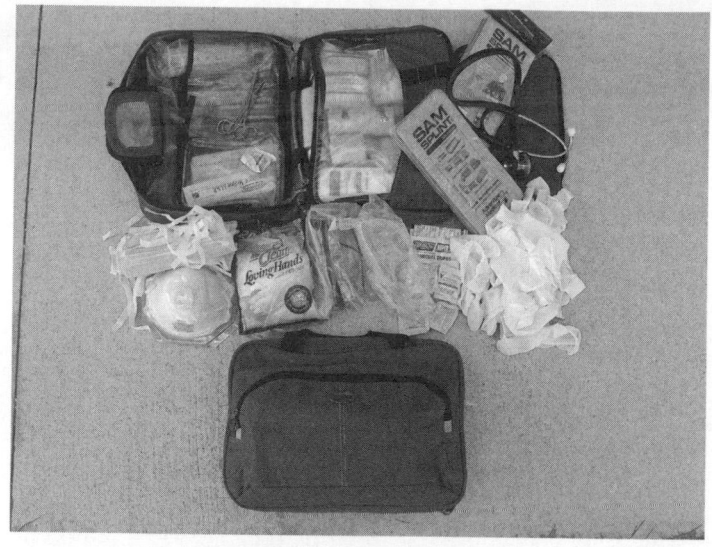

Example of a family-sized first aid kit.

- Laxative (1 bottle)
- Multi-vitamins (1 bottle)
- OTC infant medications
- Prescription medications
  - acetaminophen/codeine – oral (Tylenol-Codeine No. 3), for pain, diarrhea, cough
  - 2 different broad-spectrum antibiotics (1 course each)
  - Epinephrine pre-loaded syringe (1)
  - SAM splints (3)
- Paper & pencil
- For those who know how to use them:
  - Stethoscope (1), to listen to the heart & breathing
  - Otoscope & extra batteries, for examining eyes, ears, and nose

Chapter 13
Light Rescue

Search and Rescue operations are dangerous functions that should be reserved for trained professional or paraprofessional rescuers. It will initially be the decision of those left standing whether or not to jump in and risk their own lives, and, unfortunately, the statistics show in many cases more people are killed trying to rescue others than are killed in the initial accident. In some types of rescue scenarios, rescuers account for more than 60 percent of fatalities.

Even highly trained rescue professionals face substantial risks. Those risks are multiplied for untrained rescuers. If you witness a tragedy, contact 911 as soon as possible, and keep other people away from the hazard. Do not act impulsively. If you decide to try to help or attempt a rescue, first evaluate the risks and understand your limitations.

Usually when we think about disaster rescue, urban structural rescue comes to mind. This type of rescue involves locating, extricating, and treating victims who are trapped in the structural entanglements and confined spaces caused by structural collapse. Collapsed structures leave voids within the debris and wreckage, and there can be several victims trapped under seemingly endless heavy, unstable debris. This is a notoriously dangerous scenario for anyone.

In a mass casualty incident in which you become a rescuer, your goal is to get lightly trapped victims out first. Learn how to perform light rescue correctly by taking a

CERT course and joining your local Community Emergency Response Team. Contact your local firefighters and ask them where you can get involved with CERT.

As a lay rescuer one of your decisions will be to determine whether evacuation is needed for survivor safety. You should assist with that before attempting search or rescuer operations.

Search and rescue, or SAR, has three phases: size-up, search, and rescue.

Take some time to size up the situation and get an idea of what hazards are present, how many victims may be trapped, and where they are likely to be (e.g. where are the voids that might have been created, and where are likely areas where groups might have gathered). Continue sizing up the situation throughout the operation.

If you plan to get involved with light rescue, you'll need some basic gear: personal protective equipment, lighting, tools, communications, and marking.

The search should be accomplished using a systematic, thorough method that will not require repeating and which provides some minimal documentation.

Here's basic structure-search methodology:

- Call out and listen carefully.
- Never enter a burning or unstable structure.
- Search only stable multi-story buildings, from the bottom up or the top down. Be consistent.
- In the dark or poor visibility conditions, the wall is your lifeline. Keep your right hand on the right wall or left hand on the left wall to stay oriented.
- Triangulate (usually three people from different directions) to give a single location better scrutiny and illumination.
- Search with a buddy and do NOT go alone.
- Mark searched rooms or areas with an X on or near the door. CERT teams who enter the area will notice these markings. On top of the X write the time and date of the search. On the right side of the X write only hazard information. On the bottom of the X write how many victims are still inside. If the room or area is hazardous, draw a box around the X. These are known as FEMA X-code markings. Google "FEMA X-codes" to learn more. Be aware that in other countries different marking codes are used.
- Document the results of your searches on paper, and give the information to the CERTS or other responders when they arrive.

Once the victims have been located and triaged, they can then be removed if safety concerns permit. A dead or injured hero only adds to the chaos, so recognize your limits and be safe.

The method of extrication will depend on the number and the abilities of helpers available, the stability of the environment, and the condition of the patient. Accessing a victim often requires removal or stabilization of debris. Heavy debris can be moved or lifted by leveraging, and stabilized by cribbing. Cribbing is a framework placed under the lifted object to keep it in place and prevent it from shifting. Cribbing is often made of wooden blocks, but can be improvised from anything solid that can take the weight.

Let the victim help him or herself as much as possible. Remove obstacles and debris and allow them to get themselves out. Those who cannot get themselves out will be lifted, carried, or dragged in a fashion that avoids or limits further injury. Those with head and spine injuries should be stabilized and immobilized as much as reasonably possible before moving them. Otherwise, victims are removed to a medical area where someone in your group who has medical training can triage the injuries and prioritize first aid care to give assistance first to those with life- or limb-threatening injuries.

When lifting a patient or any heavy load, keep the back straight and keep the load close to your body. Push up with the legs and stand up with the load rather than bending over and pulling the load up with arm and back muscles.

1. Special Rescue Situations

Swift water rescue, hazmat, confined space rescue, fire rescue, collapsed building rescue, complex automobile extrication, and high angle situations require special skills and experience. Send for help and wait for the experts.

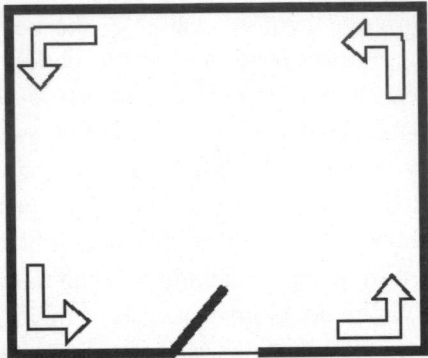

A simple room search pattern. Typically it's done along the wall going counterclockwise, keeping the right hand in constant contact with the wall. Interior portions of the room can be probed one-handed with a pole, and light can be triangulated from multiple directions to provide the best visual coverage.

MRC members practicing patient extrication using a simple two-person leverage and cribbing operation. Leverage and cribbing can be used to remove debris and avoid more injuries. Wear whatever protective gear you have available. Crib with whatever solid material you can find.

Some things you can carefully do in water scenarios include reaching out to the swimmer with a pole or stick, throwing a rope or flotation device, or paddling or rowing out on an improvised raft or boat. If you are isolated and need to swim out for help in deep but calm water, put empty plastic bottles in a backpack or bag and wear it or hold it in front of you like a swimming board. Do not enter moving water deeper than mid-calf or of unknown depth, and never tie into a rope in moving water.

Chapter 14
Specific Hazards

1. Drought

The Basics

Drought is a lack or deficiency of rainfall or snowpack over an extended period ranging from months to years or decades, resulting in a critical insufficiency in the water supply for a particular region. Drought is crushing for agriculture, and it has serious detrimental effects on industry, commerce, the economy, the environment, and social well-being. The effects of drought can include:

- Death of livestock
- Crop failure
- Famine and malnutrition, worsened by poverty
- Reduced water quality due to concentration of contaminants and pollutants
- Dehydration and disease
- Wildfires in dry vegetation
- Desertification
- Civil unrest, riots, and war
- Mass migration

The Jargon

Desertification—a process in which fertile land turns into desert.

Meteorological—pertaining to the science of weather
Hydrologic—pertaining to the study of water
Agricultural—pertaining to farming

Protecting Yourself and Your Family

Unfortunately, drought is one of those natural occurrences that's hard to be effective against. Community strategies might eventually include water restrictions and the use of alternative water sources, such as desalinization, recycling, drilling, and regulated planting of selective crops. Most of these strategies require the focus and cooperation of individuals, and that's very difficult to get. Americans have a difficult time letting go of their precious lawns and landscapes.

Unless you've had the foresight, space, and patience to store enormous quantities of water, there's little you can do about drought except being conscientious about your water use.

Adding some cash and goods to your disaster supply kit would probably be just as or more effective than trying to store and maintain huge tanks of emergency water. As drought progresses, those who have the cash or goods to barter for water will get what they need. Those who don't, won't.

2. Data Loss

The Basics

Data loss itself is a disaster, and is likely to occur during any other major disaster. We have become almost totally reliant on computers for communication, information storage, and financial management. The loss of this capability and the data already committed to it can be devastating to individuals as well as major companies and government agencies, and it could be weeks or months—maybe never—before the data can be restored or recovered.

In a nutshell, there are four basic causes of data loss. The first is **corruption** due to viruses. The second is **mechanical failure** due to power surges or failures, water damage, and the like. The third is **theft**. The fourth is **operator error**.

Dealing with potential data loss is a matter of doing a risk assessment and formulating plans to deal with those risks. Your plans should enable you to resume business without serious disruption. Your insurance policies should cover hardware and software. Large businesses should consider hacker insurance.

The Jargon

CPU—Central Processing Unit. The brains of the computer. It handles all the operations.

Data—Any type of information. In a computer, data is stored in files.

Gigabyte—G; a measurement of memory equivalent to 1,024 megabytes.

Hacker—A person who has gained unauthorized access into a computer system.

Hard drive—A device that stores data and programs, usually connected permanently to the main computer housing.

Hardware—The physical equipment that makes up the computer system: monitor, keyboard, disk drives.

Peripherals—Hardware that's added to the CPU, such as a printer, monitor, mouse, keyboard, or external drive.

Power surge—A sudden increase in power.

Server—A computer that delivers information and services to other computers linked by a network.

Software—Computer programs.

UPS—Uninterruptible power supply containing a battery that provides a continuous supply of power in case of a power failure and circuitry to protect electronic equipment from power surges.

Wi-Fi—A local area network allowing computers, smartphones, or other devices to connect to the Internet or communicate with each other wirelessly (via radio waves).

Virus—A computer program designed to attach itself to a file and replicate and spread from file to file, destroying data or interrupting computer operations.

Protecting Yourself, Your Family, and Your Business

Here are six steps you can take to ensure a comfortable level of safety for your data system.

Protect Your System

If your data systems are critical to your financial well-being, get help from an expert who can assess the threats and minimize the risks to your data systems. He/she will probably insist that you:

- Grant system access on a very selective basis. Limit access as much as possible. At your office, limit physical access to only those employees who are required to use the computer to do their jobs.
- Allow business use only on business computers. There should be no personal software allowed.
- Take extreme caution when downloading anything.

- Not load any software that isn't shrink-wrapped and from a dealer you trust.
- Use passwords and change them frequently.
- Give your computers periodic checkups and run antiviral software daily.

Protect Your Hardware

Protect your hardware by taking the following precautions:

- Don't allow food or drinks at the computer.
- Have the CPU and the peripherals cleaned by a professional on a regular basis. Dust and dirt are trouble.
- Keep waterproof tarps or covers handy to protect equipment. Elevate equipment to keep it away from flood water and secure equipment to keep it from falling to the ground.
- Have an alternative power source.
- Use surge protectors or a UPS (uninterrupted power supply). This is especially important if your power is backed up by a generator. If the power fails and the generator kicks in, the generator may have trouble keeping the power stable during the surge. Replace surge protectors every year or so. If the generator isn't automatic, switch everything off before starting it up.
- When the air crackles (close lightning, electrical shorts, etc.), disconnect the modem.
- Maintain the temperature and humidity. Excessive warmth and dampness are more trouble.
- Keep hardware and software licenses up to date. Maintain hardcopy records in a secure location.

Protect Your Files

Backing up your files is the single most important step in mitigating a data-loss disaster:

- NEVER be in a position where re-entry of data will require more than a day's work.

- Use a removable data storage device and back up your on-site data on a regular basis, preferably at least daily. You can take it with you when you evacuate. A 250G external hard drive can be purchased for under $200, 160G for around $100. A 30G iPod costs under $200 and might be used as incentive for employees to back up their files. Consider having laptops or notebook computers for employees so they can take their data and computers off-site and continue working seamlessly.

- Back up your drive and all of your data at least weekly and keep a set stored off-site. Use a secure server more than 50 miles from the office, or use an online back-up service, like the cloud. Or place the backup in a fireproof safe, at a satellite office, at home, or at a commercial data center.

- Include in your backups all key business and family or personal information, including budgets, client lists, contact information, sales and tax records, insurance policies, and banking transactions.

- Keep a clear paper trail that will allow easy re-entry of data.

Protect your inventory

Pre-analyze your supply and demand, so you'll know what you'll need to keep working.

Develop a Data Disaster
Attachment to Your Disaster Plan

In the attachment, answer the following questions:

- What concrete measures are in place and who is responsible for them?
- Even with the data backed up, how will we restore it and get it running again?
- If computers are not an option, how can paper-based systems be used and are they in place?

Stay Up to Date

A year or so after the publishing date, this material will be outdated. Both the threats and solutions will be more complicated.

3. Fire

The Basics

Fire requires three elements to exist: heat, fuel, and oxygen. This is often referred to as the fire triangle. When fire ignites, it needs all of these elements to accomplish the chain reaction required to maintain the fire. Remove any of the elements, and the fire goes out.

In many parts of the world fires are put into one of four classes:

Class A–Ordinary combustibles like wood, cloth, paper, plastics
Class B–Flammable liquids and gases
Class C–Electrical equipment
Class D–Combustible metals

The class of fire determines the method of fire suppression.

The Jargon

Arson—The crime of intentionally setting destructive fire
Combustible—Capable of igniting and burning
Conduction—The transfer of heat from one object to another when they're in contact
Convection—The transfer of heat by movement of a heated substance (e.g., heated air currents)
Crown fire—A fire that jumps along the tops of trees due to wind
Fire Triangle— Triangle defining the essential elements of fire: heat, fuel, and oxygen in a chain reaction
Flammable—Easily ignited and capable of burning quickly. Technically, the difference between flammable and combustible is defined by a material's flash point
Ground fire—Fire burning along the forest floor
Standpipe—A vertical pipe leading from a water supply, especially one that provides an emergency water resource
Structure fire—Fire in a building
Surface fire—Slow-moving fire at tree or brush level
Wildfire—An unplanned fire in forest, grass, or brush

Protecting Yourself and Your Family

Extinguishers

Each class of fire requires somewhat different methods to extinguish. Your choice of extinguishers will depend on what type of fires you expect to do battle against.

Extinguishers have a numerical rating that indicates the size of the fire it can handle. The higher the number, the more fire it can handle. A well-prepared office or home will have at least two extinguishers.

There are five types of extinguishers: water, dry chemical, halon, carbon dioxide, and foam. Water and foam remove the heat. Foam also cuts off the air supply, as does carbon dioxide. Halon and dry chemical agents break the chain reaction. The special agents used against Class D fires usually remove air. Use water, foam, or dry chemical against class A fires. Use foam, carbon dioxide, dry chemical, or halon against Class B. Electrical fires should be fought with nonconductive agents (carbon dioxide, dry chemical, or halon).

To use a portable extinguisher, follow the instructions shown on it. The basic method is:

- **PULL** the pin
- **AIM** the nozzle
- **SQUEEZE** the handle
- **SWEEP** the base of the fire

In the United States extinguishers are everywhere. In most other parts of the world a bucket of water or dirt (or sand) is still the main "extinguisher."

Alarms

Smoke alarms detect smoke and sound an alarm. Smoke alarms are cheap, and if you can't afford one you can probably get one free from your local fire department, health department, or emergency management office. If you have alarms in your home that run on house current, remember that they will not work when the power is out. Supplement them with a couple of battery-operated units. Have a smoke alarm on every level of the structure. Test them monthly and change the batteries at least once per year.

A battery-operated carbon monoxide alarm is also a good investment. Place one near the sleeping area, and if you have a designated safe room or shelter area, place one near there. Carbon monoxide is a by-product of inefficient combustion and replaces oxygen. Simply put, carbon monoxide molecules take all the oxygen parking places, and oxygen has no place to park. Any fire or fuel-burning device produces carbon monoxide.

Gas detectors are available and can be placed near the furnace and hot water heater. Test the device monthly.

Sprinkler Systems

For most of us, a sprinkler system in the home is not in our budget. For business the investment could be more worthwhile. Sprinkler systems detect heat and respond to it by spraying water from a sprinkler head.

Making a Decision to Fight a Structure Fire

In a wide-spread disaster, calling the fire department will be low on the list of priorities. Evacuate the structure first. Then make your decision about whether to fight the fire. Ask yourself these three questions: Will I be able to escape quickly if I stay to fight it and something goes wrong? Do I have the correct equipment and enough of it for the type and size of fire? Is the area free from other dangers, such as hazardous material, structural collapse? If the answer to any of these questions is no, leave immediately. Do NOT attempt to fight the fire. Shut doors behind you to contain the fire.

If You Attempt to Fight the Fire

- Wear safety equipment including helmet, goggles, dust mask, gloves, and boots.
- Work with a partner, and have a backup team standing by.
- Have two ways to get out of the fire area.
- Feel closed doors with the back of the hand, from the bottom up. Fire will be behind a hot door.
- Keep doors closed to confine the fire.
- Always worry about carbon monoxide, heated air, and toxic fire gases. Do not wear a respirator mask into an oxygen depleted atmosphere.
- Stay low to the ground. Smoke and heat will concentrate higher in the room.
- If it can be done without increasing the size of the fire, open windows for ventilation to remove smoke. Try to cross ventilate by opening windows on opposite sides of the room, or placing a fan blowing in and a fan blowing out.
- Keep a safe distance from the fire.
- Remove heat by cooling. This means using water in class A fires (typical structure fires).
- If there's an interior wet standpipe in your building, use three people to operate it: one to handle the hose, one to bleed air from the lines, and one to control the water pressure. Most interior wet standpipes will have a hundred feet of jacketed hose with a three-eighths-inch nozzle tip, using up to 125 gallons per minute. That's a lot of pressure. Hang on tightly and get a good stance before opening the nozzle.

If Inside During a Fire

- Stay low to the floor and exit the building as quickly as possible.
- Cover your nose and mouth with a wet cloth.
- When approaching a closed door, use the back of your hand to feel the lower, middle, and upper parts of the door. Never use the palm of your hand or fingers to test for heat: burning those areas could impair your ability to escape a fire (i.e., ladders and crawling).
- If the door is NOT hot, open slowly and ensure fire and/or smoke is not blocking your escape route. If your escape route is blocked, shut the door immediately and use an alternate escape route, such as a window. If clear, leave immediately through the door. Be prepared to crawl. Smoke and heat rise. The air is clearer and cooler near the floor.
- If the door is hot, do not open it. Escape through a window. If you cannot escape, hang a white or light-colored sheet outside the window, alerting firefighters to your presence.
- Heavy smoke and poisonous gases collect first along the ceiling. Stay below the smoke at all times.

Wildfires

Minimize wildfire losses by doing some pre-event preparation:

- Use fire resistant building material. Build to code.
- Build roads and driveways at least 16 feet wide.
- Maintain at least two exits in the home.
- Keep your chimney clean.
- Don't burn openly in dry weather.
- Maintain some clean space:

- Keep drains and gutters free from vegetation.
- Put a non-flammable screen over flues.
- Remove all vegetation within ten feet of any stove or chimney.
- Soak fireplace ashes and charcoal in water before disposing of it.
- Widely space landscape vegetation.
- Remove branches to a height of 15 feet.
- Maintain a fuel-free zone around all structures for a minimum of 30 feet—remove dry and excess vegetation, garbage, and any sources of tinder.
- Store propane tanks at a significant distance from buildings and maintain a fuel-free zone around them.
- Store combustibles such as firewood away from buildings.

- Leave a 100-foot garden hose connected to a freeze-proof faucet, and leave a ladder long enough to reach the roof nearby.
- Have firefighting tools handy: ladder, shovels, rakes, buckets.
- Clearly mark your address and road signs so firefighters can find your property if called.

During a Wildfire

- Listen to the media for information and instructions.
- Remove any combustibles (lawn furniture, etc.) from around the house.
- Remove flammable drapes and blinds.
- Close doors and windows.
- Close gas valves and turn off pilot lights.

- Turn on every light when needed for visibility in dense smoke.
- Put large waterproof valuables into a pool or pond.
- Leave sprinklers on, aimed at the roof and the side of the house facing the approaching fire.
- Be ready to get out fast.
- If smoke gets dense before you can evacuate, stay low to get the best air.
- If you are overcome by fire, get low or float face up in a pond or stream. Cover the head and upper chest with wet clothing. If no body of water is available, get into the large boulders, or lie flat and cover yourself with wet clothing or soil.

After the Fire

- Take great caution, hot spots can smolder for hours before flaring up.
- Check and recheck the roof and walls, then wait a few hours and check again. Get a distant look at the building to see smoke from any lingering hotspots.

4. Flood

The Basics

A flood is an abnormal expanse of water that submerges land. It occurs when the water exceeds its normal depth or it flows above or beyond the normal limits of its container.

Floods of seawater can be caused by heavy storms, high tides, and tsunamis. Seawater flooding from storm surges often combines with intense monsoon or tropical storm rains to produce devastating floods. Seawater floods are particularly devastating because of the large populations concentrated on coastlines and the long-term salt damage to farmland soils.

River flooding may occur because of heavy storms, high runoff, and sometimes due to high temperatures causing accelerated melting of the snowpack. The river overflows its banks onto the flood plain. Flash floods are often the result of intense rainfall in a particular drainage or system of drainages. The factors in a flash flood include slope, drainage, vegetation, soil and surface conditions, and saturation. Flash floods can move slowly and hit hours later when the sun is shining.

Floods can also be caused by blocked waterways. The blockages can be ice and debris jams on rivers, or clogged sewers and community water systems.

Floods are so common that flood insurance can be hard to get, and insurance companies will often find any available loophole in insurance policies to deny a flood-damage claim.

The Jargon

Dike—A low wall, ditch, or embankment.

Flash flood—A sudden flood, usually cause by a heavy rain.

Flood plain—A low plain next to a river, formed of river sediment and subject to flooding.

Flash Flood Watch—Flash flooding is possible. Tune to NOAA weather radio of other media for information.

Flash Flood Warning—A flash flood is occurring. Seek higher ground on foot immediately.

Flood Watch—Flooding is possible. Tune to NOAA weather radio or other media for information.

Flood Warning—Flooding is occurring or will occur soon. If advised to evacuate, do so immediately.

Monsoon—Seasonal wind system or the rain that accompanies that wind.

Precipitation—Solid or liquid water that falls from the air to the earth.

Storm surge—A local rise in sea level near the shore caused by strong winds from a storm.

Tide—Rise and fall of the sea happening twice each lunar day.

Tsunami—An ocean wave produced by submarine earthquake, volcano, or landslide

Protecting Yourself and Your Family

Preparing

- Find out how likely floods are in your area.
- Know the local emergency plan and evacuation routes.
- Raise the furnace, water heater, and electric appliances off the floor.
- Install sump pumps and make arrangements for backup power.
- Construct barriers to deflect water around the home.
- Anchor outdoor fuel tanks.
- Get some flood insurance.

If There's Time Before an Impending Flood

- Secure the home. Move furniture and valuables upstairs.
- Turn off the utilities at the main switches or valves if instructed to do so. Unplug appliances, but don't touch electrical equipment if you're standing in water. Don't be in water where appliances are plugged in.
- Fill your gas tank and head for high ground.

If the Flood Threat Is Immediate (A Flash Flood)

- Stay away from water courses and drainages.
- Get out of a watercourse onto high ground. If you're in a deep drainage with no escape, run like hell downstream. It will buy you some time.

Author's note: during the filming of the BBC/Discovery Channel series Planet Earth, *I chased flash floods with a camera crew for six weeks in the Southwest's slickrock canyon country. I learned that, contrary to what you are told, it is quite possible to outrun some flash floods. Running beats standing there waiting for the wall of water to swallow you up.*

- In your car, don't cross flooded roads. As little as six inches of water can push your car off.
- If you are trapped midstream, get on the car top.
- Do not wade anything above mid-calf. You risk being swept away or entrapping your foot. If you must cross a shallow but swift stream, use a stick or other people for support.
- If you MUST get into deeper swift water, swim it. Get on your back in a defensive swimming position: feet downhill, head up, steering with your arms and warding off obstacles with your feet. Angle your head toward the shore you wish to reach. This will put you at an angle that makes the current push you toward that shore (a "ferry angle").
- Never tie into a rope in moving water. It will pull you down and drown you. Do not go into the water to rescue someone. If you have a rope, throw it in small coils directly at the swimmer. If they grab it, take a strong stance and hold on. They will pendulum in toward the shore.

- For emergency flotation use anything less dense than air or that holds air. Some empty plastic bottles in a backpack make an excellent personal flotation device.

After a Flood

- Listen to the media and return when authorities say it's safe.

- Downed power lines are a hazard. Stay away from fallen lines and transformers. Report the damage to the power company.

- Floods contaminate local water supplies with oil, gasoline, and sewage. Don't play in the water. Wash your hands often and clean injuries thoroughly.

- Disinfect toys and other metal/plastic items with a 1:10 solution of bleach and water (1½ cups bleach to a gallon of water).

- Throw away any food that might have been contaminated by flood water.

5. Hurricanes and Other Cyclonic Storms

The Basics

A tropical cyclone is a storm system with a low pressure center and storms that produce high winds, tornadoes, heavy rain, and storm surges. These storms develop and grow over warm seas as moist warm air rises and water vapor condenses. Because of the Coriolis effect (remember that from ninth-grade earth science?), cyclones rotate counterclockwise in the Northern Hemisphere and clockwise in the Southern Hemisphere, and are referred to as tropical depressions, tropical storms, typhoons, cyclones, or hurricanes, depending on their location and intensity or strength.

Tropical cyclonic storms lose strength when they move over land. Coastal areas get the full brunt of the storm and suffer from the high winds, heavy rain, and storm surges, causing serious coastal flooding. Inland areas usually experience reduced winds but can still experience serious flooding from heavy rains.

The Jargon

Eye—A core of relatively calm air in the center of a hurricane.

Hurricane—A large rotating tropical weather system with winds of at least 74 miles per hour.

Hurricane categories:

Storm surge—A local rise in sea level caused by strong winds from a storm.

Hurricane/Tropical Storm Warning—Hurricane/tropical storm conditions are expected within 24 hours.

Hurricane/Tropical Storm Watch—Hurricane/tropical storm conditions are possible within 36 hours. Tune to NOAA weather radio or other media for information.

Storm Tide—A combination of normal tide and storm surge.

Tropical Storm—An organized system of strong thunderstorms with a defined circulation and maximum sustained winds of 39–73 miles per hour.

Protecting Yourself and Your Family

Before the Storm

- Know the local risks, evacuation routes, and shelter locations.
- Take in outdoor items, including furniture and awnings. Tie down large objects. Cut down and

Category	Sustained wind (mph)	Damage	Storm surge
Category 1	74–95	Minimal. None to permanent structures. Some to unanchored mobile homes and vegetation.	4–5 feet
Category 2	96–110	Moderate. Roofing, door, and window damage.	6–8 feet
Category 3	111–130	Extensive. More structural damage. Mobile homes destroyed. Some structural damage from flooding on the coast.	9–12 feet
Category 4	131–155	Extreme. Extensive damage. Beach erosion. Trees down. Inland flooding.	13–18 feet
Category 5	>155	Catastrophic. Complete roof or building failure of many structures. Major roads cut off. Major flood damage near the shore. Mass evacuations likely.	>18 feet

dispose of dead branches and any live branches that are too close to the house.

- Close and secure window shutters, or cover windows with plywood or boards.
- Check your disaster supply kit to make sure the radio and lights work and the batteries are fresh.
- Lock all doors and windows to reduce vibration. Close drapes and curtains, and tape windows to limit and contain flying glass.
- Tie/anchor down mobile homes.
- Review your insurance policy.
- Fill the car with gas and prepare to evacuate.
- Listen to the NOAA weather radio or other media for information.
- If told to evacuate, go immediately.

During the Storm

- Stay indoors and away from windows. Go to your safe room if you have one.
- Stay away from flood waters.
- Be alert for tornadoes.
- Remember, the "eye" of the storm means the storm is only half over.

After the Storm

- Listen to the media for information.
- Wait until the area is declared safe before entering.
- Use a flashlight to inspect for damage, including gas, water, electrical lines, and appliances.
- If you smell gas or fire, turn off the gas main. Switch off individual circuit breakers (or unscrew individual

fuses) and turn off the main breaker (or unscrew the main fuse).

- Stay away from downed power lines.
- Use the phone for urgent calls only.
- If the area has flooded, drink the local water only if it has been declared safe. Throw out any food contaminated by flood waters.

6. Tornadoes

The Basics

A tornado is a violent column of rotating air formed when a warm humid air mass meets a cold air mass. The column, or condensation funnel cloud, is usually in contact with a cumulonimbus cloud base above and the ground below. The bottom of the funnel is usually surrounded by a debris cloud. Tornadoes occur most often in the United States, but do occur elsewhere. A tornado over water is called a waterspout. Tornadoes move at an average speed of 30 miles per hour, but can move twice or half that speed. The internal winds can reach 300 miles per hour. The path of damage can be miles long and hundreds of feet wide.

Tornadoes are rated by the Fuijita (F) Scale or the Enhanced Fujita Scale (EF) according to the damage they cause. An F0 causes light damage and can strip some tree limbs off, but won't seriously damage structures. An F5 will cause incredible damage and will tear a building off its foundation. Tornadoes can strike without warning and can travel fast, changing directions with no warning. Knowing the potential F rating isn't important. If you hear the warning or see the funnel, take appropriate action.

The signs of a tornado are:

- A funnel cloud, sometimes difficult to see
- Dark sky with an eerie greenish tone
- Large dark low-lying clouds
- High winds becoming calm or still
- Loud roar, "like a freight train"

The Jargon

Cumulonimbus—A cumulus cloud that produces thunderstorms.

Funnel cloud—A rotating column of air working its way down from the bottom of a cumulonimbus cloud.

Water spout—A tornado over a large body of water.

Dust devil—A circular wind that picks up dust, not associated with a tornado.

Fujita scale—A scale defining tornado intensity and damage.

Tornado Warning—A tornado has been sighted or indicated by weather radar. Take shelter immediately.

Tornado Watch—Tornadoes are possible. Remain alert for approaching storms. Watch the sky and monitor NOAA weather radio or other media for information.

Protecting Yourself and Your Family

Before Tornado Season

- Find or make a low, windowless, structurally sound place to take shelter in. Consider the basement, under the stairs, a safe room, or an interior hallway or closet on the lowest floor.

- Find or make a low, windowless, structurally strong place to take shelter in. Consider the basement, under stairs, a safe room, an interior hallway or closet on the lowest floor.
- If your house is a mobile home, configure it with a tie-down system to limit damage, but avoid using it for shelter.
- Learn the siren signals in your area.
- Do drills with the family.

When a Tornado Is Imminent

- Take cover immediately. Most injuries are caused by flying debris.
- Report sighted tornadoes.
- Stay away from windows to avoid airborne glass shards.
- Go to your designated shelter or to the interior part of the basement or an interior room on the lowest floor. Avoid being near doors, windows, outside walls, and corners. Do not stay directly beneath heavy furniture or appliances on the floor above.
- Get under a heavy table or other sturdy cover. Cover yourself with a mattress or heavy blankets. Cover and protect you head and face.
- If you're in a mobile home, go to the community tornado shelter. If there is none or you don't have time, go to a sturdy nearby building, to the basement or an interior room on the lowest floor. If that's not possible, get out of the mobile home and lie flat in the nearest ground depression, preferably a ditch or culvert.
- If you're in a vehicle:
    - Stop and get out.
    - Get in a nearby ditch or low spot.

- ■ Never get under the car. Stay away from vehicles.
- ■ Protect your head under structural cover or with your arms.
- ■ Avoid areas with trees.
- • If you're in a building other than your home:
  - ■ Take the precautions given above.
  - ■ Avoid elevators.
- • If you're in a mall or large gymnasium:
  - ■ Stay away from windows and glass doors.
  - ■ Get to the lowest level.
  - ■ Get under a door frame or huddle against a structure that will deflect falling debris.

After a Tornado

- • Enter a building only after authorities have checked the foundation for shifting or cracking and the walls and ceilings for structural soundness.
- • If you smell gas, shut off the main valve immediately and call the gas company.
- • Shut off the electricity and have an electrician check for circuit shorts.

7. Winter Storms

The Basics

Winter storms are weather disturbances that combine cold temperatures with the resulting forms of precipitation (snow, sleet, ice, freezing rain). These are usually winter events, but can often occur in spring and fall. In this section we focus on the effects of precipitation or the combined effects of precipitation and cold. For heat and cold emergencies, see the next section.

Winter storms can wreak havoc:

- Disrupted traffic and increased risk of accidents due to limited visibility, icy roads, deep drifts
- Disruption in transportation and distribution of goods and supplies, resulting in depletions of food, water, and medical supplies for humans and livestock
- Cut-off of emergency response teams
- Increased risk of cold injuries (frostbite and hypothermia, exertion injuries and illnesses, and carbon monoxide poisoning)
- Structural collapse, including buildings and power lines, due to deep or heavy wet snow
- Avalanches in mountainous areas (common in Alaska, Colorado, Utah and some other mountain states)
- Flooding in low lying areas

The Jargon

Avalanche—A slide of large masses of snow or ice down a mountain slope.

Avalanche Warning—A forecast to draw attention to severe avalanche danger.

Blizzard Scale—A blizzard has winds of 35–44 miles per hour and visibility less than 500 feet. A severe blizzard has winds over 45 miles per hour and zero visibility.

Blizzard Warning—Sustained winds or gusts to 35 miles per hour or greater and considerable falling or blowing snow expected for a period of three hours or longer.

Freezing Rain—Rain that freezes when it hits the ground.

Frost or Freeze Warning—Below freezing temperatures are expected.

Heavy Snow Warning—A significant amount of snow is forecast that will make travel dangerous.

Sleet—Rain that turns to ice before it hits the ground

Travel Advisory—Weather conditions have created impassable or hazardous roads.

Wind Chill—The reason why it feels colder when the wind blows. A product of wind speed and air temperature.

Winter Storm Warning—A significant winter storm or hazardous winter weather is occurring, imminent, or likely and is a threat to life and property.

Winter Storm Watch—Significant winter weather is expected within 12 to 36 hours.

Protecting Yourself and Your Family

Before the Storm

- General preparations for winter should include draining water from sprinkler lines, draining outdoor hoses, closing inside valves that supply outdoor hose faucets, and opening outside valves to drain water and allow ice to expand.

- Protect pipes with insulating sleeves or heat tape.

- Insulate the walls and attic.

- Clean out rain gutters to allow runoff and keep them from blocking with snow and ice.

- Prepare for power loss. Maintain a disaster supply kit. Maintain a reasonable supply of heating fuel.

- Winterize your home by repairing roof damage and blocking small holes in the walls and around pipes and vents. Maintain weather-stripping around windows and doors.

- Check batteries in smoke and carbon monoxide detectors.

- Have a professional clean your furnace, flues, and chimney.
- Maintain snow removal equipment.
- Winterize your car:
  - Keep the tank full.
  - Check your battery and clean the terminals.
  - Check antifreeze levels and the thermostat.
  - Check the heater, defroster, windshield wipers, and add windshield washer fluid.
  - Check the exhaust system.
  - Change to a lightweight oil.
  - Install all-weather radials or snow tires.
  - Keep an ice scraper and a broom in the car.
  - Carry an emergency car kit.

During a Storm

- Put on warm clothes.
- Protect water pipes with insulation or an external heat source. Allow water to trickle from faucets to prevent freezing.
- Do not allow drinking water to freeze.

In the Car

- Drive only if absolutely necessary and only during the day.
- Stay on the main roads.
- Travel with a companion.
- Tell someone your destination, schedule, and route.
- Take along a cell phone or a two-way radio.
- If trapped by a blizzard:
  - Pull off and turn on the hazard lights or tie a bright tape or cloth to the antenna or window.

Raising the hood may signal distress, but you'll lose engine heat.

- Open a downwind window slightly for ventilation.
- Operate the engine and heater for only 10 minutes per hour to prevent carbon monoxide poisoning. Occasionally clear snow from the exhaust.
- Leave an overhead light on only when the engine is running.
- Insulate as much as possible and huddle together.
- Change position frequently and move around to generate body warmth and avoid cramps.
- Take turns staying awake on safety watch.
- Drink fluids to avoid dehydration. Avoid eating snow or ice. It lowers body temperature.
- When the storm clears, if you are stranded, stomp an SOS into deep snow, or burn engine oil for a smoke and fire signal.

After a Storm

- Listen to media for information and forecasts.
- Check the Internet and telephone resources for road conditions.
- Check on your neighbors, especially anyone with special needs.

8. Thunderstorms & Lightning

The Basics

All thunderstorms and lightning are dangerous. Many people are killed by lightning and the survivors of lightning strikes can suffer a variety of long-term complications. Thunderstorms can be dry or wet and are associated with tornadoes, strong winds, and flash floods.

The Jargon

Severe Thunderstorm Watch—Severe thunderstorms are likely to occur. Watch the sky and listen to NOAA weather radio or other media for information.
Severe Thunderstorm Warning—Severe weather has been reported by spotters or indicated by radar. There is imminent danger to life and property for those in the path of the storm.

Protecting Yourself and Your Family

- The 30/30 lightning safety rule: If after seeing lightning you cannot count to 30 before hearing thunder, get inside a building or an automobile (not a convertible). Stay indoors for 30 minutes after hearing the last thunder.
- Delay outdoor activities.
- Don't shower or bathe during the storm. Pipes and fixtures can conduct electrical current.
- Use your cell phone, but not your landline (POTS telephone line).
- Lightning can cause power surges. Turn off electronics and appliances.
- Monitor NOAA weather radio and other media for information.
- Avoid tall isolated trees, hilltops, beaches, open water, open fields, small isolated sheds in open areas, and anything metal.
- If in a forest, get low under a thick stand of small trees.

- If in open terrain, go to a gully or ravine. Be watchful for flash flooding.
- If on the water, get to land and find shelter.
- If you feel your hair standing or hear metal buzzing, crouch low to the ground but do not lie flat.

After the Storm

- If anyone is injured, check ABCs and seek medical help.

9. Cold & Heat Emergencies

The Basics

Here we're talking about cold waves and heat waves or unique events when the temperature is acutely and extremely colder or hotter than usual for the average climate of a region. Heat and cold waves are prolonged periods of excessively hot or cold temperature. Both conditions can be exacerbated by humidity, although it's more often a factor in heat waves. They both have common effects:

- Crop failures due to cooking or freezing of vulnerable plants.
- Deaths by hypothermia or hyperthermia ("exposure" and heat stroke), especially among the elderly, chronically ill, and homeless. Also, in the case of cold waves, there's an increase in carbon monoxide poisoning from the extensive use of fuel-burning heaters.
- Illnesses related to dehydration.
- Power outages due to increased use of heating or air conditioning.

- Structural damage, especially roads, from expansion and contraction.

- Wildfires during heat waves and structural fires during cold waves.

See Chapter 5 (Emergency Heating and Cooling) and Chapter 9 (First Aid and Light Rescue) for more detailed information on those particular aspects of heat and cold emergencies.

	Heat Wave	Cold Wave
Activity	Avoid strenuous activity. Work during the coolest parts of the day.	Do not avoid strenuous activity, except to maintain energy levels during food and water deficiencies. Get in bed to maintain warmth during the coldest part of the day.
Shelter	Move to the lowest level of the building, where cool air falls.	Move to the upper level of the building, where warm air rises.
Clothing	Strip down indoors. Outdoors, cover up with long sleeves and pants to reduce sunburn. Light colors are significantly cooler than dark in the sunlight. Moist clothing can provide a swamp-cooler effect in low-humidity heat.	Dress in layers: a weather resistant shell over insulation. Wear a hat. Cover the mouth. Stay dry or change out of wet clothes. Wear mittens.
Food and Nutrition	Drink plenty of water.	Drink plenty of water. Eat lots of carbohydrates.
Pre-Disaster Preparation	See chapter 5	See chapter 5

The Jargon

Dehydration—A condition in which the loss of body fluids exceeds the amount taken in.

Frostbite—Damage to skin and other tissues due to extreme cold.

Heat exhaustion—When the body is too hot, either from exercise or weather. The body's cooling system is still working but not keeping up.

Heat stroke—A medical emergency in which the body's cooling system has stopped working.

Hypothermia—A condition in which the body temperature falls below 95 degrees because more heat is being lost than gained.

Protecting Yourself and Your Family

Refer to the chart on page 243 and chapter 12.

10. Earthquake

The Basics

In a nutshell, an earthquake is a ground-shake that usually only lasts a few seconds. Strong earthquakes can cause massive structural damage and a high death toll. The after-effects can include massive urban fires and giant killer ocean waves (tsunamis).

Earthquakes are caused by the movement of faults generated by the constant motion of tectonic plates. Earthquakes are most common in areas along the edges of tectonic plates (California, Japan, etc.). In the United States, strong earthquakes are most common in Alaska, Hawaii, the West Coast, and the intermountain states (Nevada, Idaho, Wyoming, Montana, and Utah), although other areas of the country, such as the central Mississippi Valley, are also at risk.

Quakes send seismic waves through the ground that can be measured all over the world. The strength and intensity of earthquakes are measured using the Richter Scale and the Modified Mercalli Scale.

The Jargon

Earthquake-proofing—Modifying a structure and its contents to withstand the effects of an earthquake.

Epicenter—The surface location directly above the center of the earthquake.

Richter Scale—A scale from 1–10, used to measure the energy (magnitude) of an earthquake.

Modified Mercalli Scale—A scale of earthquake intensity measuring the severity of shaking. A scale-1 earthquake is weak, causing no damage. A scale-12 is a quake causing nearly total destruction.

Tectonic plates—Plates of the earth's outer shell in relative motion to one another.

Fault—A break in the earth's crust along which movement can take place, causing an earthquake.

Seismic waves—Waves caused by earthquakes.

Liquefaction—A process by which saturated soil behaves like liquid during an earthquake, with devastating effect on structures.

Aftershock—A weaker earthquake in the same area as the main earthquake.

Protecting Yourself and Your Family

Before the Quake

- Make structural modifications, including extra bracing and sill plate/foundation bolts, or hold-downs to secure walls to foundations. Strap the chimney in place with structural straps and angle bracing.

- Repair defective wiring. Install flexible utility connections.
- Secure fuel oil and propane tanks to the floor or ground and install flexible connections.
- Secure the fridge, furnace, and heavy appliances to wall studs with heavy strapping.
- Secure the water heater with heavy strapping or metal plumber's tape.
- Store large heavy objects and breakables on lower shelves.
- Reinforce attachments of overhead light fixtures and ceiling fans.
- Secure mirrors, shelves, and frames to the walls.
- Choose an alternate exit from each room.
- Do practice drills with the family and coworkers.

During the Quake

- Most injuries are caused by debris from collapsing structures and falling objects.
- Get under a strong doorway, against an inside wall, in a safe room, or under stable, heavy furniture such as a bed or desk.
- If in bed, stay in bed until the shaking stops.
- Avoid being near windows, outside doors, or weak walls.
- Stay inside until the shaking stops.
- If you are outdoors:
  - Stay put until the shaking stops. Crouch and protect your head and face with your arms.
  - Move away from buildings, fuel tanks, and power lines.

- ▪ Don't go into nearby buildings.
- If you are in a vehicle:
  - ▪ Pull over and stop away from utility poles, trees, wires, overpasses, and fuel tanks.
  - ▪ Set the emergency brake.
  - ▪ Stay in the vehicle.
- If you are trapped under rubble:
  - ▪ Make an airspace (a void) where you can breathe.
  - ▪ Do not use matches or lighters.
  - ▪ Keep still to avoid kicking up and breathing dust.
  - ▪ Cover your mouth and nose with clothing or a handkerchief.
  - ▪ Signal by tapping on a pipe or wall.

After the Quake

- Expect aftershocks.
- Be alert to the possibility of flooding and tsunamis. If in a low area near a large body of water, head for higher ground (for instance, in the "big one" expected along the Wasatch Fault, some experts predict the Great Salt Lake will tilt and splash up against the west slope of the Wasatch Mountains, killing thousands). Liquefaction and damage to dams may also increase the risk of local flooding. In coastal areas, tsunamis are possible. Get to higher ground.
- Enter damaged buildings as carefully as possible, preferably after authorities have inspected the foundation for shifting and the walls and ceilings for structural soundness.

- If there is structural damage or you smell gas, shut off the main gas valve.
- Shut off the electricity and have your circuits checked for shorts.
- Listen to the media for information and instructions.
- Stay away from downed power lines.
- In the home:
  - Shut off the main water valve if the pipes are damaged.
  - If you smell gas, get out. If you haven't already, shut of the gas main. Report leaks to the gas company or authorities.
  - Check the sewage lines for damage before using the toilet.
  - Open cabinets cautiously.
  - Clean up spilled flammables.
  - When possible, have a professional check the house for structural damage.
  - Be prepared to evacuate.

11. Landslides & Mass Wasting

The Basics

Landslides are down-slope movement of rock, soil, or related debris. Landslides are synonymous with the term "mass wasting," a variety of processes such as rock fall, creep, slump, mudflow, earth flow, and debris flow. In most mass wasting, water plays a key role by assisting in the decomposition and loosening of rock, lubricating rock and soil surfaces, adding weight to the soil, and giving buoyancy to the individual particles. This material will remain stationary until it exceeds its angle of repose and starts to slide. The proportions of rock, sand, clay, and water will dictate the type of slope failure, speed, and extent of a slide.

Landslides are propelled by gravity but they are often set off by other natural disasters, like volcanoes and earthquakes, or by human activity. A type of debris flow called "lahar"—a mixture of volcanic ash and water—is specific to volcanic activity. Lahars are often the major hazard experienced in a volcanic event. Although earthquakes can initiate debris flows, the major causes of landslides in the United States are rains that saturate soils.

Landslides often result directly from human activity. Modifications of surface flow and drainage can lead to landslides, as is the case in most urban landslides. Construction too close to eroding shores and vista points can lead to the loss of a structure. Over-irrigation, clear cutting, clearing vegetation by human or wildfire causes, and highway construction, especially highway cuts, can result in a landslide hazard.

Many unstable areas can be recognized from scarps, tilted and bent trees, wetlands and standing water, irregular and hummocky ground topography, over-steepened slopes with a thick soil cover, or steep slopes that have been burned clean. Mass movement can often be seen in aerial photography.

The Jargon

Angle of repose—the steepest angle that allows a material to be stationary.
Lahar—a debris flow of volcanic ash and water.

Mass wasting—the downhill movement of rock and soil under the direct influence of gravity.

Mudflow—a debris flow containing large amounts of water that usually occurs in canyons and gullies of mountainous areas.

Slump—a slide along a curved surface where unconsolidated material slips downward as a unit.

Rockslide—slide of a rock mass along planes of weakness.

Protecting Yourself and Your Family

Before a Slide

- Find out if you area has a history of slides or is considered at risk for slides by contacting the USGS, local emergency management, or the geology departments at nearby universities and colleges.
- Check the drainage patterns above your house. Watch for changes. Look for signs of ground movement. Poles and trees that lean past vertical uphill are a bad sign.
- Check and update your insurance policy.

During Wet Periods

- Listen to the NOAA weather radio and other media for information and warnings.
- Flash floods and mud flows may produce a characteristic apron of water or thin mud in front of the flow that tends to raise the level of water in front of it. If the stream rises or you detect a shallow mud flow, be suspicious and take precautions. Most streams go dirty brown during storms, so color isn't a reliable indicator when it's raining.
- Listen for unusual noises. Look for recently upslope-tilted utility poles and trees.

- Consider evacuating or moving to an upper story if you become suspicious. Be prepared to move quickly. Mud flows and flash floods can travel over 30 miles per hour.

- If you detect a debris flow, get out of its path to high ground as fast as possible.

- If caught in the flow, curl into a tight ball and cover your head.

After the Slide

- Stay away from the slide area. Stay out of the direct slide path. More slides are possible.

- Scan the area for victims and make notes of where they might be. Give the information to rescuers when they arrive.

- Report downed power lines and any other hazards you see.

12. Tsunami

A tsunami is a series of waves that occur when a large body of water is suddenly displaced on a massive scale. Tectonic activity such as earthquakes and volcanoes are often thought of as the primary origins of tsunamis, but massive landslides, ice shelf collapse, and even nuclear weapons and meteor or asteroid impacts could cause a tsunami.

An earthquake is usually the first warning of an impending tsunami. Tsunamis can pass unnoticed in the deep ocean, traveling as fast as 450 miles per hour, but as they approach land, a trough rather than a wave crest, develops and water along the shoreline recedes and exposes areas that are normally submerged. The crest usually arrives very shortly after (seconds or minutes).

Hawaii and Alaska see more tsunamis than anywhere else in the United States, although the entire West Coast is at risk. Tsunami Warning Centers in Hawaii and Alaska use a buoy monitor system to detect disturbances that might indicate a tsunami. When a tsunami is recorded, the center tracks it and issues a warning when needed.

Drowning is the most common cause of death associated with a tsunami, and the waves and the receding water are very destructive to structures. Secondary hazards include flooding, salt contamination of farming soil, contamination of drinking water, and fires from gas lines or ruptured tanks.

The Jargon

Tsunami Advisory—An earthquake has occurred and might generate a tsunami.

Tsunami Warning—A dangerous tsunami was or could have been generated and people in the warning area are strongly advised to evacuate.

Tsunami Watch—A dangerous tsunami may have been generated but it is at least two hours away from the watch area.

How to Protect Yourself and Your Family

Before and During a Tsunami

- Turn on your radio to learn whether there is a tsunami warning if an earthquake occurs and you are in a coastal area.
- Move inland to higher ground immediately and stay there.
- Stay away from the beach. Never go down to the beach to watch a tsunami come in. If you can see the wave you are too close to escape it. If there

is noticeable recession in water away from the shoreline you should move away immediately.

After the Tsunami

- Monitor the media for information and instructions.
- Stay away from flooded and damaged areas until officials say it is safe to return.
- Stay away from debris in the water; it may pose a safety hazard to boats and people.

13. Volcano

The Basics

A volcano is an opening to a pool of molten rock below the surface of the earth. When pressure builds up, eruptions occur. Gases and molten rock shoot up through the opening and spill over or fill the air with lava fragments. Eruptions can cause lateral blasts, lava flows, hot ash flows, mudslides, avalanches, falling ash, and floods. Volcanic eruptions have been known to knock down entire forests. An erupting volcano can trigger tsunamis, flash floods, earthquakes, mudflows and rockfalls.

Volcanoes usually form where tectonic plates pull apart from each other or converge with each other. They also form over hotspots away from the edges of the tectonic plates (e.g., the Hawaiian volcanoes). Active volcanoes in the US are found mainly in Hawaii, Alaska, California, Oregon, and Washington.

Volcanoes can be feisty. Buildings are destroyed and people are killed or made homeless. Fresh volcanic ash, made of pulverized rock, can be harsh, acidic, gritty, glassy, and smelly. Clouds of ash cover plants making them inedible. The ash can cause acute and chronic respiratory problems. Poisonous gases like carbon dioxide and sulfur dioxide kill people and animals. Dark skies, cold temperatures, severe winds, and heavy rains may follow an eruption for months afterward, causing famine and contributing to disease. Volcanic gases may contribute to the greenhouse effect. For a good primer on volcanoes, get a copy of the movie *Dante's Peak*. In spite of a few Hollywood moments, it's a fairly accurate depiction of what can happen.

The Jargon

Active—Erupting.
Ash—Fine particles of pulverized rock.
Bomb—A large fragment of semi-molten rock hurled from an eruption.
Dormant—Inactive but may erupt in the future.
Eruption—The process by which material is ejected from a volcano.
Lava—Magma which has reached the surface through a volcanic opening.
Pyroclastic flow—The flow of a mixture of hot gases, ash, and rock fragments that can flow of speeds up to 100 miles per hour.

Protecting Yourself and Your Family

Before an Eruption

- It's likely that there will be some advanced warning from obvious activity and geologic investigation.

- Monitor local radio and TV for information and warnings.
- In volcano areas, your disaster supplies kit should include goggles and a supply of face masks. N95 respirator masks are preferred but may clog quickly. Have some simple masks on hand.

During Volcanic Activity

- Follow the advice of local authorities. Evacuate immediately if ordered to do so. Sheltering near the volcano is dangerous.
- Avoid low-lying areas where poisonous gases can accumulate.
- Avoid streambeds where mudflows are possible.
- Bring pets and livestock into closed shelters.
- If you don't have a mask, improvise one from damp cloth.
- Wear protective clothing, including a helmet if you have one.
- If stranded in an area with a heavy accumulation of ash, stay inside and keep all doors and windows closed. Turn off all fans, heating, and air conditioning systems.
- Avoid driving in heavy ashfall. Engines clog, vehicles stall, and low visibility causes accidents.
- For an ash flow or a pyroclastic flow you may have few choices. Either shelter in an underground emergency refuge or hold your breath and submerge yourself underwater as long as possible in a river, a lake, or the sea. Chances are you'll cook anyway, but there's a slim chance the danger will pass in less than a minute.

After an Eruption

- Listen to media for information and instructions.

- Drink bottled or stored water until the local water can be tested.
- Clear the roof of ash. Ash is heavy and can cause a structural collapse.

14. Emerging Infectious Diseases & Bioterrorism

The Basics

Emerging infections are those that have recently appeared or those whose occurrence or geographic range is quickly increasing or threatening to increase. They can be caused by previously unknown pathogens, known pathogens that have spread to new locations or new populations, or re-emerging pathogens.

The factors in the emergence or re-emergence of infectious diseases can include natural processes related to the evolution of the pathogen, or the direct results of human behavior. Population growth, urbanization, international air travel, poverty, war, and environmental excesses can all contribute.

For an emerging infectious disease to flourish it must have a vulnerable population and the ability to spread easily from person to person. Many of these diseases take root when they pass from animals to humans. Examples of this are HIV and influenza.

Another critical factor in the re-emergence of infectious diseases is acquired resistance to antibiotics and antivirals. We've seen this with TB, STDs and other infections in the last couple of decades, and scientists expect it to get worse.

Bioterrorism agents are pathogens and related toxins that are used to cause death and disease in animals (including humans) and plants for terrorist purposes. These are usually "germs" that are found in nature but modified to increase their virulence, to make them resistant to antibiotics or vaccines, or to enhance the ability of the germ to spread through the environment and from person to person.

Terrorists have an interest in biological weapons because they are cheap and accessible. They can be easily produced and delivered without detection. Most bio agents have an incubation period. They can cause public chaos and panic without the terrorist even having to be present.

Pathogens and toxins that could be used as bioterrorism agents are classified into Class A, B, and C based on their ability to be disseminated, their mortality rates, their likelihood to cause public panic, and the actions that must be taken to combat them.

Category A agents are considered the worst (or the best, from a terrorist's point of view) because they can be easily disseminated or transmitted from person to person and pose the highest risk to national security because of their high mortality rates, their potential to cause panic, and the complications of controlling their spread. They have been studied by some countries for use in biological warfare and include anthrax, botulism, plague, smallpox, tularemia, and viral hemorrhagic fevers like Ebola and Marburg.

Category C includes germs that could be engineered for dissemination, and also includes some agents that are currently considered emerging infection threats, like SARS and drug resistant TB.

Bio weapons can be delivered by wet or dry aerosol sprays, by explosive devices, by vectors and direct contact with carriers, by introduction into our food and water, contamination of medications, or by contact with germ-laden objects.

The Jargon

Antibiotic—A substance that can destroy or inhibit the growth of microorganisms.

Antiviral—A substance that can destroy or inhibit the growth of viruses.

Bioterrorism agents—Pathogens and toxins that may be used for bioterrorism.

Contagious disease—Infectious disease that can be caught by a person who comes in contact with someone who is infected.

Contaminate—To make impure or unclean by contact.

Disinfection—To cleanse so as to destroy "germs."

Dissemination—To spread around or abroad.

Eradication—To eliminate completely.

Infectious disease—Diseases caused by the invasion of harmful organisms.

Incubation period—The time from exposure to a germ to the time the patient begins to have symptoms.

Isolation—Removes people who are ill with contagious diseases from the general public.

Microorganism—Microscopic organisms that may or may not cause disease.

Mortality rate—Ratio of deaths to a population.

Pandemic—Widespread epidemic disease.

Pathogens—An agent that causes disease, including bacteria, viruses, and parasites—germs.

Quarantine—Separates people who may have been exposed to a contagious disease but who are not yet ill.

Toxin—A poisonous substance produced from microorganisms.
Vaccine—A preparation of a weakened or dead pathogen that stimulates antibody production but doesn't cause disease.
Vector—An organism that carries disease-causing germs from one organism to another.
Virulence—The capacity of a germ to cause disease.
Zoonosis—A disease of animals that can be transmitted to humans.

Protecting Yourself and Your Family

There has been a lot of barely justifiable public and government paranoia about bioterrorism and emerging infections. A pandemic is a horrible concept in terms of the death toll. In modern times we've fed that fear with an endless stream of *Dawn of the Dead* and *Andromeda Strain*-style movies. Let's get realistic and practical about all of this. Biological warfare and emerging infections are nothing more than infectious diseases, and there are standard, common ways of reducing the chance that you'll be a victim of either:

- **Wash your hands often**, especially before and after preparing food, before eating and after using the toilet.

- **Get vaccinated**. Keep your and your children's vaccinations up to date. If you travel, get the recommended vaccines for your destination.

- **Use antibiotics and antivirals only when needed**. Take them exactly as directed. Don't stop taking them early because you feel better.

- **Stay at home if you feel sick or have cold symptoms**. Don't go to work with nausea, diarrhea, or a fever. Don't send your children to school if they have these symptoms.

- **Prepare food properly**. Keep counters and other kitchen surfaces clean. Promptly refrigerate leftovers.
- **Disinfect the "germiest" areas of your home**—the kitchen and bathroom.
- **Practice safe sex**.
- **Don't share** toothbrushes, combs, razor blades, towels, drinking glasses, or eating utensils.
- **Be a smart and courteous traveler**. Nobody wants to share the cabin of a plane or a ride in a taxi with somebody who's sick.
- **Keep your pets healthy**. Practice good pet nutrition and hygiene. Keep them up on their vaccinations. See a vet if they get sick.
- **In the event of an epidemic or biological terrorism event, follow the advice of the authorities**. They may tell you to shelter in place. They may put you through a decontamination process. They may quarantine you.
- Listen to the media for information and instructions.
- Contact your local and state health departments for information.

With a little common sense and the proper precautions, you can avoid infectious diseases and keep from spreading them.

15. Chemical Events

The Basics

Chemicals are found everywhere. Many cannot be seen or smelled. Hazards can occur during production, storage, transportation, use, or disposal. Sources of these hazardous materials can be chemical manufacturers, service stations, hospitals, hazardous waste sites, and chemical carriers.

Exposure can be unintentional (e.g., transportation accidents) or intentional (e.g., chemical terrorism). You and your community are at risk if a chemical is used unsafely or released in harmful amounts.

Chemical manufacturers are one source of hazardous materials, but there are many others, including service stations, hospitals, and hazardous materials waste sites.

Chemical warfare agents can be poisonous gases, liquids, or solids. They are deployed in one or more of several ways: wet or dry aerosol, vaporization by heat, application to a specific site, and contamination of food, water, or medications.

The signs of a chemical attack or a chemical accident are:

- Dead plants, animals, insects
- Pungent odor
- Unusual clouds, vapors, droplets
- Discoloration of surfaces

Chemical contamination of the air might cause the following signs and symptoms in multiple patients:

- Tightness in the chest and difficulty breathing
- Nausea and vomiting
- Watery eyes or blurry vision
- Seizures

The Jargon

Blister agent—chemical warfare agents that cause blisters (e.g., mustard gas).
Blood agent—chemical warfare agents that deprive blood and organs of oxygen.

Choking agent—chemical warfare agents that attack the respiratory system, causing difficulty breathing (e.g., chlorine).

Cold, warm, and hot zones—Operational zones set up by teams responding to a hazardous materials incident. The Hot Zone is the area at the site of the release. The perimeter is determined by the substance, the size of the spill, and ambient conditions, often using a standard reference text called the *Emergency Response Guidebook* (US Department of Transportation, ERG2004). Only trained personnel in specialized protective clothing may enter the Hot Zone. The Warm Zone is the area around the Hot Zone. It is used for decontamination, and usually requires specialized protective clothing. The Cold Zone surrounds the Warm Zone and is used for staging of responders and equipment, incident command, and medical support. It usually requires no protective clothing.

Confinement—Action taken to keep a material within a defined local area.

Corrosive—A liquid or solid that eats away another material.

Flash point—The lowest temperature at which a liquid will give off enough flammable vapor to burn.

Insecticide—A chemical made to kill insects, usually similar to nerve agents. Most can cause illness and death in humans.

Metabolic agent—A chemical warfare agent that affects the body's ability to use oxygen at the cell level (e.g., cyanide).

Nerve agent—Chemical warfare agents that affect the nervous system. These are of great concern because of the low amounts needed to cause death (e.g., sarin).

Protecting Yourself and Your Family

Before an Incident

- The Local Emergency Planning Committees (LEPCs) are responsible for collecting information about hazardous materials in the community and making this information available to the public upon request. The LEPCs also are responsible for developing an emergency plan to prepare for and respond to chemical emergencies in the community. The plan will include the ways the public will be notified and actions the public must take in the event of a release. Contact the LEPCs through your local emergency management office to find out more about chemical hazards and what needs to be done to minimize the risk to individuals and the community.
- Know the signs of a chemical incident.

During an Incident

Listen to local radio or TV for detailed information and instructions. Follow the instructions. Stay away from the area to minimize the risk of contamination. Some toxic chemicals are invisible and odorless.

- If you're told to evacuate, do so immediately. There may be very little time.
- If you're outside, stay uphill, upwind, upstream of the incident. Distance yourself at least a half a mile (8–10 blocks) from the hot zone.
- If you're in a vehicle, stop and take shelter in a building. If you can't risk leaving the vehicle, keep the windows and vents closed and shut off the heater or air conditioner.

- If you're told to stay indoors, close and lock exterior doors and windows. Close vents, fireplace dampers, and as many interior doors as possible.

  - Turn off air conditioners and ventilation systems. In larger buildings, set the ventilation system to 100 percent recirculation (no outside air) or turn it off.

  - Go into your designated shelter room or an interior room with few or no exterior windows or doors. Take your disaster supplies kit with you.

  - Seal the doors, windows, and vents with plastic sheeting and duct tape. Stuff holes and cracks with material and seal with tape. (See chapter 8, "Evacuation and Shelter.")

- If the attack or exposure is indoors:

  - Get out quickly, covering your face with your shirt or other clean material.

  - Shed your clothes. Dry decontamination (shedding the clothes) removes up to 80 percent of the toxic agent.

  - Thoroughly rinse the skin. Flush irritated eyes for several minutes if possible.

  - Stay calm and follow instructions.

What about that expensive gas mask you bought for this very event? If you have a gas mask with appropriate filters or cartridges, and you remember how to put it on and check the seal, use it. Do NOT use the mask in low-oxygen atmospheres. For instance, if you're sheltering in place and you have sealed the room with plastic and duct tape, the oxygen level in the room will soon drop below the limit recommended by the mask manufacturer.

After a Hazardous Materials Incident

- Return home only when authorities say it is safe. Open windows and vents and turn on fans to provide ventilation.

- Act quickly if you have touched or been exposed to hazardous chemicals. Many chemicals are rapidly absorbed through the skin.

  - Follow decontamination instructions from local authorities. They might advise to take a thorough shower, or you may be told to follow another procedure. If you can't get instructions from an authority, follow the following general **dry decontamination procedures**:

    - Remove clothing, jewelry, eyeglasses, and other items in contact with the skin. Place exposed clothing and shoes in a plastic garbage bag and tie a knot in it, then place that in another plastic bag and tie it. Do not allow contaminated clothing to contact other people or objects. When authorities are available, ask them how to dispose of it. Dry decontamination will remove as much as 80 percent of the chemical.

  - **If wet decontamination** is recommended:

    - Use large amounts of soap and water.
    - If the eyes are affected, flush for 10–15 minutes.
    - Remove and discard contaminated contacts.
    - Wash eyeglasses with soap and water.
    - Dispose of clothes by double bagging in plastic garbage sacks. Don't touch the

A Gas Mask Primer

You've heard a lot of talk about gas masks, but before you run out and buy one, it's important to know some basic information. A mask is no guarantee against the effects of a chemical or biological exposure. Only what's called Class A protective equipment (fully encapsulating protective suit with self-contained breathing apparatus, or SCBA) can provide total protection. Unless you plan to spend over a thousand dollars and carry this bulky equipment around with you, it's not something you should consider.

Gas masks come in several types. Half-masks cover the nose and mouth but not the eyes, and some chemical agents attack through or target the eyes. A full face masks covers the eyes, nose, and mouth. These can be effective if the seal is good. Half- and full-face filtered-air masks are called air purifying respirators (APR).

A PAPR, or positive pressure air-purifying respirator, pulls air through a filter and pumps it into the respirator, pressurizing it so leaks blow filtered air out rather than allowing contaminated air into the mask. Some APRs can be turned into PAPRs, but not all PAPRs can be used as APRs if the pump batteries run out.

Different filters provide different kinds of protection. Particulate filters filter out small airborne particles (e.g., fine particulate filters that are used against asbestos or biologic agents). Activated charcoal filters remove some chemical vapors and mists. Other chemicals can be removed by filters that neutralize chemical agents with a chemical reaction. Modern APR and PAPR filters use a combination of these methods. The filters are color-coded for specific groups of chemicals or particulate hazards according to NIOSH standards. Refer to the owner's manual for recommendations on which filters you will need to keep on hand.

If you don't have a gas mask, use a piece of cloth (bandana, T-shirt, etc.) or surgical mask snugly over nose and mouth. This will provide some protection against larger particulates and limited protection against vapors. It will not neutralize chemicals.

clothes. Use gloves and tongs and place them in the bag, too. Seal the bags.
- ◆ Ask the health department about disposal.
- ◆ Dress in clean clothes. If it was stored in a closet or drawers, it's probably safe.

- Seek medical care for unusual symptoms as soon as possible.
- Tell everyone who comes into contact with you that you may have been exposed.
- As soon as possible find out from local authorities how to clean up your land and property.
- Report any lingering vapors, unusual smells, or other hazards to your local law enforcement, fire department, or health department.

16. Nuclear & Radiological Emergencies

The Basics

A nuclear or radiological emergency is an event that poses a nuclear a radiological threat to public health and safety, property, or the environment.

Nuclear or radiological emergencies could include:

- An emergency at a nuclear facility, such as a nuclear power station.
- An emergency involving a nuclear-powered vessel.
- A transportation accident involving the shipment of radioactive material.
- An incident involving the loss, theft, or discovery of radioactive material.

- A terrorist attack utilizing radioactive materials, such as a "dirty bomb" or an RDD (radiological dispersion device using common explosives to spread radioactive material—this is NOT the same thing as a nuclear blast).
- A nuclear blast.

A nuclear blast is produced by a nuclear detonation. It involves the joining or splitting of atoms (called fusion and fission) to produce an intense pulse or wave of heat, light, air pressure, and radiation. It creates a large fireball, and everything inside of this fireball vaporizes and is carried upwards, creating a mushroom cloud. Radioactive material from the nuclear device mixes with the vaporized material in the mushroom cloud. It cools and condenses and forms particles. The condensed radioactive "dust" then falls back to the earth and is known as fallout. Radioactive fallout can be carried for many miles on wind currents and can contaminate anything on which it lands on. The effects on humans will depend on the size of the bomb and the distance the person is from the explosion. Injury or death may occur as a result of the blast itself, airborne debris, or burns. The intense light of the blast can cause serious eye damage. Victims near the blast site will be exposed to high levels of radiation and will develop radiation sickness (called acute radiation syndrome, or ARS). Burns will appear quickly but other signs and symptoms can take days to appear.

Two types of exposure from radioactive materials can occur from a nuclear blast: external exposure from the blast and fallout and internal exposure from contaminated air, food, and water. Exposure to very large doses of radiation may cause death within a few days or weeks. Exposure to lower doses may lead to cancer.

A nuclear power plant accident would not cause the same kind of destruction as a nuclear blast. Some radioactive material might be released in a plume, but no fallout is produced. The radiation hazard in the local area will depend on the type of accident, the amount of radiation released, and the weather. In case of an accident, plant and local authorities would monitor the situation and issue instructions to the surrounding communities. If you hear news about an accident at a nearby nuclear plant, don't panic. Not all accidents will result in a release of radiation.

Every level of government responds in the event of a nuclear or radiological emergency. The response starts at the local level, and progresses to state and federal levels, depending upon the location, type, and size of the emergency.

The key to surviving a radiation emergency is to limit the amount of radiation you are exposed to. Use shielding, distance, and time.

- **Shielding:** A thick shield between yourself and the source will absorb some of the radiation.
- **Distance:** The farther away you are away from the source, the lower your exposure.
- **Time:** Less time near the source means less exposure.

The Jargon

Alpha and Beta particles—Forms of radiation that can be stopped by thin shielding (for Alpha) to moderate shielding (for Beta).

Blast shelter—A shelter that offers protection from blast pressure, radiation, heat, and fire.

Fallout shelter—Any protected space with an encasing structure thick and dense enough to block or absorb the radiation given off by fallout.

Gamma waves—A penetrating form of radiation that requires thick, dense shielding for protection.

Ionizing radiation—Radiation that can cause other atoms, including those in human tissue, to become charged.

Nuclear event—Nuclear detonation involving fusion and fission, leaving radioactivity and fallout behind.

Nuclear plant warnings—

> *Unusual Event:* A small problem with no expected radiation leak. No action necessary.
>
> *Alert:* A small problem with minor radiation leakage inside the plant. No action necessary.
>
> *Site Area Emergency:* Sirens may be sounded. Listen to media for information and instructions.
>
> *General Emergency:* Radiation leaks possible outside the plant and off the plant site. Listen to media for information and instructions. Follow instructions promptly.

Radiation—Electromagnetic energy released from a radioactive material.

Radioactive contamination—Deposition of radioactive material on surfaces.

Radioactive exposure—Penetration of the body by radiation. Exposed patients aren't necessarily contaminated (e.g., X-rays).

Radiological event—An event that may involve explosion and release of radioactivity but no fission or fusion.

RDD—Radiation dispersal device, or "dirty bomb."

Radiation units—*Roentgen* and the *rad* are measures of the effect radiation has on the absorbing material. The *rem* is a measure of biological damage to humans.

Protecting Yourself and Your Family

Prepare for these incidents the way you would prepare for other hazardous materials emergencies:

- Ask local authorities and plant officials about the hazards. Get specific information about the hazards to children and the chronically ill or pregnant. Ask where hazardous waste dumps are located and other questions you might have about transportation and storage of materials in your community. Attend public information meetings.

- Learn the community warning system and likely evacuation routes.

- Learn emergency plans for schools, daycares, nursing homes, and workplaces where your family members may be.

- Maintain a disaster supplies kit.

- Use your family communication plan.

Dirty Bomb or RDD

- If you are inside and there is an explosion inside or you are warned of a radiation release inside your building, cover your nose and mouth and go outside immediately. Find an undamaged building or other shelter and quickly get inside. Once inside, move to an interior room and close windows and doors. Turn off air conditioners, heaters, or other ventilation systems.

- If you are inside an undamaged building and there has been an explosion outside or authorities have warned of an outside release check, stay in the building. Move to an interior room. Close windows and doors, and turn off air conditioners, heaters or other ventilation systems.

- If you are outside and there is an explosion or authorities warn of a radiation release nearby, cover your nose and mouth and quickly go inside an undamaged building. If you think you have been exposed to radiation, take off your clothes, shower and wash your body with soap as soon as possible.
- Stay where you are, watch TV, listen to the radio, or check the Internet for official news as it becomes available.

Nuclear Blast

(recommendations from the World Health Organization)

If You Are Near the Blast When it Occurs

- Turn away and close and cover your eyes to prevent damage to your sight.
- Drop to the ground face down and place your hands under your body.
- Remain flat until the heat and two shock waves have passed.

If You Are Outside When the Blast Occurs

- Find something to cover your mouth and nose, such as a scarf, handkerchief, or other cloth.
- Remove any dust from your clothes by brushing, shaking, and wiping in a ventilated area—however, cover your mouth and nose while you do this.
- Move to a shelter, basement, or other underground area, preferably located away from the direction that the wind is blowing.
- Remove clothing since it may be contaminated. If possible, take a shower, wash your hair, and change clothes before you enter the shelter.

If You Are Already in a Shelter or Basement

- Cover your mouth and nose with a face mask or other material (such as a scarf or handkerchief) until the fallout cloud has passed.
- Shut off ventilation systems and seal doors or windows until the fallout cloud has passed. After the fallout cloud has passed, unseal the doors and windows to allow for some air circulation.
- Stay inside until authorities say it is safe to come out.
- Listen to the local radio or television for information and advice. Authorities may direct you to stay in your shelter or evacuate to a safer place away from the area.
- If you must go out, cover your mouth and nose with a damp towel.
- Use stored food and drinking water. Do not eat local fresh food or drink water from open water supplies.
- Clean and cover any open wounds on your body.

If You Are Advised to Evacuate

- Listen to the radio or television for information about evacuation routes, temporary shelters, and procedures to follow.
- Before you leave, close and lock windows and doors and turn off air conditioning, vents, fans, and furnace. Close fireplace and dampers.
- Take disaster supplies with you (such as a flashlight and extra batteries, battery-operated radio, first aid kit and manual, emergency food and water, non-electric can opener, essential medicines, cash, credit cards, and sturdy shoes).

A Radiation Detector Primer

This is another device that preparedness salesmen want to sell to you, but that most of us are not going to need or want. Aside from being expensive and bulky, chances are you're not going to have it with you when you need it.

The common detector is the Geiger counter. It has a tube that produces a clicking sound or a flash of light when alpha or beta particles enter it. The old bulky Cold War–era Geigers are still available. Some modern Geigers are available that plug into your laptop. A more sensible idea would be something like the RadDetect, a keychain-size device that has an alarm and flashing light that warn of high level radiation, a directional sensor, and a simple diagnostic feature that shows approximate roentgens per hour. It sells for under $230. The RadTriageTM Radiation Detector sells for under $50 and is a credit card sized personal dosimeter. It uses a sensor strip that instantly detects radiation, turning darker when it detects harmful levels. The darker the sensor strip, the higher the radiation dose. A few smartphone rad detector apps have popped up in the last few years. Avoid taking these too seriously yet. Accurate radiation detection still requires specialized technology.

- Remember your neighbors may require special assistance, especially infants, elderly people, and people with disabilities.
- Evacuate to an emergency shelter immediately. Your children in school will be taken care of at school. Do not rush to get them.

Nuclear Power Plant Accident

- If you hear rumors of an accident, monitor local media for information and instructions.

- Unless instructed otherwise, bring family and pets inside and close and lock all doors and windows. Cover your mouth and nose while you're outside.
- Get in an interior room on a lower level and close and all doors and windows. Turn off air conditioning, fans, and furnace. Cover vents. Close fireplace dampers.
- Be prepared to evacuate immediately if told to do so by authorities. Remember neighbors with special needs.

When the Danger Has Passed

- Avoid using foods from the garden or milk from local animals until they are cleared by local authorities.
- Potassium Iodine, if taken soon enough after exposure, can block thyroid uptake of radioactive iodine and prevent thyroid cancer and other thyroid problems caused by inhaling or ingesting radioactive iodine. The decision to use and distribute potassium iodine to the community is up to the state. If you have potassium iodine in your kit, get the OK from local health authorities or emergency management personnel before taking it.

17. Terrorism

The Basics

The specific tools of terrorism are covered in other sections of this chapter. Also, refer to the section on Civil Unrest.

Terrorism is the use of force or violence against persons or property for purposes of intimidation, coercion, or ransom. Terrorists often use threats to:

- Create fear among the public.
- Try to convince citizens that their government is powerless to prevent terrorism.

- Get immediate publicity for their causes.

Acts of terrorism include threats of attacks, assassinations, kidnappings, hijackings, bomb scares and bombings, cyber attacks (computer-based), and the use of chemical, biological, nuclear and radiological weapons.

High-risk targets for acts of terrorism include military and civilian government facilities, international airports, large cities, high-profile landmarks, large public gatherings, water and food supplies, utilities, corporate centers, and mail and mass transit systems.

During a terrorist attack you would need to rely on local police, fire, and other officials for instructions. Eventually state and federal agencies will become involved in the response.

The Jargon

CBRNE—The likely weapons of terrorism and mass destruction: chemical, biological, radiological, nuclear, and explosive; arson should be added.

Homeland Security Advisory—

> *Red* (severe risk)—terrorist attack has occurred or is imminent.
> *Orange* (high risk)—Attack likely, target not identified.
> *Yellow* (elevated, significant risk)—Elevated risk, specific region or target not identified.
> *Blue* (guarded, general risk)—No credible threats or specific targets.
> *Green* (low risk)—Routine security advised.

Secondary device—A device set to detonate after police, fire, and emergency medical services are on the scene, or in safe areas where evacuees have gathered.

Terrorism—The use of violence or threats of violence to achieve a goal or to intimidate.

WMD—Weapon of mass destruction; any agent or weapon designed to cause mass casualties or massive infrastructure and property damage.

Protecting Yourself and Your Family

You can prepare in much the same way you would prepare for other crisis events.

The following are general guidelines recommended by FEMA:

- Be aware of your surroundings.
- Be aware of likely targets: skyscrapers and high rises, bridges and tunnels, pipelines, harbors, symbolic and religious landmarks, schools, government buildings, churches, malls, computer networks and data systems, power systems, vehicles of mass transit, and food and water supplies.
- Move or leave if you feel uncomfortable or if something does not seem right.
- Take precautions when traveling. Be aware of conspicuous or unusual behavior. Do not accept packages from strangers. Do not leave luggage unattended. You should promptly report unusual behavior, suspicious or unattended packages, and strange devices to the police or security personnel.
- Learn where emergency exits are located in buildings you frequent. Plan how to get out in the event of an emergency.
- Be prepared to do without services you normally depend on: electricity, telephone, natural gas, gasoline pumps, cash registers, ATMs, and Internet transactions.
- Work with building owners to ensure the following items are located on each floor of the building:

- Portable, battery-operated radio and extra batteries.
- Several flashlights and extra batteries.
- First aid kit and manual.
- Hard hats and dust masks.
- Fluorescent tape to rope off dangerous areas.

When the threat level is Orange or Red:

- Report suspicious activities to 911 or your law enforcement services number.
- Expect delays, searches, and denial of access to public buildings.
- Expect traffic delays and restrictions.
- Avoid crowded areas or large crowds.
- Monitor media and be prepared to evacuate or shelter in place.
- Do not start or help circulate rumors.

18. Civil Unrest & Armed Conflict

> *"Go to hell! It's every man for himself!"*
> —A New Orleans policeman to a stranded
> tourist in the chaos of Hurricane Katrina

The Basics

Civil unrest covers a big list of public disturbances by groups, often because of protest or outrage. It includes riots, strikes, uprising and rebellion, looting, sit-ins, demonstrations, parades, sabotage, kidnapping, shootouts and sniping, executions, bombings, and other forms of terrorism, street fighting, and civil war. In most places both the police and the military will be involved, often clashing violently with the dissident groups. Things can get particularly ugly because the motives are usually hate, resentment, and fear. Fortunately most civil unrest and armed conflict results from tensions that build up over a period of time, and we can sense when the time is right to leave for safer turf. Occasionally a single event results in a sudden rampage. The best way to avoid getting captured, injured, or killed in these situations is to avoid them entirely by getting out before they escalate or evacuating as soon as the opportunity presents itself. Once you're caught in the middle of it, getting out can be tough.

The Jargon

Boycott—A refusal by a group to use a service or product of a business or government as a form of protest or pressure.

Curfew—An order requiring the public or certain groups to get off and stay off the streets at a certain hour.

Looting—The criminal act of taking things from homes and buildings by forceful means.

Martial law—Temporary military rule imposed in an emergency.

Protest—A public gathering to express opposition.

Rebellion—An uprising meant to overthrow a government or ruling authority, or to oppose it by force.

Riot—A chaotic disturbance caused by a large number of people.

Strike—An event in which workers stop working in support or protest of decisions by their employers or government.

Protecting Yourself and Your Family

Before an Incident

- Make the basic preparations recommended in chapter 3. If you're in an exotic or foreign location your evacuation plan should include your likely evacuations destinations (e.g., the airport, the embassy, the closest border crossing, etc.) and some safe haven you can go to if you're unable to get to your evacuation destination. Include your family in the planning process so they know where to go. On your contact list include the phone numbers and locations of friendly embassies or consulates, police stations, hospitals, and airports. Keep a "hasty" pack of disaster supplies for each member of the family that they can grab at a moments notice. With your passports and other essential papers keep some emergency cash in the currency of the country you're in as well as the universal cash—the US dollar. If you get cut off and stuck in the middle of the mess, money will be your key to safety. It doesn't hurt to have an emergency credit card, but I don't think rioters, terrorists, and crooked cops accept them.

- Stay informed and alert. There is usually some indication in the news that there are potential problems. There may be travel advisories issued from your embassy or the Department of State. Postpone or reroute your travel plans.

- Contact your embassy and let them know where you are. Give your itinerary to some friends who aren't traveling with you. *Authors note: I personally have had nothing but bad service from US embassies abroad. This has ranged from outright refusal to assist a large group of US missionaries during South American riots and the ensuing violent revolution, to being scoffed at by embassy staff in the Republic of Georgia when the stairs to my hotel room in Kutaisi were rigged with a phone bomb, to being overruled by pencil-pushing embassy white-shirts in my field investigation of a suspicious death of an American advisor in the Middle East. I did learn some tricks when I was living in the Middle East: shmooze and brown nose with the embassy staff and make friends there. Do the same with the international NGOs. You'll get access to all kinds of things, the most valuable of which might be information and protection when you need it the most.*

- Know the local laws and customs. Dress conservatively, and consider dressing like the locals.
- Be vigilant with personal and family security by:
    - Traveling in groups.
    - Keeping personal information secret.
    - Protecting your passport.
    - Being polite.
    - Keeping an emergency contact list with you.
    - Varying your routine so potential criminals or terrorists cannot predict your movements. Avoid walking slow and loitering or browsing.
    - Leaving when your gut tells you something bad is imminent.

- Be aware of current events and the local environment. The tension often builds over a period of days or weeks. When the tension is near the breaking point, there will be a palpable sense that something is about to happen. Your ability to tune into this will depend on your understanding of the culture, the routines, and the normal activity of the community you're in. Local residents will seem nervous. If asked, they might tell you what's going on. If locals warn you that the shit is about to hit the fan, get out.

- Travel with a small group of people for protection, but avoid other groups of people, especially large groups. Do not go near demonstrations, meetings, or parades you don't know the meaning of. If there's palpable tension, avoid being in the street, even for parties or shopping in the open markets.

- Don't rubberneck. If something suspicious is happening, don't stop to see what's going on.

- Avoid mass transit and other forms of public transportation. Train stations and airports can get dangerously crowded when everyone is trying to get out at the same time. Your embassy might be able to suggest alternatives.

- If you're leaving a home or office behind, secure it. Looting is often the result of civil unrest. Lock doors and windows. Board them up from the inside and outside if possible. If there's time, take smaller valuables with you or stash them in a safe location.

- *Do not panic.* A calm demeanor will get you through some of the most tense confrontations.

- If rioting or street warfare breaks out while you're inside, stay there. Lock doors and windows and barricade them. Move to interior rooms to avoid bullets and rocks. Define two ways out for rapid escape in case of fire or inside attack. Call the embassy and the police.

- If you're outside and fighting is imminent or in progress, move away. Move slowly to avoid attention, and move diagonally with the flow of the crowd to eventually make your way to the side of the crowd. There are lots of things to think about. If you leave the crowd, will you be an easy target? If you stay with the crowd, will police and military mistake you for a participant? Some other recommendations:

  - Avoid major roads and public squares. Take the road less traveled.

  - Avoid public transportation. It naturally draws crowds and can be a target. It can also be difficult to escape from.

  - If you're in a car, keep driving. Do not stop. Be suspicious of cars following you and cars slowing down in front of you. Do not stop if someone tries to wave you down. Go around crowds to avoid having to slow down.

- If you're caught in a rushing crowd, avoid getting crushed by moving away from points of escape and exits. Do whatever you can to avoid tripping or falling. Climb something to get above the crowd.

- Do NOT confront groups. Do not be insulting, combative, or defiant. And don't plead American citizenship. In today's world it's not a "Get Out of Jail Free" card, and it's likely to get you in deeper trouble.

- Be suspicious about police, military, and roadblocks. Act confident but not defiant. Ask for ID, but be polite.

- If you are confronted with an armed military, police, or paramilitary roadblock, stay calm. Cooperate but act confident, respectfully, and with a controlled

A Body Armor Primer

I almost laughed when the county authorities insisted I wear body armor when I signed on to run an ambulance service in northeast Wyoming almost 30 years ago. It was a rough, Wild West environment to work in, and after the first couple of life-threatening incidents I wore the armor faithfully and felt vulnerable without it.

For most of us body armor is just another gadget the salesmen are trying to sell a paranoid public. There are those who actually do have reasons for concern, including wealthy business executives, government VIPs, body guards, security officers, law enforcement, and in some areas, fire and EMS personnel. Lately even teachers are starting to look at wearing body armor.

Body armor has changed over the decades to the point where now it's possible to get reasonable protection in a vest made from soft woven fibers. This "soft armor" is more tailored than traditional armor, making it easy to conceal and comfortable to wear.

Body armor's protection capability is rated I through IV, sometimes with an –A suffix that indicates soft armor. Class I armor will stop small caliber handgun bullets. Class IV can stop a close blast from a large-gauge shotgun.

As with any other gadget, don't bother buying it if you're not going to lug it around with you. The time you will need it will be the time you don't have it. For most of us, body armor will be a waste of money.

A Small Weapons Primer

I believe in the right to bear arms. It's a fundamental constitutional right. It's just too bad that some people can't control their weapons. From personal experience I can tell you that any handgun you keep in the home is more likely to be a weapon of homicide or suicide in your home and by family or friends than to be a weapon of self-defense against a criminal, a rioting crowd, or an intruder. Aside from the demise of two brothers and a nephew at the hands of their own weapons, my own experience on the street can't lie: In 17 years of paramedic practice I saw a few hundred suicides and homicides with personal weapons, but only a single incident where a weapon was used for personal protection. That should be a major deterrent to keeping guns in a family home, but in reality most people live under the delusion that something like that just can't happen to them.

A gun is another one of those gadgets the Chicken-Little salesmen want to sell us. If you decide to buy one, do it legally and get some training and a permit. Realize that pulling a weapon out during civil unrest implies you are committed to a violent act. Your actions will elicit one of two emotions: fear or anger. If your foes are afraid, you've probably won the battle. If your foes are pissed off, you may have made the worst mistake of your life.

If you decide you can't live without a firearm for personal protection, choose a handgun that is of sufficient caliber to neutralize a large adult. Experts pretty much agree that 9 mm is as small as you should go, and anything larger than a .38 Special or .357 Magnum is too big. Other considerations to make are price, your physical size, and hand strength. Revolvers are safer than semi-automatics, but semi-automatics are quicker to load and easier to conceal.

Once you've decided on a weapon, you'll need some training from experienced professionals who are street-smart. Plinking at cans isn't sufficient training for the close combat that typically occurs in armed urban unrest.

degree of friendliness. The author's opinion is that it's better to act as though you are traveling to complete important but friendly business rather than letting on that you are fleeing and in panic mode. If you can convince them that they have a reason to let you go, you will be allowed to pass. If that ultimately means bribing them with money without implying that the bribe is immoral or unethical, so be it. If they're corrupt but not violently criminal, they'll take your money and let you pass.

Another experienced-based opinion from the author: I have found myself facing the muzzle of a police or military machine gun more often than I care to remember. In all cases the gunman has either been more scared than me, or a fearless bully with a grudge or agenda. In the first situation I felt like it was best to calm the gunman's fears and sympathize with the frightening job he has to do. In the second, I found that respect is what the gunman is looking for. Neither of these gunmen would be inclined to sympathize with a wailing idiot tearfully pleading for his own life. It's better to give them what they need and want, and maintain your demeanor.

19. Explosives & Bombs

The Basics

An explosion is the sudden release of energy and the accompanying pressure (shock waves) exerted on surrounding materials by the expanding gas. An explosion can be the result of natural causes (volcanoes, for instance) or accidental or intentional causes such as hazardous materials, accidents, or terrorism. A bomb is a man-made explosive device. Destruction and injury are caused by the blast wave and the impact of fragments propelled by the blast.

The most common explosion injuries are penetrating and blunt trauma. Death is often caused by lung injuries ("blast lung"). Burns are also common. Explosions in confined spaces (buildings, mines, vehicles) and structural collapse will increase the injuries and damage.

The Jargon

Detonator—a device used to set off an explosive charge.
Explosives—prepared chemicals that produce a rapid, violent chemical change on being heated or impacted.
High explosives—an explosive that produces gas and pressure at a very high rate.
IED—improvised explosive device (including "pipe bombs").
Propellants—an explosive used to propel projectiles.

How to Protect Yourself and Your Family

Preparing for a Building Explosion

Explosions can collapse buildings and cause fires. People who live or work in a multi-level building can do the following:

- Know emergency evacuation procedures. Know where emergency exits are located.
- Keep fire extinguishers in working order. Know where they are located and learn how to use them.
- Learn first aid.

- Building owners should keep a disaster supplies kit on each floor of the building. It should contain the following items:
  - The basic items listed in chapter 2
  - Several additional flashlights and extra batteries
  - First aid kit
  - Several hard hats
  - Fluorescent tape to rope off dangerous areas

Bomb Threats

If you receive a bomb threat, get as much information from the caller as possible. Keep the caller on the line and record everything that is said. Then notify the police and the building management.

If you are notified of a bomb threat, do not touch any suspicious mail or packages. Clear the area around suspicious mail, packages, or unidentified unattended bags or boxes and notify the police immediately. While evacuating the building, don't stand in front of windows, glass doors, or other potentially hazardous areas. Do not block doorways, sidewalks, or streets to be used by emergency officials or others still exiting the building.

Suspicious Parcels and Letters

Be wary of suspicious packages and letters. They can contain explosives, chemical, or biological agents. Be suspicious of mail and packages that:

- Are unexpected or from someone unfamiliar to you.
- Have no return address, or have one that can't be verified as legitimate.

- Are marked with restrictive endorsements, such as "Personal," "Confidential," or "Do not x-ray."
- Have protruding wires or aluminum foil, strange odors, or stains.
- Show a city or state in the postmark that doesn't match the return address.
- Are of unusual weight, given their size, or are lopsided or oddly shaped.
- Are marked with any threatening language.
- Have inappropriate or unusual labeling.
- Have excessive postage or excessive packaging material such as masking tape and string.
- Have misspellings of common words.
- Are addressed to someone no longer with your organization or are otherwise outdated.
- Have incorrect titles or title without a name.
- Are not addressed to a specific person.
- Have handwritten or poorly typed addresses.

With suspicious envelopes and packages other than those that might contain explosives, take these additional steps against possible biological and chemical agents:

- Refrain from eating or drinking in a designated mail handling area.
- Place suspicious envelopes or packages in a plastic bag or some other type of container to prevent leakage of contents. Never sniff or smell suspect mail.
- If you do not have a container, then cover the envelope or package with anything available (e.g., clothing, paper, trash can) and do not remove the cover.
- Leave the room and close the door, or section off the area to prevent others from entering.

- Wash your hands with soap and water to prevent spreading any powder to your face.

- If you are at work, report the incident to your building security official or an available supervisor, who should notify police and other authorities without delay.

- List all people who were in the room or area when this suspicious letter or package was recognized. Give a copy of this list to both the local public health authorities and law enforcement officials for follow-up investigations and advice.

- If you are at home, report the incident to local police.

- Leave the building as quickly as possible. Do not stop to retrieve personal possessions or make phone calls.

- If there's an explosion and things are falling around you, get under a sturdy table or desk until they stop falling. Then leave quickly, watching for weakened floors and stairs and falling debris as you exit.

- Keep in mind that a second device or threat may be planted by the bomber. When you get out of the building, move away from the area. Do not stand in the open to watch the activity.

If There Is a Fire

- Stay low to the floor and exit the building as quickly as possible.

- Cover your nose and mouth with a wet cloth.

- When approaching a closed door, use the back of your hand to feel the lower, middle, and upper parts of the door. Never use the palm of your hand or fingers to test for heat: burning those areas could impair your ability to escape a fire (i.e., ladders and crawling).

- If the door is NOT hot, open slowly and ensure fire and/or smoke is not blocking your escape route. If your escape route is blocked, shut the door immediately and use an alternate escape route, such as a window. If clear, leave immediately through the door. Be prepared to crawl. Smoke and heat rise. The air is clearer and cooler near the floor.

- If the door is hot, do not open it. Escape through a window. If you cannot escape, hang a white or light-colored sheet outside the window, alerting firefighters to your presence.

- Heavy smoke and poisonous gases collect first along the ceiling. Stay below the smoke at all times.

- Do not light a match.

- Do not move about or kick up dust. Cover your mouth with a handkerchief or clothing.

- Rhythmically tap on a pipe or wall so that rescuers can hear where you are. Use a whistle if one is available. Shout only as a last resort when you hear sounds and think someone will hear you—shouting can cause a person to inhale dangerous amounts of dust.

20. Threats From Space

We all know from watching *Armageddon* over and over again on the cable channels that when the big asteroid comes to get us, we'll send up a band of renegade oil drillers to blow it up with giant nuclear bombs. I feel so safe now.

In actuality, we do have at least two worries from space: comets and asteroids. Comets are immense collections of dust, ice, and gas. Theoretically a comet could sneak up on us before we saw it and leave us less than a year to figure out what to do with it. In our neck of the cosmic woods comets are rare. We're about a hundred times more likely to get smacked with an asteroid.

Asteroids are largely composed of stone and iron. We can see them coming because they're more dense. The problem is that there are millions of them in the asteroid belt between Mars and Jupiter, and sometimes they come close to earth. We've been hit before. Sooner or later we'll be hit again.

An asteroid spotted in 2004 is a good example. Scientists and computers predict that in 2029 it will come as close as 15,000 miles from earth. That is a long way out from our perspective, but in astronomical terms it's very close. Some scientists think it will get close again a few years later, possibly much closer. If it were to hit us, say in an ocean, it would cause the tsunami from hell, drowning millions and destroying farmlands a hundred or so miles inland, resulting in crop failure, famine, and disease. If it hit land, the impact would pulverize an area the size of Utah and Nevada combined and send a dust cloud into the atmosphere that would cause serious global cooling, crop failure, and resulting famine and disease.

We have options. Strategies include nuclear explosive devices, tractors and tugs of various types, and the use of focused energy to push it off course.

Before the Collision

Let's go back to the scenario. We've spotted the doomsday asteroid heading our way. We've got a few years to get ready. If we're seriously worried about it, we build a two year disaster supplies kit. We pack a lot of thick books, because with our neighbors all dead and civilization in total collapse, it's going to be a long two years. Oh, guys, pack some Viagra, because you'll be busy trying to repopulate the planet.

During the Collision Event

If you're lucky enough to be on the other side of the planet when it hits, your short-term survival is relatively secure. If not, kiss your ass good-bye.

Appendix 1
Informational Resources

1. Web-based

www.redcross.org—American Red Cross
www.salvationarmyusa.org—Salvation Army
www.usafreedomcorps.gov—USA Freedom Corps
www.medicalreservecorps.gov—Medical Reserve Corps
www.arrl.org—Amateur Radio Emergency Service (ARES)
www.races.net—Radio Amateur Civil Emergency Service (RACES)
www.nvoad.org—National Voluntary Organizations Active in Disaster
www.citizencorps.gov/programs/—Community Emergency Response Team Program (CERT), Medical Reserve Corps, Fire Corps, USAonWatch, Volunteers in Police Service
www.reliefweb.int—the U.N. Office for the Coordination of Humanitarian Affairs—Centers for Disease Control and Prevention
www.pandemicflu.gov—for pandemic flu information
http://hhs.gov/emergency/—Department of Health and Human Services
http://disasterhelp/portaljhtml/index.jhtml—for assistance information
http://epa.gov—Environmental Protection Agency
www.fema.gov—Federal Emergency Management Agency
www.travel.state.gov—Department of State
www.nih.gov—National Institute of Health

www.fda.gov—Food and Drug Administration
www.doe.gov—Department of Energy
www.fbi.gov—Federal Bureau of Investigation

2. And Some Phone Numbers . . .

Federal Emergency Management Agency: 1-800-621-3362 (621-FEMA)

Federal Citizen Information Center (FCIC): 1-800-333-4636 (FED-INFO)

American Red Cross National Headquarters: 1-866-438-4636 (GET-INFO)

Appendix 2
Simple Unknown Substance Hazard Identification

In a large-scale disaster it may be hours or days before an emergency response unit can respond to a hazardous materials incident that isn't producing casualties. Some simple tests can provide you with some information about the hazards of unknown substances spilled or deposited in your community. It can also tell you if the substance might present a live germ hazard (e.g., a mysterious "white powder" event).

Even though material is not producing casualties you should evacuate the area for several hundred feet.

Be aware that these tests provide only basic information about the hazards of the substance. The tests are not comprehensive, and there is no test to determine if a substance is poison, unless you want to feed it to your pet rat, in which case the kids will hate you.

Take appropriate precautions and use personal protective equipment if you decide to handle any of the unknown material. You only need a small sample. Take notes on what you find and give them to the responders.

1. Physical Description and Air Reactivity

- What's the state of the material (solid, liquid, or gas)?
- What color is it?

- What consistency is it (for solids: powder, grains, chunk, etc.) and what viscosity (for liquids: like water, like oil, like cold molasses)?
- What clarity does it have (transparent, translucent, opaque)?
- Does it react when exposed to air (heat, smoke, gas, flame, etc.)? If so, it's **air reactive. Bad stuff**.

2. Water Reactivity Test

- In a glass dish or test tube, carefully add a few drops of the unknown to a few drops of water. If there's heat, gas, or flame generated, it's **water reactive**. Don't try to wash it away.

3. Water Solubility

- Does it dissolve in water? If not:
- Does it sink or float (is it less or more dense than water)?

4. pH

- Test a liquid or a dissolved solution with pH paper. If it's less than 3 or greater than 12, it's highly **corrosive.** Note: "Germs" (biologic agents) will not survive in low or high pH (<5 or >9).

5. Ignitability or Flammability

- Use a lighter or wooden match. Touch it to a few drops or small chunks of the unknown. If it lights, pull the lighter away. If it reacts violently, it's **explosive**. **Evacuate an appropriate area**. If it supports its own combustion, it's **flammable (a major fire**

hazard). If it goes out, hold the lighter to it for one second. If it burns, it's **combustible**.

6. Oxidizer Test

- You'll need some weak hydrochloric acid and some starch-iodine paper for this test. Purchase the paper commercially or have the local chemistry teacher make it for you ahead of time. Wet a tiny piece of the paper with a drop or two of the acid. Then touch it to a drop or tiny piece of the unknown. If the paper turns dark purple or black, the unknown is an oxidizer. It can react with other substances and cause or accelerate a fire. Note: oxidizers kill "germs."

So what has all this told you? You've determined if the substance is a fire or explosion hazard and if it's dangerously corrosive. Many corrosives are also respiratory hazards. You also know what will happen if you add water to the unknown in an attempt to dilute it or wash it way. And if the pH was high or low and/or it's an oxidizer, it's not likely that your unknown has any live germs in it. But you never know. Stay away from the stuff anyway until the professionals can test and dispose of it.

There are some problems with these tests. As mentioned before they don't tell you if a substance is poison. Some very potent acids will not show extreme pH on the strip, and some oxidizers cannot be identified with the starch-iodine paper. Germs may not survive in low or high pH or in oxidizers, but bio-toxins (e.g., ricin) might.

If nothing else, learning these tests will give you an awareness of the potential hazards of unknown substances.

Appendix 3
Rappelling/Lowering for High Rise Evacuation

Of the extreme high-rise evacuation methods mentioned in Chapter 15, it's the author's opinion that rappelling and lowering are the most practical means of getting yourself and others down in a "last resort" situation.

Assumptions:

1. Over two-thirds of high-rise fires start below the fifth floor.
2. Heat and sharps (glass and metal) are the primary threats to rope evac equipment. Regular nylon, polyester, and polypropylene climbing and rescue ropes may not be able to withstand the damage.
3. Smoke and operator error are the primary threats to rope evacuees.

Based on these assumptions, the following conclusions can be made:

1. Most high-rise rope evacs should only require 120 feet or less of rope (20 feet per floor plus 20 feet for anchoring). If the fire is above the 5th floor, the rope can be used to get evacuees to the floors below the fire, or a rope of appropriate length can be used to land evacuees on the ground (again, 20 feet per floor, plus 20 feet for anchoring).
2. a. Most nylon, polyester, and polypropylene ropes lose half their strength by the time they are exposed to temperatures between 250 to 350 degrees. Testing has shown that some newer

high-tensile fibers, Technora, for example, are two to three times as resistant to heat and significantly more resistant to abrasion than the fibers used in standard ropes.

b. Evacuate on the side least exposed to glass and metal sharps. This will be the side that's not in flames or that hasn't been blown out in the explosion. One of the advantages of simple rappel systems is that you can put your anchors anywhere.

3. a. Again, set your anchors on the side of the building that has the least amount of smoke exposure.

b. Because smoke, poisonous gases, and heat can cause you to disorient or pass out on rappel, do not use an "autoblock" backup (e.g., Grigri, Sum, autoblock knots) unless you are the last or only person using the rope to evacuate. Learn to rely on fireman's belays for backup. Fireman's belays are described later in the appendix.

c. There are two common operator errors that can ruin your day:

1. Misjudging the amount of friction you need to control the belay. The amount of friction you need increases as you get closer to the ground. Rappellers often find themselves going faster and faster, then losing control entirely.

2. Getting something caught in the rappel device. This will bring the evacuation to a screeching halt.

4. In order to prevent bad things from happening and to take advantage of the versatility and simplicity of rope evacuation systems, the author recommends taking rappelling courses from experienced, qualified trainers. In general, experienced canyoneers and

cavers know far more about the "ups and downs" of rappelling than the average climber or firefighter does. At a minimum your business or building security office should establish and train a "captain" for each floor. Even better, two captains for each floor. The captains should become an expert at anchoring and controlling the rope evacuations.

1. Basic Rope Evacuation Systems

There are three basic systems that can be used to evacuate:

	Pros	Cons
1. **Lowering systems** in which each evacuee is secured to the rope and lowered directly to the ground by somebody who controls the rope from above.	If there's enough time, everyone can get down, even if they don't have any rappelling experience. There's no chance of rappel devices becoming jammed. 2:1 lowering systems can be used to quickly lower evacuees and recover the rope without them having to de-rig.	If evacuee is injured or otherwise unable to remove himself from the tie-in, the entire system comes to a standstill.
2. **Rappel systems** in which each evacuee rigs the rope to a rappel brake on his or her harness and controls their own descent directly to the ground.		Requires prior rappelling experience. There will NOT be enough time to do a group rappelling class during an incident. A jammed rappel device will bring the entire system to a standstill.
3. **"Guided" rappels and lowers** in which the bottom end of the rope is anchored well away from the base of the building and evacuees are lowered or rappel along the guideline to a safe location.	Areas of heat, smoke, and dangerous debris can be avoided, and evacuees are landed in safe areas away from danger. Pros of rappelling or lowering apply.	Cons of rappelling or lowering apply.

Equipment For High-Rise Rope Evacuation

- **Rope.** Use static (low or no-stretch) canyoneering, caving, or rescue rope. Several companies (e.g., PMI and Bluewater) are producing static ropes with Technora and other high-tensile fibers. These are stronger, more abrasion resistant, and less susceptible to heat damage than standard fiber ropes. Ropes with a diameter of 9 to 13 mm (three-eighths to one-half-inch) are preferable if the drop can be kept under 120 feet. These fat diameters are easy to control. If the drop is going to be more than 120 feet, consider 8 mm or 9.2 mm ropes made with high-tensile fibers. 8 to 9.2 mm ropes do not give the control of fatter ropes, but they are considerably less bulky. You'll need at least 120 feet for simple lowers and rappels, 240 feet if you plan to use 2:1 lowering systems or to double the rope and rappel or lower on both strands simultaneously.

- **Rope Bag.** Rope bags are the best way to store and deploy a bag. Do not use rope-coiling techniques commonly used by climbers and firefighters. They are likely to tangle when you need them the most. A properly bagged rope can easily be anchored on one end and dropped, bag and all, directly to the ground without snarls or kinks.

- **Harness.** If you're going to be the only person using your rope evac system, get a good, simple climbing or canyoneering harness. If you plan to help others get down, you'll want to have a number of 12- to 14-foot slings made of one-inch tubular webbing. These slings are tied with a water knot and used as a "diaper seat" harness. Buy this webbing from a climbing store.

- **Carabiners.** These are strong snaplinks used to clip into the rope for various purposes. They come in various shapes and in locking and non-locking varieties. Locking varieties are by far more safe than

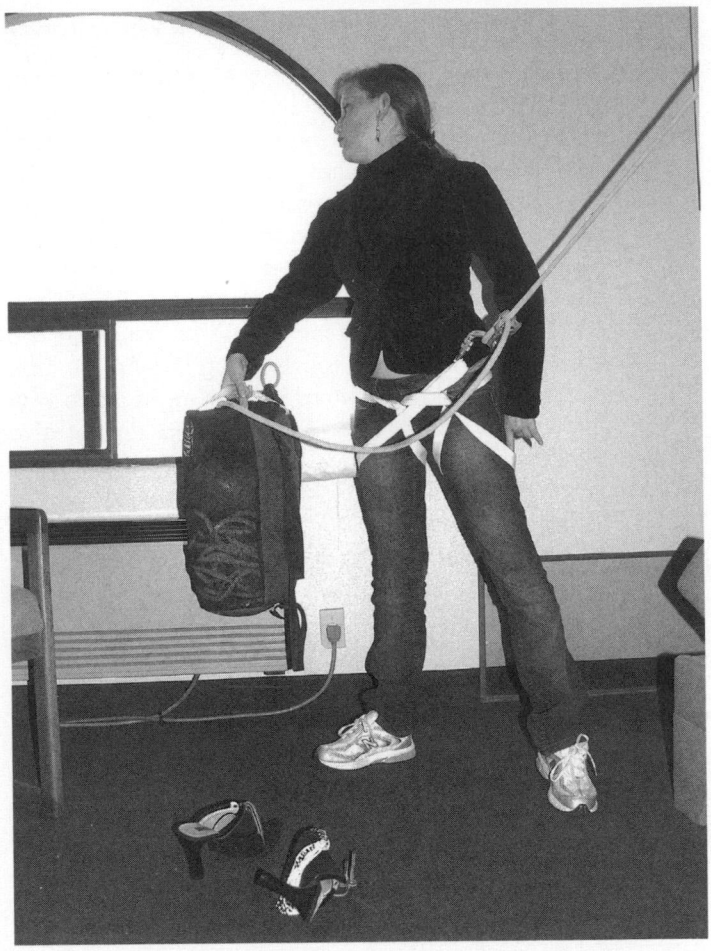

Before tossing the bag over the edge, make sure the edge is padded. Remove anything that could get jammed in the rappel device (ties, necklaces) and tuck away long hair. If you're wearing heels, get into a pair of tennis shoes. Wear a helmet if one is available.

non-locking when using them to secure an evacuee to a rope or rappel device, but people in panic mode seem to have a difficult time with locking carabiners. Also, when you've got 20 people to evacuate and 15 minutes to do it, the extra 10 seconds it takes to lock and unlock the 'biner each time can eat up a lot of seriously precious time. Use your discretion. Try keeping at least three lockers and three non-lockers in your kit.

- **Rappel/Lowering Device.** The author recommends a simple rappel device, like an ATC made by Black Diamond Equipment or an SBG II from Omega, that can be used to rappel or control lowering and that is easy to vary friction on. Avoid spring-loaded devices that will automatically lock you to the rope if you pass out and let go.

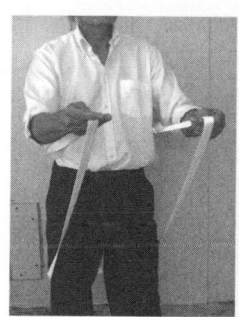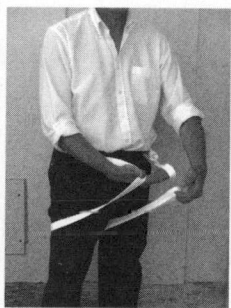

A diaper harness made from 14 feet of webbing. An expedient method of rigging a "diaper seat" harness using a 14-foot piece of one inch tubular webbing. Tie the ends together with a *water knot* (aka ring bend, left. The wings are brought up through the loop pulled up from between the legs, center. Attach the carabiner and rappel device to the wings, right. Snug up the harness and don't let it loosen and fall off the waist and down the thighs.

- **Anchor Material.** The rope can be tied directly into the anchor, or clipped into an anchor sling with a carabiner. Use one of your 12-foot tubular webbings, or keep a 15-foot piece of Omni-sling in your kit specifically for anchors.

- **Helmet and Gloves.** If a helmet is available, wear it. But don't waste time ferrying a single helmet up and down between evacuees. Gloves are not necessary if you know how to rappel and control your friction device. Gloves are often used by inexperienced rappellers. While a glove can protect the hand from rope burns, it's difficult to grip the rope correctly with a glove, and wearing gloves can ultimately result in less control. If you use gloves, make sure they are soft and ergonomic—pre-curved to the shape of a semi-clenched hand.

Techniques

Anchors

Escape anchors are probably going to be one of two types. They might be **wrapped** around a stout structure or **jammed** in a choke-point. For an entertaining primer on structural anchors, watch the classic Eastwood-Burton war movie *Where Eagles Dare.*

Anchor Basics

- Make sure the anchor is solid against the direction of pull (usually the fall-line).
- Pad the anchor and the rope against broken glass and abrasion.

Lowering Technique

Before sending each evacuee down, make sure they understand that when they reach the ground they are to step out of the harness without disconnecting the carabiner so the belayer can retrieve rope, 'biner, and harness. Here are two methods of lowering:

1. Clip a carabiner into the end of a rope (figure 8 knot) and to the diaper seat of an evacuee. Set the rappel device on an anchor as indicated on its decals or owner's manual. Send the evacuee off and control the rate of descent. Having a "spotter" on the edge to watch the evacuee and relay instructions will make the operation smoother.

2. Use a 2:1 lowering system (doubled rope through the evacuee's carabiner). One end of the rope is tied to the anchor, the other controlled by the belayer. The advantage of this system is that if anything goes wrong, the rope can be pulled through the evacuee's carabiner and retrieved.

By doubling the rope and securing the middle to the anchor, two 2:1 lowering systems can be operated at the same time. This is a fast, efficient way of getting people to safety.

Rappelling Technique

Contrary to the way it looks in the movies, rappelling is seriously complicated in terms of the various methods and devices used to descend and the physics and dynamics of the procedure. Don't try anything heroic or stupid. Upside-down-and-backward and bounding commando rappels are ridiculous and excessively dangerous.

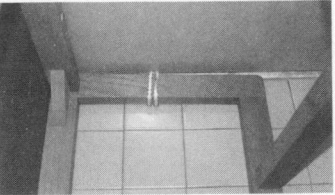

Fig. B, A runner girth hitched
around a stout chair leg and
blocked by the same door.

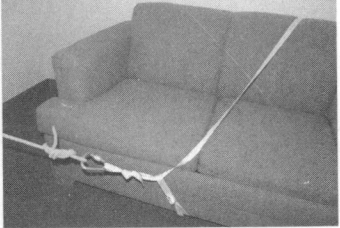

Fig. A, A runner knot jammed
behind a snugly closed door on the
hinged side, opposite the latch.

Fig. C, A runner girth hitched
around a heavy sofa.

Fig. D, A rappel rope tied directly to a structural feature.
Anchors are everywhere.

Here's the basic procedure:

1.   Attach the end of the rope to the anchor and drop the other end to the ground, the next roof, or alongside a target ledge or balcony.

2.   Attach the rope to your rappel device and your rappel device to your harness according to the manufacturers' instructions. If you're using locking carabiners, lock them. Remember when you're rigging your device that you will be sliding faster as you get closer to the ground. It's critical that you have lots of friction in your device at the top so there will be enough friction to control the descent closer to the ground.

3.   Quickly secure anything loose that could jam in the rappel device. Remove necklaces and chains, tuck away hair, button sleeves, tuck in shirt-tails. This is important. If you screw up and jam your device, you will die hanging on the rope and no one above you will be able to use the rope for rappelling.

4.   Grab the rope with your "guide" hand about a foot above the rappel device. Use this for support and balance only, but not to control the rappel.

5.   Grab the rope with your brake hand just below the rappel device and slide the hand back and wrap the rope across the hip. From this point, do not remove your brake hand from the rope until you have reached your destination safely.

6.   Sit on the edge of the building, balcony, or window ledge and ease carefully but quickly over.

7.   Face the wall and put both feet on the wall, shoulder-width apart, then lean back and let out a few inches of rope until you're in the proper position.

8.   Rappel down by carefully but smoothly letting the rope in your brake hand slide through the rappel device, walking backward down the wall.

9. Stay leaning out as pictured, while rappelling. Leaning in can cause items to get caught and jam the rappel device. Leaning out keeps the rope farther away from sharp edges, shattered glass, and items that might have absorbed radiated heat. It also keeps the sole of the foot on the wall and prevents slipping. Leaning too far back can cause you to tip upside down.

10. If you are dangling from overhanging eaves, just sit comfortably upright in the harness and rappel smoothly.

11. Stay in the fall-line directly below your anchor. Moving too far to either side of the fall-line can cause you to tip over, swing, or severely damage the rope.

12. When you are safely on the ground or at your target location, release the rope from your rappel device, then look upward and yell "OFF RAPPEL!" as loudly as possible to anyone above who is waiting to get on the rope. Chances are there will be too much noise for anyone to hear voices and too much smoke to see, so use your FRS radios or pre-arrange some rope signals beforehand (e.g., two very hard tugs for "off rappel").

Fireman's Belay

If you're in a group of people who plan to rappel, send someone down first who is a competent rappeller and who knows how to do a fireman's belay. With a fireman's belay the belayer can stop the fall of a rappeller who lets go of the rope for any reason.

To perform a fireman's belay:

- The belayer takes cover behind whatever cover he/she can find, out of the direct fall-line, that

A climber showing the proper body position for rappelling on a wall.

shields him/her from falling debris but allows an unobstructed view of the rappeller.

- The belayer holds the rope loosely while the rappeller descends. There must be enough slack in the rope at the bottom so the belay does not interfere with the rope moving through the rappel device.

- If the rappeller loses control, the belayer pulls down and back to tighten the rope, which applies friction at the rappel device and stops the fall.

- The belayer can hold the rappeller securely in position until the rappeller regains control, or lower the rappeller by varying the tension on the rope.

A climber using a Fireman's Belay. By pulling down on
the rope she can stop or slow the rappeller above.

Guided Systems

A guided system directs a rappeller or a lowered victim to a particular landing spot away from the fall-line, smoke, sharps, and heat. The first person down simply rappels or is lowered to the ground and then pulls the rope away from the building to the preferred site. Then he/she pulls tightly to remove the slack and anchors the rope to a stout anchor. In an urban situation this bottom anchor will be anything that won't move: a tree, a truck, a column. When the bottom anchor is secure, each person in turn attaches the "cows tails" of their harness to the guideline and they are lowered along the guideline with a second line (usually the other half of the rappel rope). Or, each person can rappel along the guideline using the second rope in their rappel device. Whichever method is employed, when the person reaches the bottom he/she must unclip from the guide rope and step out of the harness without unclipping the carabiner from the second line, so the harness, carabiner, and rope can all be pulled back up for the next person.

Adjusting Friction

Probably the two easiest ways for a layman to add additional friction to his device during a rappel are:

1. Pass the rope around the back to the opposite hand.
2. Before starting the rappel, put an additional carabiner to the leg loop on the brake-hand side, and when the time is right pass the rope through that carabiner. Note that this will then require the rappel to be controlled out front rather than back at the hip.

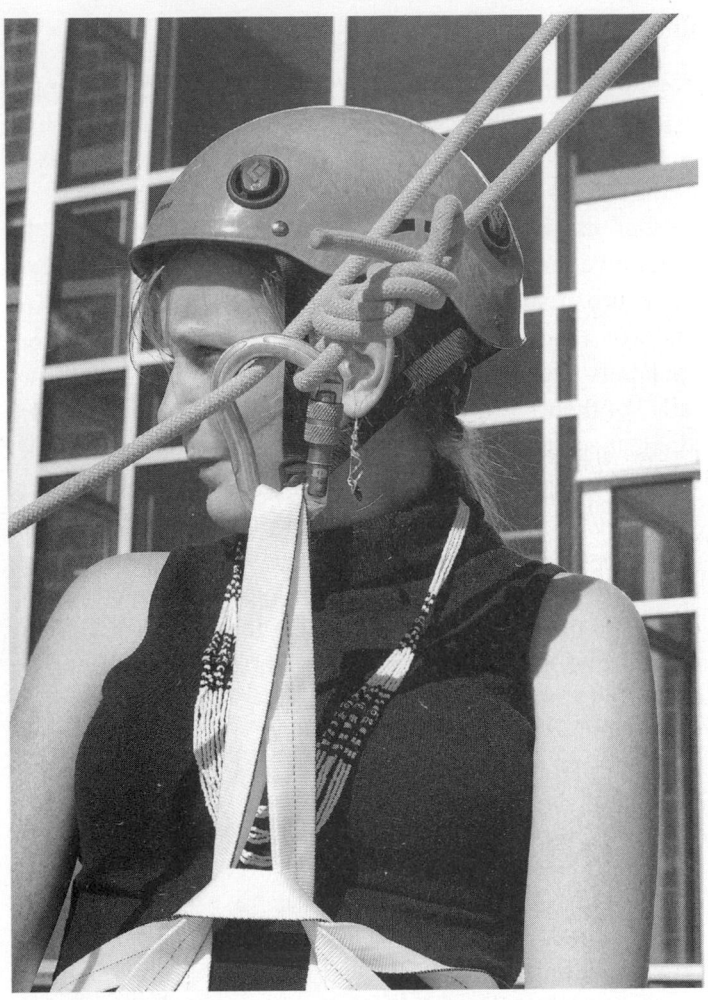

Rigging for a guided lower. Lowers can be controlled with the friction of the lowering rope through a rappel/belay device attached to an anchor, or from wrapping the rope around a structurally-sound feature such as a solid rail, a stair frame, or column.

Contingencies for Screw-Ups

Other than not knowing *how* to rappel, the most common problem encountered will be getting something jammed in the rappel/belay device. A third problem will be the tendency for a rappeller to freeze up while attempting to pass hazardous sections of the rappel. Having an extra rappel device for a contingency anchor can prevent the tragic failure of the rappel system due to someone getting jammed or stranded on the rope.

A contingency anchor is rigged as follows:

1. The middle of the rope is attached to the extra rappel device and the device is then attached to the rappel anchor sling in the same manner it would be attached to your harness if you were rappelling with it.

2. A loop of the "brake" side of the rope is pulled through the carabiner and then brought forward in front of the device and a slip knot is applied across both strands. Further secure the slip knot by tying the end of the loop in an overhand knot around the strands.

If the rappeller gets jammed or stops for some unknown reason, the overhand and slip knots can be released and the rope controlled through the rappel device to lower the rappeller to the ground. The ability to do this is increasingly important as more smoke and heat pervade the fall-line.

There are other methods of setting up contingency systems with just carabiners and special knots. This takes training and competence to set up correctly and efficiently.

One excellent source of this type of training—easily modified to urban rappels—is the American Canyoneering Association (*www.canyoneering.net*).

Appendix 4
An Improvised Level C Exposure Suit

Protective clothing for hazardous materials operations provides varying levels of protection from chemical and biological agents, radiation exposure, and extremes of temperature. Level A is the highest level of protection and uses a fully encapsulating chemical-resistant suit with a self-contained breathing apparatus (SCBA) inside the suit. Level B also uses a chemical resistant one-piece suit which may or may not be totally encapsulating, and an SCBA that may be inside or outside the suit. If the suit is not totally encapsulating, the sleeves and cuffs are usually taped to the gloves and booties to make a seal and minimize chem/bio/rad penetration. Level C includes a one or two piece chemically resistant suit and an APR (air purifying respirator, aka "gas mask"). Level D usually consists of a simple coverall and general safety gear (goggles, gloves, etc.).

Commercial hazmat suits are expensive and bulky. In the worst case scenario, and only when you are truly convinced that you cannot safely evacuate or shelter in place, and your life depends on it, you can improvise protective clothing approaching the C level from the following equipment:

- Gas mask, or even a quality smoke hood (available from a safety supply store).
- Rain pant and hooded top that are completely waterproof, preferably made of heavy-duty vinyl or a rubberized fabric that will not absorb liquids. A cheap vinyl rain suit is well suited for this purpose.

Do not use breathable fabrics. Non-breathable and un-vented is best.

- Dishwashing gloves
- Rain overboots ("galoshes") or plastic trash bags
- Duct tape

Notice that all of these items are on the list of items recommended for a comprehensive disaster supply kit. Here's the sequence for "suiting-up":

1. If exposure is in progress in close proximity, hold your breath and place a new filter on the mask. If this procedure is going to take longer than you can hold your breath, immediately cover your mouth and nose with a surgical mask or soft material (e.g., pull your T-shirt collar up over your face).

2. Put on your mask or your smoke hood. We'll assume here you have preplanned this, and that your mask is the right size and the straps are loosened. Follow the instructions that came with the mask or hood. The general procedure for donning a mask is as follows:

   a. With the headstraps pulled back, put your chin in its place in the mask and pull the mask onto the face and the straps over the head. Tighten the straps as directed.

   b. Exhale, then cover the PAPR air tube connector or the APR air intake on the filter with a hand and keep it there for a few seconds. Breathe in. The mask should make an obvious vacuum seal on the face, and the vacuum should remain while you keep your hand over the intake. If the vacuum releases, the seal is bad. Reposition the mask and retighten the straps, then check the seal again. If you're using a PAPR (powered or positive pressure air purifying respirator), connect the air tube and turn the unit on.

3. Pull on the shell pants and don the jacket and zip it fully closed. Pull the hood up over the mask and tighten the hood closure.

4. Pull on the galoshes or pull two garbage bags over each foot (leave your shoes on).

5. Duct tape the juncture of your pants cuffs and the galoshes or garbage bag. Run a strip of duct tape around the foot to secure the bag tightly close to the foot.

6. Tape the hem of the coat to the waist of the pants, and the edge of the hood to the mask (but only if the hood is big enough to prevent the mask from pulling away from the face when the head is turned).

7. Put on gloves.

8. Tape the gloves to the cuff of the sleeve.

How long can this suit be relied on? It depends on what it's made of and what kind of exposure is occurring. The function of this suit is to get you out of an exposure hazard that cannot be handled by shelter in place. It's going to provide a modicum of protection for a limited amount of time—minutes, not hours. Remember that this suit provides only temporary protection from chemicals, biologicals, and ingestion or inhalation of radioactive particles. It does not provide significant protection from heat extremes. It is sweaty, unventilated, and uncomfortable. Remember the following points:

- Get out and get away. Don't hang around, expecting your suit to protect you for hours.

- If you truly needed this suit, you will need to be properly decontaminated and everything you wear will need to be handled properly to prevent secondary exposures.

- Anything you carry with you will also need to be protected—covered by plastic garbage bags and sealed. These will also need to be decontaminated properly.

- If you don't have this gear, don't panic. Some protection is better than none. During brief exposures—and most exposures are going to be brief—normal clothing and some form of face protection (anything ranging from an N95 mask and swim goggles to a scarf over the face,) may provide enough protection to make the difference between being sick and being dead. As soon as the exposure has ended, remove clothing, decontaminate, and seek medical advice.

Appendix 5
Potty Matters

In an emergency during which sewage systems are not functioning, it will be necessary to create emergency toilets. The other option is to have everyone running around, pooping at any random location that suits his or her fancy. It's messy, smelly, and very unhealthy. Latrines and toilets are needed to allow for safe collection and handling of human waste.

Here are the basics of emergency toilets and latrines:

- Provide some privacy if possible, using barriers (walls) or any sort. Most of the population will not use a latrine that's in open view.
- Locate toilets and latrines away from food preparation or eating areas.
- Locate toilets and latrines at least 100 feet away from bodies of surface water (lakes, rivers, etc.), and at least 100 feet downhill or downstream from drinking water resources and inhabitations.
- If possible, provide running water, soap, paper towels, and a garbage container next to the toilet(s). If that's not possible, make hand sanitizer available. Encourage (by whatever means) hand washing or sanitizing to prevent the spread of severe gastrointestinal diseases.
- If the toilet or latrine has a door or covers of any sort, keep them closed when not in use to minimize insects, animals, and stench.
- In an urban disaster setting, use the following hierarchy of toilets: functioning flush toilets; personal

porta-potties or public portable toilets; emergency bucket/bowl toilets and garbage bags; hole and pit latrines.

Making an Emergency Toilet from a Flush Toilet or Bucket

- Line the inside of a five-gallon bucket or toilet bowl with two heavy-duty plastic garbage bags.
- Once daily add a cup of 1:10 bleach (3–6 percent sodium hypochlorite) and water to control pathogens and odor. Or, put a cup or two of kitty litter, ashes, sawdust, or sand into the bags. If you have a limited amount of kitty litter, mix with a filler like ashes, sand, or sawdust first.
- At the end of the day, seal the bags and store them in a protected area, out of the sun, where animals and insects will not disturb them and smell will not pervade living and dining areas.
- Listen to area media and speak with health or sanitation department officials for instructions on what to do with the stored waste.

Latrines

A latrine is basically a hole that's dug to collect human waste. These can range from "catholes" (a simple one-use hole) to large pit and trench latrines for public use. Since it's difficult to know where the hard pan or water table is without digging into it, latrines are not appropriate for urban locations that will continue to be areas of inhabitation or commerce. The carry-over hygiene problems will be unpleasant.

Here are the latrine basics:

- Public-use latrines should be at least three feet deep but at least one foot above the hard pan or the water table.
- After each use, the "doodie" should be covered with dirt, lime, or ash to keep the odor down and to minimize infestation by insects and animals.
- Consider covering the latrine with a piece of scrap board between uses.

The Web is full of sites that can give you the poop on latrine science. Get on your browser and type in "latrine."

Appendix 6
Simple Self Defense

If you find yourself in a situation where you have that feeling that you are at risk of attack, stay attentive and aware of your surroundings. Here are some suggestions:

- Keep your eyes alternately on the hands and eyes of anyone nearby. If someone catches you looking and quickly looks away or hides the hands, be suspicious and take another path.
- Cross the street or go around the block to avoid suspicious groups.
- Avoid speaking to anyone, and when you do speak make certain you don't say anything that could be misinterpreted as insulting, inflammatory, or threatening.

If someone produces a weapon and threatens you, you really only have three choices: 1) Do what they tell you to do. 2) Run like hell. 3) Fight and be injured, possibly killed. When no weapon is involved, you have more options.

Once a weaponless act of violence has begun, be prepared to defend yourself to minimize the damage.

- Make noise and yell for help.
- Put your hands in front of your face, with the forearms and elbows drawn in to protect your neck, chest, and upper abdomen. Tuck your chin in. Close your mouth tightly and clench your teeth to prevent broken teeth and a busted jawbone.

- Circle away and to the opposite side of the dominant hand and foot of an attacker. A fighter will usually stand with the dominant hand pulled back, ready to strike, and the dominant foot slightly behind the other. If he swings with the dominant hand, pull back and lean or move to one side or another. The non-dominant hand will likely be used to threaten and distract you from blocking the real power punch that will be coming from his dominant hand or foot.

- Stay as far away from the attacker as possible. Get something in between you and your attackers—a parked car, a pile of garbage. If your attacker gets your back against a wall and closes in, step in next to him and wrap your arms around him to keep him from landing heavy blows.

Aggression can be an effective means of defense, but should be a last resort since it's likely to anger your attackers even more. Sometimes an aggressive move will distract an attacker and allow a quick escape.

- Beforehand get some coaching from a martial arts expert on how to properly kick and strike without injuring yourself or losing your balance.

- Use a foot, elbow, or knee to the groin, abdomen, face, or throat. Gouge eyes. If it looks grim, grab and use any weapon at hand.

- If you get knocked to the ground and can't get up quickly, get onto your side in a tight fetal position. Protect your head, neck, and face with your arms and hands, and your internal organs with tightly drawn-up knees.

Here's another bit of honesty that will ruin some of your vigilante fantasies: becoming a kung fu expert is not going to make you invincible. In fact, a black belt pitted against a professional boxer will almost always end up on the sharp end of the stick. Why? Because as soon as your enemy does something you haven't seen in the dojo, you've lost the advantage and the match then goes to the meanest. This isn't to say you shouldn't take karate. It does mean that you should include a wide range of weapon-based and weaponless fighting forms in your training if you intend to be serious about defending yourself against street fighters or groups of enraged pitchfork-wielding campesinos.

> "Perfect wisdom is unplanned. Perfect living offers no guarantee of a peaceful death."
> —Master Po, from the TV series *Kung Fu*